MEDIA *AND* POWER
IN POST-SOVIET
RUSSIA

MEDIA *AND* POWER *IN* POST-SOVIET RUSSIA

Ivan Zassoursky

M.E. Sharpe
Armonk, New York
London, England

Library of Congress Cataloging-in-Publication Data

Zasurskii, Ivan.
   [Rekonstruktsiia Rossii. English]
   Media and power in post-Soviet Russia / by Ivan Zassoursky.
     p. cm.
   "Published in cooperation with the Transnational Institute, Amsterdam".
   Includes bibliographical references and index.
   ISBN 0-7656-0863-4 (cloth: alk. paper) — ISBN 0-7656-0864-2 (pbk.: alk. paper)
     1. Mass media—Political aspects—Russia (Federation). 2. Russia (Federation)—
Politics and government—1991– I. Title.

P95.82.R9Z3713 2002
302.23′0947—dc21

                         2001058177

Table of Contents

List of Tables and Figure

Tables

Figure

Preface: A Decade of Freedom

Every epoch has its pace of changes. Sometimes change is slow. This is when one is tempted to think long-term. The actions of any individual seem to carry little weight compared to the mighty machinery of history. When one deals with small periods of extremely intensive change, it is hardly possible to provide such an easy solution. In the second (1910–1920) and the last (1990–2000) decades of the twentieth century in Russia, the change was rapid and far-reaching, leading to enormous consequences, programming large chunks of the future. Yet as everyone who has witnessed times like these can tell, while living through such turbulent periods one is never sure what will happen next. The laws of historical development, if they exist outside of our heads, seem to be suspended. This basic, existential uncertainty comes with anxiety and freedom of action. At times like these, when no one knows what will happen next, it is up to individuals to act and make the future happen the way they want it to be. What matters in times like these, however, are not words, but deeds.

Media and Power in Post-Soviet Russia is based on the decade-long observation of Russian media, politics, and economy documented in two books (in Russian): *Mass Media of the Second Republic* and *Re-Constructing Russia: Mass Media and Politics in the Nineties*, published in 1999 and 2001, respectively, and sold out. It is a book one can shelve both as media research and as political history of the nineties. It is also a nonfiction story of how the media have been shaped by Russian history and how media in turn have shaped Russian history.

This book pays its dues to the discourse of the nineties and even goes out of its way to explain where it came from. Yet all rhetoric is treated jointly with the strategies of the political actors, journalists, and media moguls who have used it for their own ends. Following the logic of history thus means tracing the strategies of the historical actors involved.

In twentieth-century Russia, theory was very important, binding, blinding, and extremely misleading. It laid the foundation for the Soviet state. Then, in the beginning of the nineties, it became the weapon of that state's demise, leading again to great debacles and, quite possibly, to a lot of unnecessary suffering. The power of theory in Russia declined in the nineties as a result of the great demise of the printed press and the rise of television with its image-based capacity for emotional involvement. Tracing the logic of events in media, power, and politics, this book strives to provide an answer to what the new Russian identity is and how it emerged, where it comes from, and what role the media play in it.

I hope you will enjoy reading this book!

Ivan Zassoursky

Acknowledgments

Grateful acknowledgment is made here by the author to all those who have contributed to this story, which is woven from many others. Aside from the plentitude of books listed at the end of this volume this goes to individuals who not only advised but also inspired and motivated me.

I would like to thank all those who have communicated important ideas to me in the long process of building the narrative: Yassen Zassoursky, Boris Kagarlitsky, Elena Kustova, Svetlana Sherlaimova, Kaarle Nordenstreng, Elena Vartanova, Artemy Levedev, Mikhail Yakubov, Maria Loukina, Rafail Ovsepyan, and many others.

I will also use this rare opportunity to thank Irina Makarova, Alexander Gagua, and Vitaly Portnikov, Vitaly Tretiakov and Michael Leontiev, Viktor and Nina Gerashchenko, Yegor Yakovlev and Gleb Pavlovsky, Marat Guelman and Yury Lopatinsky, Grigory Yavlinsky, and Boris Nemtsov, my friend, for professional guidance that has provided me with the perspective needed to complete this endeavor.

There are also people who supported me on this journey: Larisa Zasurskaya, Julia Makarova, Robert Gosende and M.B., Jana, Inga, Oleg, Inna, and Fyodor. Their energy has been decisive. Special thanks are reserved for Barbara Jancar-Webster, Fiona Dove, and Annelies Borsboom from the Transnational Institute, and translator Renfrey Clarke, without whom the publication of this book would have been impossible.

Although I will stop short of naming all the people dear to me and listing their contributions, let it be said that this list could have been a better, and much more adventurous one.

Ivan Zassoursky

MEDIA *AND* POWER *IN* POST-SOVIET RUSSIA

Word and Deed

Politicization of the Mass Media

It cannot be said that the ruling apparatus of the USSR was unaware of the problems of the Soviet economy. The numerous reforms that were implemented under successive general secretaries of the Communist Party were always intended to reduce the degree to which the USSR lagged behind the capitalist countries.

At the April 1985 plenum meeting of the CPSU Central Committee, a new general secretary, Mikhail S. Gorbachev, put forth his strategy for sweeping change. In one account:

> The key word of the reform strategy was "acceleration." Seized upon immediately by the party propaganda organs and the mass media, it was repeated like an incantation. Everything had to be "accelerated" Gorbachev-style: production, the social sphere, the activity of the party organs, and most importantly, scientific and technological progress. Eventually, "glasnost" and "perestroika" were added to the strategic concepts. *Glasnost* meant revealing all the shortcomings that were hindering acceleration, and the criticism and self-criticism of the executive "from top to bottom." *Perestroika* involved making structural and organizational changes to the economic, social, and political mechanisms, and also to the ideology, with the aim of achieving the same acceleration of social development. Gradually, however, as it became apparent that "acceleration" was not occurring, the stress came to be placed on "perestroika," and it was this word that came to symbolize Gorbachev's policies.[1]

In his book *Glasnost and Soviet Television*, Reino Paasilinna, the former head of the Finnish television and radio broadcasting corporation, explains how events unfolded in the late 1980s, and the role that glasnost played in the overall scheme of the reforms. He also examines the new role that television came to play in society as a result of these policies.

Glasnost at first was not a goal in its own right, but a tool for the democratization and political reforms that were supposed to strengthen the socialist system in the USSR. A freed-up (but still controlled) press was in essence the only reliable ally Gorbachev possessed in his struggle with conservative forces in the party apparatus. Television played a special role. Gorbachev was the first Soviet politician to understand fully the power of this medium as a political weapon and a means of creating a personal image—a power that would allow him to circumvent the party hierarchy and appeal directly to the country's citizens. According to Paasilinna, Gorbachev's awareness of the possibilities of television was apparent in everything, right down to small details. Noticing a camera in the hall, for example, Gorbachev would orient himself carefully toward it—a skill acquired by politicians throughout the world.

The significance of television emerged during the broadcasts of the proceedings of the Congress of People's Deputies in the late 1980s. The first sitting of the congress became a huge soap opera that held the country spellbound to such an extent that the streets were emptied. But unlike the Latin American television serials they were competing with, the direct broadcasts of political events, along with a stream of documentary and artistic films on the crimes of communism, helped to politicize the masses:

> Television was discovered to have a power whose existence no one had suspected, or perhaps, in which no one had believed. . . . A unique dethroning of political officials took place on the television screen. No important historical events or individuals, nor the party, nor the system, nor even the most carefully fostered beliefs withstood the gaze of public opinion; everything was blown apart or annihilated. People learned about the mechanisms of power, which had been kept in such stringent secrecy. Earlier, changes of such scope would have been impossible without physical violence, but now television became the nation's judge.[2]

During his 1990 election campaign, Boris Yeltsin enjoyed the support of several print publications and of Leningrad television. It was Leningrad television (which could be viewed in Moscow with the help of an indoor antenna) that, for example, broadcast footage of the dispersing of a demonstration in Tbilisi, in the Georgian Republic, and the storming of the television center in Vilnius, Lithuania, where the station, headed by a committee set up by local officials, tried to maintain an anti-Moscow position. In the winter of 1990–91, soon after Yeltsin's victory in the Russian Republic's first presidential election, the Russian government established its own television system, which began news broadcasts in May 1991.

During the 1991 putsch, Russian television broadcast news programs that reflected the positions of the legitimate government. This was also the case with the CNN broadcasts, which were retransmitted over the Russian state television channel. The other channels were controlled by the putschists, but their GKChP, the "emergency" committee formed by the Soviet vice-president and leaders of the Communist Party hierarchy, failed to make use of the news potential at its disposal.

The committee was thus unable to find a way out of the contradiction between the need to impose its control over flows of information, and the need to provide people with information about its goals in order to gain their support. Without the support of journalists, the putschists appeared to the public like monsters. Throughout the day on August 19, 1991, after all the publications that could be considered part of the "democratic press" had been shut down, Russian television broadcast the ballet *Swan Lake* and symphonic music. For citizens used to reading between the lines, this in itself was a sign of trouble. To keep society informed, the GKChP issued a short communiqué that was read over the radio by announcers and published in pro-government newspapers. A press conference was also held, to which journalists from the suppressed publications were, inexplicably, invited. Moreover, the press conference was broadcast live, with the result that it turned into a real-time drama. The journalists accused the top-ranking hierarchs of carrying out a coup d'état. The hands of Soviet vice-president Gennady Yanaev trembled constantly, betraying the putschist's extreme nervousness and lack of self-confidence. Going live to air (a recording was later rebroadcast with the most serious blunders edited out), the press conference to a large degree determined the attitude that society adopted toward the GKChP. Even people who in principle supported the idea of strengthening the Soviet regime and imposing order were obliged to recognize that the GKChP was not the force that could bring this about.

Paasilinna's book *Glasnost and Soviet Television* describes how television affects an audience compared with the print media. Television exercises a profound emotional (and irrational) attraction on the viewer, acting with almost hypnotic power. This is illustrated by the popularity throughout the USSR of the psychics Kashpirovsky and Chumak (the first "conducted sessions" on television; the other "charged water" with healing power). For several years, these two had great success using their reputed extrasensory powers to cure viewers of any imaginable illness, and regularly put their huge audiences into trances. It could even be said that the enthusiasm of state television for curative hypnosis, like its purchases of Mexican television serials,[3] represented desperate attempts by the directors of State Television and Radio to direct the politically destabilizing impact of television into comparatively safe channels.

At the time, fortunately or otherwise, this attempt failed. But it is now succeeding.[4]

The Newspaper as an Ideological Space

The Soviet propaganda system was based mainly on the use of two media, newspapers and radio. Movies were added later. Russia in the nineteenth century was a book-reading culture, but the ideology of the revolution was born primarily in newspaper polemics, against the backdrop—as Marshall McLuhan noted in *Understanding Media*[5]—of the oral culture still prevailing in the illiterate provinces.

Every medium has its own peculiarities that aid in affirming one or another modality of perception. While Christianity and other great religions are founded on manuscript texts, and the movements of the Reformation and the logical reductionism of Descartes on the printing press, newspapers are linked to mass industrial society, and to the epoch of the rise of nationalism and of the great ideologies. The newspaper page is ideally suited to schematic exposition and publicistic simplifications, which have always aided the propagation of ideas among the mass public. At the same time, the mosaic of articles creates a sense of the representation of reality due to the range of subjects covered.

In all Soviet-era textbooks, authors always stressed the importance of newspapers, which served as the foundation and the primary information source of the propaganda system. Radio performed a special function in the everyday organization of reality around rituals, whose planning and direction took place in a centralized fashion. Until the reformist 1980s, for example, radio programs began at 6 a.m., and in many hotels, hostels, communal apartments, and even residential complexes the radio could not be turned off; it was as inescapable as the factory whistle.[6] In apartments, the radio could be turned off, but the apparatus itself had the character of an obligatory listening-post, usually with three programs. Until the advent of transistor receivers, and even for some time afterward, there was no possibility of listening to other stations. The broadcasts ended at midnight with the playing of the Soviet anthem. Of course, there was also Radio Mayak, broadcasting on the medium-wave band, but on the whole radio broadcasting had a compulsory quality.

Cinematography in the USSR underwent a prolonged evolution from the experimental-propagandist school of Vertov, Dovzhenko, and Kuleshov early in the century to a triumphant "golden age" under Stalin. The epoch of totalitarianism began with musicals promising the fulfillment of the Soviet dream and a happy life in general, before moving on during the war to historical epics (*Alexander Nevsky* and *Ivan the Terrible*). Following the war came more complex films like *The Cranes are Flying* and the so-called old cinema films, which to a degree retained the triumphalist note of their prewar counterparts. Passing through heroic-epic, triumphal, and popular phases of development, the cinema approximated the complex worldview of the urban middle layers in the USSR. Its development far outstripped that of Soviet television, not to mention the newspapers, frozen in their monumental forms.

In the second half of the century, books and films purely for entertainment were permitted, while newspapers were not only censored, but served as a tool for the propagation of an ideologized reality to which, in everyday life, radio and television lent formal shape. Radio and television differed little from one another in this respect. In the Soviet media system, television (which fortunately was not interactive as Orwell imagined it) in essence became something like radio with pictures: The same morning exercise drill could now be seen, with a person demonstrating the exercises. After the death of a state leader, just as the radio played symphonic music, the television channels showed ballet programs. Radio plays became television dramas, and so forth. The live picture did, of course, have its strengths—as when the program "International Panorama" showed footage of life in war-torn Lebanon or on the streets of Western cities. In many ways it was television that was responsible for creating the magical aura that surrounded anything foreign. To inhabitants of the USSR, the modern Western urban space seemed enticing and alluring. Compared with the wholesome dullness of Soviet reality, the neon advertising on the streets and the interior of a bar created a sense of danger and adventure—an atmosphere so popular that attempts

Table 1.1

Circulation of Newspapers in Russia

Year	Number of titles	Number of issues	Daily circulation (thousand copies)	Total circulation (thousand copies)	Average daily circulation of a newspaper (thousand copies)
1940	5,730	604,268	25,156	5,094,619	4.4
1960	4,474	585,561	5,629	11,053,327	10.2
1980	4,413	502,822	119,574	29,245,100	27.1
1990	4,808	523,886	165,546	37,848,556	34.4
1998	5,436	395,764	112,483	7,507,715	20.7

Source: Yelena Vartanova, "Media in Post-Soviet Russia: Shifts in Structures and Access to Contents, paper presented at conference" (Singapore: IAMCR conference, 2000).

were often made to counterfeit it. For example, in footage of the Baltic republics filmed to order for television, Riga and Tallinn became show-pieces of "Western life."

Small pleasures also awaited newspaper readers, who sometimes encountered features written in good literary style.[7] Nevertheless, the function of mass "propagandist, agitator, and organizer," which Lenin prescribed for the party press, held sway over the newspaper industry.

Newspapers, in fact, were the most favorable ambient medium for Soviet ideology (see Table 1.1 for details), and every publication that did not break out of this mold grew rigid, turning into its own monument, its clumsy, conventional ideologies recalling the tombs of unknown soldiers and the statues of Lenin with outstretched arm that were scattered across the urban landscape. It is not surprising that conceptualist artists found in newspapers ideal material for their compositions. Shifting the grey newspaper columns was the equivalent of moving slabs of concrete; breaking up the rigid ideological language of the party documents that often occupied more than half of the space in newspapers was tantamount to committing an outrage against the social system. Only falling readership, and the influence throughout the 1990s of changing "central" newspapers (communist, democratic, and later commercial), would put an end to ideological reality, and to the dream of the public sphere at the same time. Along with the epoch of television, the era of the political spectacle had dawned in Russia.

Soviet newspapers, radio, and television were divorced from reality in the same way as, and to a significantly greater degree than, cinematography or the book publishing industry. In the case of radio and television, however, this abyss was somewhat hidden by the fact that, although these media addressed their audience in a didactic tone, individuals ultimately could ignore them and construct their daily lives differently. They might watch only such piquant offerings as "Travelers' Club," "In the World of Animals," or "Connoisseurs' Club," or read an interesting feature or literary essay in an otherwise boring newspaper.

The pages of the newspapers served as the main arena for instilling ideology in mass consciousness both directly and indirectly via the system of local party committees, including the base-level organizations in the enterprises. The real propagandist unit in the Soviet Union was not so much the mass media per se, but the meeting, at which a representative of the party's ideological apparatus was invariably present. Or, if the meeting was too petty and routine, there was someone in attendance who assumed this role. As a rule, this person was the real or informal leader of the collective, or someone who was interested in gaining promotion, to which social activism was considered a sure path. The modern generation of managers, represented by former prime minister Sergei Kirienko, Mikhail Khodorkovsky (from Menatep Bank), and many of the heads of financial-industrial groups, advertising companies, and personnel consultancies, are former members of the Communist Party's youth organization, the Komsomol, who began their careers with such activities.

> Indeed, the Soviet regime was extremely garrulous, and sought to accompany its functioning with a lengthy and strictly hierarchical process of linguistic brainwashing (local committee, trade union committee, pioneer troop, the Komsomol, and party meetings of the class, group, school, college, plant, region, city, province, and republic—a multitude of pyramids where people were required to listen and speak). For all this, however, the real process of regulation proceeded on other, prelinguistic levels (the question of which levels these were is a separate one). If this had not been so, why would the Soviet regime in its last thirty-odd years have existed in a state of schism between (a) what I say at the meeting, and (b) what I really think about everything concerned?[8]

The assimilation of social norms, as this author implies, proceeded internally as people encountered the real possibility of repression that characterized Soviet history right up to its final pages. In the USSR, as in the countries of Eastern Europe within the Soviet protectorate, there was a tank standing behind every monument, even if only figuratively. And just as the internal censor was chased away from people's kitchens, it remained a constant in any public space.

In exactly the same way, journalism too was unthinkable without ideology. The revival that took place as a result of the wave of reporting in the late 1980s ended with one ideology replacing another, allowing the mass media, dazzled by contact with unalloyed reality, once again to "recover its sight" and return to its habitual, ideological mode of operation.

Revolt of the Propagandists

In 1990, pure liberalism appeared as a means to hand by which communist ideology could be vanquished and the CPSU crushed. The radicals seized on it as their main political weapon. Not only were the Democratic Russia movement and its member parties at that time professing their faith in anti-communism and liberalism, so too were the most influential mass media. In the mass social consciousness, which had turned sharply to the right since 1989, the cult of liberal Western civilization and the simultaneous rejection of real socialism reached its high point in 1990.[9]

As glasnost picked up speed, the well-being of Soviet citizens continued to deteriorate. Supported by intense public interest, the politicization of the mass public, and an unprecedented increase in readership, the press—that unconditional ally of the Soviet leader—turned against Gorbachev.

The mass media in the USSR were deeply embedded in the ruling apparatus and conducted business within the framework of the existing social system, whereas the freeing of the press as an ally of Gorbachev gave journalists the chance to take their own positions. At first this contradiction was smoothed over by the unwavering control exercised by the Communist Party, a control expressed through collaboration with the most important media organs in implementing the new policies of the Central Committee leadership, glasnost and perestroika. Examples include the television program "Spotlight on Perestroika" and exposés approved by the general secretary published in the newspaper *Moskovskie Novosti*, edited by Yegor Yakovlev. The most sensational topics were investigations, based on archival materials that touched on "crimes of the CPSU." Again with the sanction of the general secretary, journalists also attacked the party establishment. In principle, the Soviet press already carried out the function of investigating how decisions of the party were being implemented. What was new in this situation was the scale of the changes envisioned by Gorbachev, as a result of which the opportunities for coming out with critical materials were noticeably enhanced.

In time, the control exercised by the party leadership over the press and even television began to slacken. The new policy of democratization significantly reduced the possibilities for the Central Committee and even the general secretary to control the press, because at a certain point it became clear that banning a publication or sacking a journalist (especially a chief editor) was impossible without threatening the party's new political line on democratic change.

In the late 1980s, the concept of the "fourth estate" was becoming increasingly popular in journalistic circles. According to this concept, the press was an independent, self-sufficient social institution, which in parallel with the three branches of power (legislative, executive, and judicial) took part in governing society, including carrying out certain functions in the system of checks and balances. The war in Afghanistan played an especially important role in shaping this ideology. The withdrawal of troops from Afghanistan in 1989 became a source of inspiration for many journalists. The war had been unpopular, of course, but it was considered improper to mention this until journalists took up the topic. Unless one has a grasp of how dependent the press was on the regime before Gorbachev,[10] it is difficult to appreciate the importance of having a representative of the people that was able to force one or another decision from the authorities—the major idea of the "fourth estate." In general, the end of the Afghan war was an important stage in the reevaluation of the Soviet system, aiding as it did in the politicization of the mass public.

For journalists, the importance of the concept of the "fourth estate" was the fact that it helped to lay an ideological foundation beneath the prevailing state of affairs; that is, it helped to legitimate the independent status of the mass media. Also, the concept helped define the new tasks of the media more clearly. To Soviet journalists, however, the idea of the fourth estate had a special meaning. In line with a tradition of the mass media that had deep historical roots, they saw their task not as to inform the public or to come up with a reliable picture of reality, but to enlighten, agitate, and organize in the name of true values and ideals.

At first, this was not especially important. The opening of archives, the appearance in the newspapers of new versions of Soviet history, open discussion of the economic problems of the Soviet system, the emergence of the first radical writers, and the turbulent political scene all helped to foster an unprecedented rise in the authority and popularity of the print media.

Freedom of the press marked the beginning of an intensive spiritual quest, in the course of which society searched for new ideals and values, and journalists for a new doctrine. The result of these quests was a radicalization of views, and the rise of market fundamentalism and a transformationist utopia. The formulation of a new dogma, and its zealous, uncompromising propagation, allowed journalists to lay claim to the position of spiritual leaders of the nation. Ultimately, this led to a significant section of the population being indoctrinated with market fundamentalist teachings.

If television acted in response to the politicization of society, it was in the "democratic" press that this seething mixture, pouring out through city streets in large spontaneous demonstrations, acquired form and content, values and convictions. In other words, the influence of television was powerful, but excessively superficial and irrational, until a new system of meanings, a new ideology, and new definitions of what was good and what was bad, issued forth from the pages of the newspapers.

Television created a crowd, a highly charged, destructive mass constantly at the boiling point in its expectation of new ideas. The press, and through it the intelligentsia (described by the leader of the liberal "Yabloko" party, Grigory Yavlinsky, as the "generation of the eighties"), who considered the "democratic" newspapers their territory, transmitted these ideas in the form of the ideal of capitalism and democracy—a free and abundant society. As the mouthpiece for its hopes, the press chose that fighter-against-privilege Boris Yeltsin, making him its hero and, in return, demanding that he implement the project of reconstructing Russia, forcing him to learn by heart the words market and democracy, and showing that by using these words frequently he would acquire magical power over the masses and would put himself on the road to power.

To these ends, it was essential to "polish" the new political leader and then to closely monitor and direct him, aiding him in the struggle against the foes of the reforms. This was how the "democratic" press saw its task and also how it saw the realization of the concept of the "fourth estate."

Another key task of the press was considered to be educating, and, if necessary, overcoming the resistance of the inert masses who were presumed to be supporters of either the communists or the nationalists. Messianic convictions were characteristic of numerous journalists during those years. In the best traditions of the Russian intelligentsia, Russian journalists did not trust the views of the majority, giving precedence to doctrine over good sense. It is curious that with few exceptions the "democratic" press, just like the Russian intelligentsia, supported the disintegration of the USSR even though an absolute majority of the country's citizens wanted it preserved and voted overwhelmingly for the USSR in the all-union referendum of 1990.

Market Fundamentalism: The "Conspiracy" of the Elites and the Dilettantes

Journalists of the older generation did not take to the role of prophets of the new utopia; after years of working within the framework of the Soviet system, they had become cynics and realists. Consequently, the late 1980s and early 1990s saw a rise in the importance of new writers and of people who exchanged their earlier professions for journalism—in other words, dilettantes.[11] The cornerstone of modern society is professional specialization and expertise, but this vanished from newspaper discussions about the fate of Soviet society and about events abroad. A simple example of the consequences of this absence of professionalism was the popular argument about suburban garden plots, which in the estimate of kitchen gossips (and later, of newspaper commentators) supplied as much as 70 percent of the overall value of agricultural production in the USSR. Largely because of the secrecy that surrounded most information pertaining to the Soviet economy, such theories were not subjected to the test of statistics, and, given the shortage of food, became facts on which convictions were founded.

Soviet journalists of the old school did not, of course, believe the Soviet propaganda about everything, but they did know more about the country's real economy. Where the West was concerned, they at least understood that the official criticism of the Western "cash society" contained a kernel of truth. For others, all these subtleties merged into the "white noise" of Soviet propaganda, which everyone learned to ignore from an early age.

To young dilettantes who had grown up listening to the broadcasts of

Radio Liberty and the BBC and reading samizdat and the novels of Vladimir Voinovich, the whole world looked distinctly different. To this new generation, American cigarettes, French perfume, Western magazines, and household electronics were all weighty proof that communism was unattainable, and that the USSR's path of development led to a dead end. Educated in the Soviet style—with an abundance of ideology and little information—the "generation of the eighties" considered all the achievements of modern civilization to be theirs by right; hence their desire to forget the socialist nightmare as soon as possible and to join in the harmonious international family served as an underlying motive for radicalism.

The attraction of market fundamentalism as a new political ideology lay in the fact that it answered the need of poorly informed people to solve all their problems at once. The "marketeers," it seemed, had no need of knowledge because they knew the main thing—that a market was necessary. The relationship of the "democrats" to democracy was similar. The radicalism of the young economists and commentators blended well with the ambitions of local party leaders and the managers of state enterprises to legalize their political power and managerial prerogatives in the form of independent states and private property; democratic rhetoric, meanwhile, was used by politicians on the make as a battering ram against the Soviet establishment.

In any case, the fact is that the dilettantes, in Vitaly Tretyakov's apt phrase, with one quick stroke outdid the entire old guard. The new generation of journalists was not afraid of the authorities; they wrote and acted according to the code "say whatever's on your mind," and this vital spontaneity was a far better match for the spirit of the age, the pressure of events, and the sea of new information. While journalists of the old school tried to weigh and evaluate everything, the young were saved by their confidence in the facts, by translations of economics and political science textbooks, and by openness to communication. While the "golden pens" of the Soviet epoch were unable to adapt themselves to the new situation, the neophytes soared, reveling in their freedom and observing a brave new world being born from the ashes.

Now that the transformational utopia has collapsed and the Yeltsin era has come to an end, the neophytes have cause for nostalgia. As the depression that followed the crisis of August 1998 brought us closer to uncertainty, it already seemed to many people that the nineties, despite their contradictoriness, harshness, and in some ways even pointlessness, were above all a Russian *belle époque*: a time of passion and opportunity open to all.

The "Fourth Estate"

It is usually supposed that the closeness of the press and those in power in the first half of the 1990s was due to their ideological kinship. In reality, the "fourth estate" (that is, the leading "democratic" publications, which felt themselves to be in the vanguard of the Russian intelligentsia) could not have implemented their conception of reform had they not had political allies, that is, people capable of putting these ideas into practice. As in the case of market fundamentalism, however, there were important mutual interests to be taken into account.

The end of the Soviet epoch brought a very important change to the political system—the process of democratic elections. In the late 1980s, elections for people's deputies saw a redistribution of real political power for the first time in Soviet history. Amid the collapse of the Soviet system, only the mass media could influence the way electors voted. Consequently, it was the media on whom the question of who would rule the country depended.

The question of who ruled the country would in turn decide who owned the mass media. The chief editors and influential journalists were agitated above all by the question of whether their assets would be nationalized by the communists. It is worth recalling that the first secret privatization of the mass media occurred under Gorbachev, when party control over the press first weakened and then evaporated. Various legislative organs, private enterprises, and editorial work collectives became the "founders"—that is, the institutional sponsors—of the editorial offices. If we consider, however, that under the law adopted in 1990 to govern the activity of the media, the rights of founders in relation to editorial offices were strictly regulated (and the concept of "owner" was completely lacking), it will be clear that by that time the editorial offices were already independent. Later, many publications rejected having outside founders altogether, naming instead their editorial offices or work collectives, which under the law could act in this capacity. After the August 1991 putsch, for example, the newspaper *Moskovsky Komsomolets* underwent reregistration with the Russian Press Ministry. Taking advantage of the fact that the newspaper had been registered without its name in quotation marks, as required, the editors reregistered it with quotation marks, thus snatching the newspaper from the demoralized city and provincial committees of the Komsomol. With similar finesse, a large section of the Russian press secured its independence, *Izvestia* from the Supreme Soviet, *Pravda* from the Central Committee of the CPSU, and *Literaturnaya Gazeta* and *Znamya* from the Union of Writers.

At times these changes went through without conflict. For example, the editor of *Moskovskie Novosti*, Yegor Yakovlev, managed to convince the management of the Novosti Press Agency to "release" the weekly. In other cases, the story was quite different; the journalists of the Leningrad newspaper *Smena*, for example, went on a hunger strike, demanding to be set free from their founder, the city committee of the Komsomol. The Russian government intervened in the affair, reregistering the newspaper without a founder. Some publications, such as the magazine *Ogonek*, had to negotiate with their founders. *Ogonek* was forced to pay 30 percent of its profits (and 70 percent of the profits from books it published) to its erstwhile founder, the Pravda publishing combine.

Throughout the final years of the Gorbachev administration and during the first years under Yeltsin, the press was a genuinely independent institution and, in an environment of weak political authority and a chaotic economy, had enormous power. At the height of the economic crisis of 1992, the alliance between the government and the "democratic" mass media (in other words, the old Soviet publications that were supporting Boris Yeltsin) became even closer thanks to the development of a system of subsidies and economic assistance for official publications. When *Trud* and *Komsomolskaya Pravda* were not published for several consecutive days in February 1992, the president signed a decree restoring fixed prices for paper. The state took responsibility for reimbursing part of the production costs of publications with particularly large printruns (the choice of these was up to the Ministry of the Press and Mass Information). In addition (and this was the only "market" position taken by the decree), orders were issued to begin the process of privatizing the distribution network for print publications. As Elena Androunas writes:

> The reaction of the press to the decree was far from being universally enthusiastic. On the whole, traditional publications such as *Komsomolskaya Pravda* and *Izvestia* were satisfied, although it was not hard to detect a certain embarrassment in their commentaries on the decree.

The independent press, naturally, criticized it. For the press, the decree acted as a kind of test: What price was it ready to pay for freedom—or for survival? It seemed that economic realities, rather than political differences, would be the feature distinguishing the genuinely independent press from publications that agreed to be controlled.

This difference had already become obvious. While *Izvestia* wrote about the "jealous rage of the commercial press," *Nezavisimaya Gazeta* criticized the "official press" that was obstinately pumping money out of the budget. *Nezavisimaya Gazeta* termed the decree "the result of hysterical lobbying" by the official mass newspapers and magazines. It seems that the use of populist pressure developed during the years of "early glasnost"—when newspapers achieved astronomical readerships because of low prices and then obtained subsidies from the budget, blackmailing the authorities with their "millions of subscribers"—has again proven effective.[12]

Immediately after the decree was signed, the most prominent newspaper editors met with press minister Mikhail Poltoranin to discuss how it would be implemented. It is significant that in the report by *Izvestia* on this historic meeting (the article was titled "The 'Fourth Estate' Should Rule"), particular attention was devoted to showing that the press could be financed by the government and be independent of it at the same time. The importance of this problem, according to *Izvestia*, lay in the fact that during the transition period the press had lost its material independence, but did not want to part with its moral independence, while the representatives of the authorities were not always ready to understand and accept that for the press, it was "natural to criticize the government, even though the government found money for the press."[13]

These complaints by the newspaper sound like the next generation of propaganda. Under the communists, the press pretended that it was free of ideological pressure. Now it pretends that it can be free of pressure from the government while being supported by government subsidies.

As *Izvestia* relates, during the meeting with Poltoranin the chief editors managed to "arrive at a single point of view not only on tactical but also on strategic questions." The fact that they have common problems "allowed them to formulate a common policy with the three other institutions of power—the legislative, the executive, and the judicial."

In the view of *Izvestia* correspondent Irina Demchenko, this agreement means that if the mass media chiefs do not yet consider themselves a "fourth estate," they are undoubtedly moving in this direction.[14]

It was not only the journalists for *Izvestia* who had it wrong. Curiously, Yelena Androunas concluded a chapter of her 1993 book as follows:

> Will the press be able to survive in a democratic society, based on a market economy, when it has such an unnatural conception of the "fourth estate"? The question is a rhetorical one. The mass media did a good deal to help bring down the communist system. Now that the system has collapsed, the media are trying to perpetuate their existence, but nothing is working for them. They are simply a part of the old system, and they are doomed to disappear along with it. They will survive just as long as the post-communist governments consider it necessary to keep them alive with injections of cash.[15]

As was later made apparent, there were more than enough people who wanted to finance these publications even without direct government intervention. Given a choice between the ideals of democracy and support for Boris Yeltsin (and the politicians loyal to him), the "democratic press," time after time (in October 1993, and in the elections of 1995 and 1996) ultimately favored the latter.

The concept of the "fourth estate" was dead even before real economic difficulties made it unviable. Its demise was not the result of political pressure, which the newspapers condemn even today. The concept was stillborn; while still in its Soviet womb, it was killed by the terror that the new owners of the mass media felt at the prospect of a review by a future communist government of the semilegal privatization of publications. This terror turned out to be even stronger than the fear of losing the exalted, independent status of the press and its freedom to choose its political position.

It would be unjust to see the role of journalists in Russia's recent history as only the revolt of a privatized propaganda machine that, freed from Communist Party control and reinforcing its claims to independence through the concept of the "fourth estate," joined with the new Russian leadership in dealing the final blow to its decrepit master. To limit oneself to this generalization would be to throw the baby out with the bathwater, to fail to appreciate the astonishing atmosphere of those years, when Soviet society came close to the ideal of the "public space," and the journalists who were engaged in a real quest. They were seeking not dogma, not the idea of a "fourth estate," but the realization of an independent press. We will discuss this further in Chapter 2.

Formation of the Russian Media System

Brian McNair distinguishes three phases in the development of the Russian mass media.[16] The first lasted from 1986 to 1990, culminating in the adoption of the Law of the USSR on the Mass Media. The next period, which he describes as the "golden age of the Russian press," continued until the August 1991 putsch. Then, after the events of August 1991, a new phase in the evolution of a media market began. During this phase, economic difficulties forced all publications to raise their prices, and the collapse of the USSR further narrowed the market for the press.

Yassen Zassoursky and Yegor Yakovlev concur on a different periodization, although each defines the phases somewhat differently. The period from 1985 to 1990 was that of glasnost, when the party still controlled the mass media, albeit in accordance with Gorbachev's new course of democratizing Soviet society. Later, until some time between 1993 and 1995, the press played the role of an independent institution. Yassen Zassoursky sees this period as culminating with the campaign against the war in Chechnya, which demonstrated the ability of the press to put pressure on the government. Then began a period defined by Zassoursky as one of "ownership concentration," and by Yakovlev as "rule of the press by capital." Table 1.2 divides the history of the years examined in the present study (from the late 1980s through 2000) into five periods. The most eventful of them is the third, from 1992 to 1996; this period in turn can be divided into three stages. More attention is devoted to this period, since it was during this time that the system of mass media of the Yeltsin era became established.

With the help of this detailed periodization, we shall first outline the history of the Russian media, after which we shall focus on the turning points, which we shall examine in detail.

The first period, until 1990 and the adoption of the law on the press, was the time of glasnost, perestroika, and the end of the war in Afghanistan. In principle, there was no independent press during this time except for *samizdat*, but among Soviet journalists the ideology of the "fourth estate" and the myth of an independent press were crystallizing. Periodicals were at the high point of their popularity, with the growth in their readership reaching its peak. The first live programs, "Viewpoint" and others, were appearing on television. This period represents the prehistory of the Russian media system, and a brief sketch of it has already been provided earlier in this chapter.

Table 1.2

The Media-Political History of Russia Since 1970

	1970–1985	1986–1990	1991–1995	1996–2000	2000–?
Political system	USSR, Inc.–unified management. One power center.	Shifting and shaking. Democratic reforms coincide with "dry" law and tobacco shortages.	No system. Struggle. Complete decentralization. Strong opposition.	Mediated, strong regional leaders; media holdings function as political parties. Elected monarchy.	Centralized system based on law enforcement agencies and army. Weak opposition. Political system emerges.
State of economy	Planned, highly structured, hierarchical, rigid. Strong black market and industrial lobbies.	Shifting–disintegrating. Rise in production coincides with consumer goods shortage.	Trade capital boom, industrial crisis (monopolies dominate). Capital-accumulation stage.	State and private monopolies, often both. Boom in telecoms. Bank crisis, industrial growth.	Economic growth projected, monopolies intact.
War consciousness	Great Patriotic War, expeditions abroad (Asia, Africa, Afghanistan).	Afghan war	Two coups d'état in Moscow. First Chechen war	Information wars, second Chechen war	War on terrorism and drugs
A widely shared social dream	Welfare consumer society, or "capitalism"	Public sphere + the West	Welfare state	Law and order	Great Russia

Media system type	Propaganda machine	Glasnost-oriented propaganda machine	"Fourth power," independent media	Media-political system, society of the spectacle	Instrumental media model, ("Social responsibility" concept is introduced)
Media system structure	Newspaper-based, radio very important, state-controlled TV (3 channels)	Newspaper-based, stronger TV, strong radio	Transforming: printed press in decline, broadcasting on the rise (TV and FM radio)	Media-political system in the commercial media environment	State-controlled media system in the commercial media environment vs. the Internet
Bias and means of control	Strong ideology, rituals. Direct control, propaganda, manipulation, repression.	Ideology. Soft persuasion, alliance with power.	Ideology, soft persuasion, alliance with power.	Strong manipulation using the laws of drama	Strict control by the press ministry over TV licenses and advertising
The role of journalists	Instrumental	Important, especially in the printed press	Extremely important	Almost completely instrumental	Defined in professional terms
Interest in politics among the people	Weak	Increasing	Strong	Decreasing	Sporadic
Ideology	Communist-imperialist, evidently false but pervasive. Stable	Democratization, socialist reforms. Optimistic.	Market fundamentalism, democratic reforms, anti-communism. Utopia	No coherent belief system. Symbolic space is built around dramatic conflicts.	Emerging national identity (strong state + capitalism) vs. flexible identities

(continued)

Table 2.1 (continued)

	1970–1985	1986–1990	1991–1995	1996–2000	2000–?
Social reality	Highly organized, based on a highly developed system of rituals and social institutions.	Shifting, transforming	Chaotic, disintegrating with islands of growth	Fragmented according to new social stratification. Uncertain	Structured in the hierarchy of signs, supported by war, rituals, and strong leader vs. different social realities
Change	Totally new media system built from scratch and perfected over the years	Video boom. Unprecedented increase in print press circulation, first live broadcasts of political events and news shows on TV. Politicization of the masses	Registered independently of their owners, the media become independent. Printing press is losing circulation due to high prices on paper and delivery	Sophisticated manipulative techniques are introduced. Media are used in info wars and profoundly discredited. Satellite TV and Internet are introduced	While state becomes the dominating power center, the control over symbolic reality becomes almost complete. Internet enters rapid growth
Means of control	Party and Soviet social institutions	Party and Soviet social institutions, unifying reform policy.	Fear return of Communists, subsidies, press law	Politicized capital invested through media holdings, media owners	The new power system built around law enforcement agencies, press law. SORM2 for the Internet

Leaders	*Pravda, Izvestia* newspapers, Radio 1 and Radio "Mayak". Strong state-controlled publishing and film industry	*Moskovskie Novosti, Ogonyok,* literary and intellectual almanacs. Radio "Liberty"	*Izvestia, Moskovsky Komsomolets, Nezavisimaya Gazeta. Kommersant,* Russian TV (2nd channel), NTV (4th channel)	Public Russian Television (ORT, 1st channel), NTV (4th channel), FM radio, elite press (*Kommersant* publications), magazines *Cosmopolitan* etc. Emerging film industry	ORT (1st channel), entertainment TV, FM radio, mass newspapers (*Komsomolskaya Pravda, Izvestia*), commercial magazines, film industry. On-line newspapers and communities, entertainment
Opposition	*Samizdat,* oral speech (anecdotes), Russian-language radio stations and newspapers based abroad.	Radical *samizdat* & conservative communists (*Sovetskaya Rossiya* daily, etc.)	Communist newspapers (*Pravda, Sovetskaya Rossiya*), nationalist publication (*Den*)	Communist, nationalist and alternative media ("Trava i volya," "Radek")	Alternative press and emerging Internet counter-culture. The party press, private communications, new social movements

The second period, from 1990 until early 1992, was the "golden age" of the Russian press. This was also the period of the "first privatization" of the mass media. With the assistance of the government, some publications received the premises where their editorial offices were located as their own property, or received long-term leases at favorable rents. Relations between the government and the press entered a honeymoon period, except in the case of a few ultraconservative publications. Sharing in and reflecting the public enthusiasm of the reformist eighties and nineties, the mass media became natural allies of the rising star of Russian politics, Boris Yeltsin. Amid the unceasing political struggle and the collapse of every traditional social institution, the mass media in the early 1990s essentially retained the status they had acquired in the late 1980s: that of the regime's sole basis of support.

New publications, television channels, and radio stations appeared in the Russian media market. These new media made use of the models and formats of contemporary Western journalism. An effort was made to keep information separate from commentary. Newspapers were designed around the principle of thematic sections. Live broadcasts became the norm on radio and television.

The third period, from 1992 to 1996, is that of the formation of the new Russian media system. It can be divided into three stages. The first, covering 1992 and 1993, was a time of political resistance and of the first economic difficulties faced by the media. Then, in 1994 and the first half of 1995, came a temporary political stabilization. It was characterized on the one hand by an outflow of politicized capital and by the consequent closure of a number of publications, and on the other hand by rapid development of the commercial press. The final stage, from mid-1995 to mid-1996, saw the activation of politicized capital and the formation of a propaganda system prior to the 1996 presidential elections. This period needs to be dwelled upon in more detail.

At the very beginning of 1992, a clear difference appeared for the first time in the development of the central and regional press, a difference that was to grow stronger over time. The press in the capital was splitting into three camps, consisting of "democratic" (*Izvestia, Komsomolskaya Pravda*, and *Moskovsky Komsomolets*), "oppositional" (*Pravda* and *Sovetskaya Rossiya*), and new publications (*Nezavisimaya Gazeta* and *Kommersant*).

The speaker of the Russian Supreme Soviet, Ruslan Khasbulatov, tried unsuccessfully to take control of *Izvestia* and Russian state television. Deliberately or otherwise, Khasbulatov's actions made all journalists worry about the fate of their own publications and aided the politicization of the journalistic community. The regional press, except for the communist and nationalist publications, kept its distance from politics, occupying the position of spectator rather than participant in political battles.

By the end of 1992, even the most solid publications were taking big losses, from 15 million rubles in the case of *Komsomolskaya Pravda* to 6 million by *Sovetskaya Rossiya*. They were able to keep publishing thanks to the government subsidies that paid their debts. The newspaper *Izvestia* also received a huge building on Pushkin Square as a present from the Gaidar government, allowing it to retain its independence longer than the other newspapers. All the same, the results of the 1993 subscription campaign showed that *Izvestia* retained only 25 percent of its subscribers (800,000 of 3.2 million); *Komsomolskaya Pravda* less than 15 percent (1.8 million of 13 million); *Nezavisimaya Gazeta* slightly less than 39 percent (27,000 of 70,000); and the weekly *Argumenty i Fakty* less than 35 percent (8.8 million of 25.7 million).[17]

Under the dictate of the postal service monopoly, the cost of delivering newspapers was rising, and as a result the regional publications came to stand more firmly on their feet. The closeness of the provincial press to readers' real problems and needs, which were incompatible with the abstract political rhetoric of those years, began to make its effects felt. The plummeting of the print runs of the central newspapers led to a fragmentation in the readership of all-Russian publications and a change in their status and role. Beginning with the third period, the unity of the information space was provided solely by television.

In late 1992 and early 1993 when many newspapers and journals were on the verge of financial catastrophe, the Moscow market for quality politicized publications saw the simultaneous appearance of three new daily newspapers—*Kommersant Daily*, *Segodnya*, and *Novaya Yezhednevnaya Gazeta*. Of those three only *Kommersant Daily* is still in operation. *Segodnya*, the first media enterprise of Vladimir Gusinsky, was closed down after the fall of this media empire. *Novaya Yezhednevnaya Gazeta* is still in business as a political alternative, but now it is published weekly.

The political crisis of 1993 reached its peak with the October clash of the executive and legislative branches of power. As the historian Sogrin observes, the president managed to win the March 1993 referendum on support for his administration only thanks to the fact that he was able to conduct a broader and more intensive propaganda campaign in the press than was the opposition. The same could be said of the October 1993 events in Moscow.

To the very last, the basis of the parliamentary crisis that continued from late 1992 through October 1993 was the quite legitimate dislike expressed by the deputies for the government's economic policies. Nevertheless, the "democratic" press supported the president, and state television remained under Yeltsin's control. Vice-President Aleksandr Rutskoi, who supported the parliament's position, was propelled, by awareness of his powerlessness, to orchestrate the storming of the Ostankino television complex, which marked the beginning of the bloody denouement of the parliamentary crisis of October 1993. The outcome was the adoption, during the new general elections in December that year, of a constitution that consolidated the dominant position of the president in the power structure of Russia's "Second Republic." In the process, the possibility of such crises occurring in the future was eliminated—at the cost of a substantially diminished role for the legislature and increased powers for the president.[18]

The October events had an unexpectedly powerful impact on the mass media, largely destroying any illusions held by journalists in the new regime. When the authorities smelled gunpowder, they effectively followed the example of the plotters of 1991, shutting down large numbers of newspapers and introducing censorship.

On October 14, 1993, by decision of the Ministry of the Press and Mass Information, the following publications were officially suppressed for printing materials which "significantly increased the destabilization of the situation during the mass disorders in Moscow": *Den* (which resumed publication under the new name *Zavtra*); *Glasnost*; *Narodnaya Pravda*; *Za Rus*; *Nash Marsh*; *Natsionalist*; *Russkoe Delo*; *Russkoe Voskresenye*; *Russkie Vedomosti*; *Russky Puls*; *Russky Poryadok*; *Russkoe Slovo*; *Moskovsky Traktor*; *Russky Soyuz*; and *K Toporu*.

Criminal prosecutions were launched against them, and also against the St. Petersburg television news program *600 Sekund* (600 Seconds). Publication of *Rabochaya Tribuna*, *Pravda*, and *Sovetskaya Rossiya* was suspended. *Rabochaya Tribuna* resumed publication after three days. The Ministry of Press and Mass Information took a quite different attitude to the other two newspapers, establishing conditions for their reappearance that reportedly included name changes, reregistration, and the replacement of the chief editors. *Pravda* nevertheless reappeared on November 2, 1993, following a compromise with the ministry, but again failed to publish due to financial problems. It next appeared only on December 10, 1993, two days before the elections.

Nezavisimaya Gazeta, forced to undergo reregistration after the dissolution of its founder, the Moscow City Soviet, ran into problems in the process, because the editorial board rejected two candidates proposed for the status of founder from higher up. On November 4, 1993, in accordance with the law on the Russian mass media, the editorial board itself became the founder.

Control over the parliament's newspaper *Rossiyskaya Gazeta*, and its television channel RTV, passed into the hands of the government. Censors appeared at a number of newspapers, at the news agency ITAR-TASS, and in television studios. The following publications experienced problems with censorship of their materials: *Nezavisimaya Gazeta, Segodnya, Moskovskaya Pravda, Kommersant Daily*, and *Literaturnaya Gazeta*.[19]

The next stage of the third period, from late 1993 to mid-1995, was marked by a degree of political stabilization. This occurred while industrial output continued to fall to a level that in 1994 was only about half that of 1990. For all practical purposes, the media market ceased to expand; readership of most publications continued to decline, though a few publishing companies managed to turn themselves around. In particular, the market for business publications was flourishing, and the first "glossy" magazines, financed by advertising and meant for purchasers with high incomes, made their appearance. The period also saw the rapid development of the *Kommersant* publishing house, which launched projects for new publications one after another; the Independent Media group; and the *Segodnya-KP* holding company.

The process of strengthening the mass media was beginning, and the first information magnates were consolidating their strategic hold on the market. The key figures were Vladimir Gusinsky with his Most group, and Vladimir Yakovlev with his *Kommersant* publishing house. At that time, the war in Chechnya was affording the press an opportunity to take an independent position, even if it diverged from the policies of the regime (provided, of course, that it did not contradict the interests of the media owners). On the eve of the presidential elections, however, the antiwar position of the media seemed like the last call of Roland.

The final stage in this period, from mid-1995 until mid-1996, was distinguished by the return of politicized capital, brought back to life by the closeness of the parliamentary elections, after which the fateful presidential elections now loomed. The start of this period can be dated from the founding of ORT, the story of which begins in February–March 1995. (For political reasons, the formation of ORT occurred expeditiously, to ensure that the real state of affairs surrounding the first television channel as a joint-stock company was obscured.) Vladislav Listyev became the initiator and the victim of the process through which the spheres of influence in the television advertising market were redistributed. The founding of ORT marks the beginning of the history of Boris Berezovsky's media holding company, which was formed as a result of the mandate given by the president's family for the creation of a favorable news environment for the presidential elections. In order for Berezovsky to carry out this task, he was given the oil company Sibneft as a cash cow.

On the eve of the elections, a torrent of politicized capital once again began pouring into the mass media. The new holding companies simultaneously expressed the interests of the new owners in seeing the situation in the country stabilized and provided the party of the authorities with channels for communication, in exchange for their tolerating the distribution of state property that was occurring in the course of privatization. On both counts, the decision by the new owners to invest their stake in the mass media was strategically justified.

During the presidential election campaign, the main media outlets were almost unanimous in their support of Boris Yeltsin and became willing tools for orchestrating public opinion. In line with the scenarios worked out by the president's campaign ideologues, state-of-the-art propaganda techniques were employed. The media owners went through a process of learning the latest methods for swaying votes.

The fourth period in the history of the Russian press began after the 1996 presidential election and lasted until mid-1998. Prior to the elections, the role of the mass media in determining the outcome of political conflicts had been significant; now, on the basis of the results of the presidential campaign, this role was universally recognized as decisive. The mass media were becoming the principal means of political communication. At the same time, the role of the press was declining in importance, while that of television was at its peak. News and analysis programs on television were becoming the arena for the political spec-tacle.[20] Politics and the mass media were becoming totally intertwined, making it possible to speak of the formation of a media-political system.

The control of social life by the media was a natural development in a society without social institutions and can be traced from Yeltsin's first deliberate efforts to use television to enhance his popularity. Yeltsin's entire political career had been built on use of the media, as opposed to party and Soviet institutions. The 1993 referendum concern-ing confidence in the president was won in exactly the same fashion, with powerful support from the mass media, and so was the vote on the constitution. In the struggle for power, the events of October 1993, were the last to occur in an urban setting. This struggle continued until the end of the 1990s, but the setting in which it was fought was not institu-tional or legislative so much as symbolic. The intensity of the struggle was no less for that; it was simply that the role that might have been played by tanks was assumed by the media holding companies. Instead of people dying in this undeclared war, the victims were reputations, images, political careers, political scenarios, and symbolic constructs of all kinds.

The takeover of politics by the media in the second half of the 1990s was different from the politicization of the mass media begun at the start of the decade, because now the role of the media in the information system ceased to be independent. The mass media became a channel of communication for politicians and specialists in information techniques who used the predictability of the media (which in the case of politi-cized media organs flowed from their ownership by one or another hold-ing company, and in the case of the commercial mass media from their adherence to particular standards) in order to get their messages across. The various strategies of the media players developed and came into conflict on a symbolic stage, unfolding like a drama. The structure and logic of the political spectacle was becoming a decisive factor in the area of politics.

Impressed by the effectiveness of the media techniques used in the presidential election campaigns, powerful business groups entered into an "information arms race." Large-scale investments were made in the mass media, leading to the emergence of additional big media groups formed through takeovers of "democratic" publications such as *Literaturnaya Gazeta*, *Izvestia*, and *Komsomolskaya Pravda*, all of which had managed to retain their independence until that time. During 1997, these three publications became part of large holding companies. The political investors launched new media projects, in particular, "influence newspapers" such as *Russky Telegraf*, owned by OneksimBank, and the Luzhkov holding company's *Rossiya*. (Both newspapers were later closed when the holding companies decided to put their resources behind other publications, *Izvestia* and *Literaturnaya Gazeta*, respectively.)

It is difficult to draw the line between political investments and the new economic strategy of the large business groups. When the foreign-owned Independent Media Group sold a 10 percent share to Menatep Bank, this was most likely an ordinary investment, though in private conversations, employees of the *Moscow Times* newspaper later complained of the pressure exerted by their Russian partners. In this case, it appears, what was involved was a particular style of treating media property; the cynicism of the 1990s did not allow for the possibility of real editorial independence even in the most commercially sound publications.

Once perfected, the system of running the press with the help of media experts, compromising materials, and information campaigns figured not merely as a basic tool in political conflicts, but as a weapon in competitive struggles. In essence, the interests of the immediate owners of the mass media became the political positions of their publications; this was especially obvious during the privatization scandals, when the new owners first violated their unspoken pledge of partnership with the "young reformers" and with one another.

During the spring and summer of 1998, when miners' struggles were followed by financial and political crises, many observers saw the role of the mass media in the country's political life as that of provocateur. Those in power waged one media campaign after another. It was obvious that the earlier alliance between the Yeltsin regime and the media owners had disintegrated. The founding of a unified television and radio holding company based on the All-Russian State Television and Radio Company, or VGTRK, at first seemed less like a dangerous attempt by the state to usurp the mass media than a desperate effort by government officials to retain a presence in the information space.

A few publications, such as *Moskovsky Komsomolets*, *Argumenty i Fakty*, and those of the *Kommersant* publishing house, managed to keep their independence, while an increasingly significant number of entities, including the *Ekonomicheskaya Gazeta* publishing house, the publications of Independent Media Group, the television channels REN-TV,

CTC, and others operated quite outside the context of political life. The Russian press was thus divided into the sphere of influence of politicized capital in control of the most influential central newspapers and television channels, and the sphere of the commercial mass media. Along with central and regional publishing groups, this latter sphere included new television projects and regional television channels as well as large numbers of radio stations. During this stage, the logic of politicized and commercial capital in the mass media was diverging. If the purpose of politicized capital was to capture the greatest audience, commercial capital aimed at making profits, and as a result was decentralized. The commercial media often ignored the political context, since concentrating on meeting particular audience demands attracted advertisers and made it possible to hold an audience, which even if small, was constant, and often had a high average income.

In fairness, it should be noted that the commercial press also took one side or another in the information wars. The fondness of the mass-circulation commercial press for scandals and sensations made publishing exposés and exaggerating scandals a favorite negative promotional strategy. Of course, the commercial press seemed superior due to the fact that at times it was hard to predict whose side it would take. As a rule, all sides in any information conflict called for defending national interests, obeying the law, and preserving stability.

One characteristic of this period was a heightened effort by the Moscow newspapers and television companies to penetrate regional markets. This was supported to a large degree by politicized investments prompted by the need to form new propaganda systems in the period preceding the parliamentary elections of 1999 and the presidential elections of 2000.

The month of August 1998 forms a clear boundary between the processes that had been unfolding in Russia over the previous eight years and subsequent events. For Russia of the Yeltsin era, it was the beginning of the end, and for us it marks the beginning of *the fifth period* of media political history.

The debt crisis hurt the incipient rise of the commercial mass media most of all. With the number of new projects launched, the summer of 1998 had been a turning point for them. As a result of the prevailing uncertainty, all the new projects were shut down, and additional investments in existing mass media were frozen.

The financial crisis became a political one as well when the Kirienko government was sacked, and the lower house of parliament refused to endorse Viktor Chernomyrdin, nominated by Yeltsin for the job of prime minister. Former foreign minister and head of the Foreign Intelligence Service Yevgeny Primakov became prime minister as a result.

An important difference between the new epoch and the preceding one was the more prominent role played by the state in the media system, although for the sake of fairness it should be noted that the process of concentrating control of information flows in the hands of the executive powers had a long history. To be precise, the state during the new stage no longer relied on the large holding companies of politicized capital but on its own state media organs. A powerful government, supported by a parliamentary majority, was in open conflict with large financial groups that had been weakened by the crisis, although many of them controlled influential media organs with large audiences. Unless the government had essential media backing, it could not depend on the success of its policies, especially since the closeness of the presidential elections caused these conflicts to become extremely acute.

The situation was also complicated by the fact that Yevgeny Primakov, unlike his predecessors, was an independent political figure. This made his sacking inevitable once Yeltsin began looking seriously for a "successor," but also prompted the rise of an alternative party of government officials in the 1999 parliamentary elections. In these elections, the Kremlin group was confronted with an alliance of Primakov, Moscow mayor Yury Luzhkov, and a number of regional leaders who together formed the powerful electoral bloc Fatherland–All Russia.

For its propaganda backing, this bloc relied on a powerful media group controlled by Yury Luzhkov and his partners from the company AFK Sistema, as well as on regional newspapers and television channels, which in most cases had always been controlled more or less by the provincial administrations. The 1999 elections turned into a veritable brawl in which the various sides swapped media blows, and in which the Kremlin's control of state television acted as the decisive instrument for crushing the Primakov-Luzhkov bloc. Along with the mass media, a vital role in the elections was played by "administrative resources"—the use of powerful levers to exert direct pressure on voters at the local level, both via the directors of large enterprises and via aid to regional newspapers and factory newspapers, which as a rule were controlled by local authorities. The influence of these local and regional publications far exceeded that of the central newspapers and was comparable to that of the first television channel, ORT.

The election victory of the Unity bloc, formed hastily by the Kremlin administration, turned out to be crushing. Yeltsin's resignation and the early elections made victory for his protégé Vladimir Putin so completely inevitable that Primakov even refused to run against Putin, thus crowning the Kremlin's triumph.

Once elected president, Putin began a vigorous reform of the ruling apparatus, the aim of which was centralization of the administration and "perestroika" of the media-political system. Right before the eyes of the public, the pendulum of history was again gathering speed, and soon we found ourselves on the threshold of a new transformation of Russia's symbolic image. The hopes and dreams of the rebellious nineties were somehow transformed into the image of "Great Russia" once again coming together to meet challenges and combat enemies at home and abroad. The main difference between the new system and the preceding one was the monopolization of control over television, the node of the national information space. The pressure by the government, exerted via threats to cancel licenses or to begin criminal prosecutions, proved able without particular difficulty to bring the media-political system under control. Yet this monopolization coincided with the fragmentation of the media audience and the rise of the Internet, whose significance for the communications system has so far been difficult to assess.

Only two things can be said in relation to the present situation. In the first place, the Internet has already made definite advances in the information system, and its role is continuing to grow. Second, the Internet is far less subject to control than the traditional mass media, and does not have as high an entry barrier. The Internet is a complex phenomenon and it demands special treatment. Later, we shall have the opportunity to examine this question in more detail.

The Case of *Nezavisimaya Gazeta*

After the adoption in 1990 of the Soviet law on the mass information media, the legal operation of private media outlets, functioning outside the Soviet propaganda system, was permitted for the first time. The most important new organs were the radio station Ekho Moskvy, the newspaper *Nezavisimaya Gazeta* (*NG*), the weekly *Kommersant*, and the magazine *Stolitsa*.

These organs were all independent and extremely radical. The difference between them was that Ekho Moskvy and *Stolitsa* subsequently retained their radical-democratic enthusiasm (in the case of *Stolitsa*, this lasted until the magazine was bought by the *Kommersant* publishing house). The newspapers *NG* and *Kommersant*, meanwhile, continued to evolve gradually; each of them took its own direction, and, from the standpoint of independent journalism, often opposed the positions taken by the "democratic media."

The Independent Newspaper

Let us focus for the moment on *Nezavisimaya Gazeta*. It would be hard to find a clearer illustration of the way in which the Russian system of mass communications was transformed and of the contradictory role that journalists and newspaper staffs played in this process, than the advances and setbacks experienced by this Moscow daily. Behind the setbacks, in particular, lies the dramatic history of the Russian idealism of the 1990s.

The history of *NG* resembles a scientific experiment; it is as though the hypothesis that a genuinely independent press can exist in Russia had been put to the test. The results of this experiment are not encouraging, but at least we have gained an idea of the various possibilities. Besides teaching us about the markets for news and advertising, the case of

Nezavisimaya Gazeta reveals the existence of another market—the market of influence. Under the "Second Republic," as Yeltsin-era Russia came to be known, success in this market became decisive in determining the fate of newspapers in the Russian capital.

Throughout the history of *Nezavisimaya Gazeta* (until it was swallowed by Berezovsky), the lack of a firm financial base meant that the newspaper swung around like a weathervane indicating the direction in which the political and economic situation in the country was headed. This means that the example of *NG* can now be used to provide a periodization of the entire process through which the Russian media system came into being.

Where the Idea for Nezavisimaya Gazeta Came From

Although *NG* did not have the characteristics of a mass-circulation publication, it was initially in heavy demand. The reason perhaps was that it managed better than other newspapers to embody the mood of optimistic politicization of the early 1990s. It would have been hard to pick a better time to launch a new newspaper; the USSR in 1990 was at the peak of a reading boom that heralded the revolution of 1991. Journalists joked among themselves that if someone were to type at random and publish the result in a print run of 50,000 copies, the edition would probably sell out. The first issue of *NG* had a press run of 150,000 copies.

The epoch when *NG* arose was that of the flowering of glasnost, and also that of the first de facto privatization of the print media. This period, described earlier, was marked by a certain perception by the press of the concept of the "fourth estate." According to this concept, the press had an important and independent role in the life of society, and quality journalism thus took precedence over its commercial and mass-circulation counterparts.

The ideal of *NG* did not coincide entirely with that of the fourth estate. It could be described more accurately as involving a shift in other reference points—above all, a shift toward the popular conception of what a quality newspaper ought to be, the principles it should uphold, and the role it was called upon to play in society. In a secondary sense, the ideal of *NG* involved a direct appeal to the publications that best embodied these ideas and that clearly served as a source of inspiration for the founders of *NG*—the newspapers *Le Monde* and the *Independent* (*Nezasimaya Gazeta* means Independent Newspaper).

As the precursor of the modern quality press and as a source of ideas about what constitutes a good newspaper, scholars turn to the elite press of the second half of the nineteenth century. Denis McQuail sees the quality newspaper as the most reputable element in the history of the press and as a high point—even a turning point—in the development of print media. He defines the characteristics of the quality newspapers of the late nineteenth century compared with earlier newspapers and with the commercial publications that appeared later as follows:

> formal independence from the state and from other institutions pursuing their own goals; recognition of the crucial role of newspapers in the political and social life of the community; a highly developed sense of social and ethical responsibility; the rise of the profession of journalism, by which is understood reportage—the providing of objective information; at the same time, a consciousness of [the newspaper's] role in creating and shaping opinions; often, a striving to identify itself with national interests. Many modern concepts of what constitutes a "good" or "elite" newspaper reflect some of the ideas listed above, ideas which also serve as the basis for criticism of forms of the press which diverge from the ideal in the direction of excessive partisanship or sensationalism.[1]

The cornerstones on which *Nezavisimaya Gazeta* was founded can be defined more or less as follows: resistance to the ossified Soviet journalistic style; a name borrowed in part from the London intellectual daily the *Independent*; the highbrow tone of *Le Monde*; and a distancing from the concept of the "fourth estate."

There is nothing astonishing about the fact that in the process of producing a newspaper *NG*'s chief editor Vitaly Tretyakov strove to fulfill an ideal. Nor is it surprising that as a man gifted with outstanding creative talents, but little commercial sense, Tretyakov pursued his ideal of a newspaper rather than the ideal of a flourishing commercial enterprise. It should also be said that if his work is regarded as an effort to attain the results suggested above, he achieved a great deal—perhaps all—of what he might have accomplished. Gathering money from friends and acquaintances among the "creative intelligentsia," Tretyakov did in fact establish a reputable independent newspaper in the Russia of the late twentieth century and continued to put it out for almost four and a half years.

From Tretyakov's editorial in the first issue of the newspaper, we can gain an idea of how the chief editor of *NG* saw the tasks that faced his publication.

1. Full information.
   "Unfortunately," he wrote, "we in the Soviet Union have not until now had a single national newspaper that has given us full—that is, thorough, without any deletions [in material] concerning various events or individuals—information about what is happening in our own country." Clearly, he envisaged *NG* as filling this role.
2. Free commentary and the presentation of all points of view.
   "All points of view are reflected on the pages of Soviet publications, and all opinions are present. This of course is correct, but one important clarification is needed: in order to discover the different points of view on a particular event, it is necessary to read various newspapers. *NG* plans to publish different opinions about a topic on its pages, not under a special heading, not as an exception, but as a matter of course, that is, constantly."
3. "No" to editorials with a "united opinion."
   "A newspaper is obliged—and *NG* will strive to do this—to present first and foremost the views of eyewitnesses and experts. In any but exceptional cases, however, it should not declare that there is any common view shared by the editorial staff as a whole."
4. Independence, and not only from those in power.
   "Independence merely from the official authorities is not independence at all, but merely an oppositional stance. Real independence is independence from the opposition as well."

It is this last point that most starkly reveals the difference between Tretyakov's views and those of supporters of the "fourth estate" concept. Unlike Tretyakov, the editors and staffers of the "democratic" newspapers saw themselves as part of the establishment; this was confirmed after the opposition in the USSR became the regime in Russia.

Not surprisingly, the chief editor of *NG* was viewed by his counterparts at the major traditional newspapers (*Izvestia*, *Komsomolskaya Pravda*, and *Moskovsky Komsomolets*) as an upstart, an *enfant terrible*. This was why none of the "big brothers" regarded the clinical death of *NG* in 1995 as a tragedy. Later, when one after another they shared the same fate, it came as an enormous surprise to the editors and journalists.

It seemed to Tretyakov that there were grounds for hoping that *NG* would succeed; after all, the structure of the newspaper had been copied from *Le Monde* and the *Independent*. The path traversed by these "model" newspapers, however, had been a rocky one.

Foreign Analogues of NG

The newspaper *Le Monde*, "in the manner of its financing, the most curious publication in France,"[2] was assigned the premises of the collaborationist newspaper *Tan* and for its first issue even borrowed its format, design, layout, and a number of writers. The first issue was published on December 18, 1944, forty-six years and three days before the appearance of *NG*.

In 1951, following the dismissal of chief editor Hubert Beuve-Méry, the assets of *Le Monde* were placed under the control of a joint-stock company, in which a considerable number of shares belonged to the newspaper's journalists, allowing them to influence the choice of directors and editorial policy.

The association of *Le Monde* journalists won the reinstatement of Beuve-Méry to his post. In 1963 came a change of chief editors (Beuve-Méry held the post of director of the newspaper and retired in 1969). The new chief editor, Jacques Fauvet, who became director of the newspaper in 1969, continued the policy of the former head of *Le Monde*. After Fauvet retired in 1982, the newspaper, which had just spent huge sums on modernization, underwent a serious crisis. André Laurens, who succeeded Fauvet, was unable to find a way out of the situation. André Fontaine, who replaced Laurens in 1985, succeeded only by implementing a harsh rescue package. *Le Monde* was forced to sell its building on the Rue des Italiens, to seek extra capital from outside, and to set up a new printing complex. This period saw the founding of a society of *Le Monde* readers, who received a share of the newspaper's capital.[3]

In 1994 the newspaper again ran into difficulties. With the arrival Jean-Marie Colombani, a decision was made to change the structure of the *Le Monde* publishing enterprise, to improve the situation by attracting new investors, and to work out a new formula for the newspaper, one based on high-quality information, objectivity, and a neutral position.

Late in 1994, a general meeting of journalists and other employees of the newspaper accepted the principle of expanding its capital by selling shares to outside investors, and approved a change in the legal status of the enterprise from that of a limited liability company to that of a joint-stock company with a supervisory council and a board of directors.

Meanwhile, in the words of chairperson of the board of directors Jean-Marie Colombani, the fundamental principle of the newspaper's financing remained intact: the majority of the shares would remain with inside shareholders and the journalists would hold a blocking minority.[4]

The *Independent* is a publication aimed at the younger generation of the British elite, and at one stage it was even stepping on the heels of the *London Times*. Its fate resembles what was to happen a little later to its Russian namesake. The publication was founded in 1986 by Newspaper Publishing, and in the view of Professor S.I. Beglov, counted on a section of the readership of the *Times* being interested in a fresh style of analytical journalism.[5] At first the new undertaking was successful, but after *Times* owner Rupert Murdoch began a price war in 1990, the *Independent* was on the verge of bankruptcy. The newspaper was no longer profitable enough to operate in the saturated market for the British prestige press. The publishers of the *Independent* tried to buy the old British newspaper the *Observer*, evidently with the aim of shutting it down. This attempt was blocked, however, by the directors of the *Guardian's* joint-stock company (the *Observer* is now published as the Sunday edition of the *Guardian*).

The company was forced to solve the problem of finances in a different fashion. The newspaper was first supported by Spanish colleagues from *El Pais* and by the Italian *Repubblica*, taking a third of the shares between them. Later, the Irish millionaire Tom O'Reilly bought 24.9 percent. The decisive move, however, was made by Mirror Group Newspapers (belonging to Robert Maxwell until his death on November 5, 1991, and later passing under the control of a consortium of banks), which bought 40 percent of the shares in Newspaper Publishing. The founder and chief editor of the *Independent*, Andreas Whittam Smith, was forced to resign. His position was taken by Ian Hargreaves, who earlier had been deputy chief editor of the *Financial Times*. In the view of observers, the post that the founder of the *Independent* retained, that of honorary director of the publishing house, allowed him no real influence on editorial policy.[6]

Such were the origins of the consortium that ran the newspaper throughout the 1990s. In March 1998, Tom O'Reilly, who had made his fortune in America as manager of the Heinz Corporation, bought out the Mirror Group's shares, thus winning control of the *Independent* and the *Independent on Sunday*. Some observers argue that for O'Reilly, the publications were of interest as a source of personal prestige and political influence.

Others, however, claim that the takeover of the flagship London newspapers was a move to transform the local publishing group into the global Independent News and Media PLC with over 160 editions worldwide.

The Golden Years of NG

The first issue of *NG* appeared on December 21, 1990. During 1991, the newspaper appeared three times a week. Later, *NG* managed to increase its frequency of publication to the point where it appeared daily, while maintaining the size of eight pages, which was substantial and even outstanding for a daily newspaper at that time.

It is curious that Tretyakov succeeded in finding eighty-three shareholders among the Moscow intelligentsia who supported the idea of *Nezavisimaya Gazeta* and were prepared to contribute a thousand rubles each to its capital. Later, during the events of October 1993 when the newspaper declared its "armed neutrality," several of these people renounced their shares in the newspaper and demanded their money back. Others remain shareholders to this day, although without any formal status.

A favorable conjunction of the price of newsprint, rent charges, and a demand for periodical publications helped ensure the success of the initiative, and the newspaper took off like a rocket. In the space of only a few weeks, *NG* won a secure place in the market.

While the established newspapers were characterized by a "Soviet" style of writing in which moralizing and stereotyped constructs were used to make up for a lack of factual material, *NG* offered its readers an informative, analytic style of writing. The commentaries by its observers were rated among the best examples of analytical journalism.

The cacophony of radical viewpoints in the newspaper was such that the first page might carry an exposé of the Soviet security forces, while the second published materials defending the right to autonomy of the union republics and Russia's autonomous republics. On the third one could find a copy of the new draft Treaty of Union for the USSR, with handwritten corrections by Gorbachev, that had been spirited out of Ruslan Khasbulatov's office; accompanying it would be comments by the newspaper's observer. On the fourth page, an analyst from the Gaidar team might set out to prove the advantages of "shock therapy" and total price liberalization, while the entire fifth page would be given over to a review of the classic works of Adam Smith. On the sixth page, a city chronicle might be published, on the seventh literary critics would dissect the latest work by the writer Vladimir Sorokin, and on the eighth a calendar of historical events would be printed next to a long essay "on time and on the self," by a member of the reflective intelligentsia.

At first, *NG* differed from the traditional "democratic" publications only in being more politicized, more heterogeneous, and on the whole more lively. The general ideology of market fundamentalism and transformational utopianism was preached by the newspaper's journalists with all the fervor of which young, talented dilettantes, raised on samizdat, were capable. In other words, the newspaper confidently took its place at the vanguard of the liberal project of the Second Republic, and on some issues (for example, the national question and economic policy), was the most radical of all the print publications.

The backbone of *NG*'s staff consisted of journalism novices, people who had come to *NG* from small-circulation and even underground publications. They were bolder and more consistent in their views than the journalists of the old school. They did not bear the weight of past errors and had no doubts as to their own vision. The "golden pens" of *NG* quickly gained a place among the journalistic elite, heroes of the new epoch. The first of the newspaper's employees to acquire real fame was Tatyana Malkina, who raised a scandal at the press conference given by the GKChP in August 1991. "Do you understand that you have staged a coup d'état?" she shouted at the gloomy, nervous Vice-President Yanaev, as the Ostankino television channel broadcast her courageous attack live.

In 1991, the newspaper's press run passed the 200,000 mark, the highest it ever reached. *NG* was a success even as a commercial enterprise.

Economic Realities and the Price of Independence

The first financial difficulties began after the collapse of the USSR and the implementation of so-called price liberalization. Justified on the basis of the need to put an end to shortages of goods and price disparities, the liberalization resulted in an explosion of inflation without precedent in peacetime. The savings of the population were wiped out, along with the greater part of effective consumer demand. The result of the reform was to create a "scissors effect," in which one blade consisted of monopolies that were now freed from any control, while the other was made up of the plummeting buying power of the population. All of Russian industry was caught between the blades.

The press was faced with rising prices for paper and increased costs for printing services, as well as unprecedented rises in the cost of delivery to subscribers. This coincided with the loss by the Russian press of its readership in the countries of the former USSR. Despite the fact that "democrats" and "marketeers" were in power in Russia, the monopoly on the press distribution network was not regulated, even though its ability to dictate prices for the delivery of publications caused enormous harm to the press, and consequently, to democracy and democrats. On the whole, the government preferred other ways of backing its supporters within the "fourth estate"; government subsidies were a more precise mechanism for directing aid to publications closest to the regime. The media market, in which stiff competition denied newspapers any chance to transfer rising costs onto the consumer, continued inexorably to contract. The "golden age" of the Russian press was over.

The most saturated of the various markets for the press at that time, and the one in which competition was most intense, was precisely the one in which *NG* operated—the market for daily political newspapers of a democratic bent. *NG* began losing readership.

Various spin-off enterprises of *NG* that had been founded in the expectation that the newspaper would prosper—the supplement *NG Meeting*, the news agency NeGa, and a book-publishing firm—were losing money. *NG Meeting* was shut down without really having managed to turn itself into an independent publication.

Of the other major Moscow newspapers, several found a way out of the situation through state subsidies, most of them due to their reputation as traditional pillars of the Russian press (*Komsomolskaya Pravda*) or their links with the government (*Izvestia*). No subsidies had been offered to *NG*, and when they were eventually extended, the newspaper was already actively criticizing the authorities. Tretyakov publicly expressed his unwillingness to accept them, considering correctly that in an acute political crisis, to take money from the Russian government was to accept a bribe from the executive power. This merely confirmed his reputation in journalistic circles as a nonconformist and a "spoiler."

By this time, the press run of *NG* had fallen below 100,000. The newspaper was running at a loss. Unlike the situation with traditional publications, the management did not have any capital reserves. Nor was there any real estate that might have been sacrificed to allow the enterprise to be reorganized or expanded.

Although the position of *NG* in the market stabilized, it was clear that the newspaper was not destined for the commercial success that the most energetic members of its editorial staff were seeking. Their inability to influence the policies of the chief editor (that is, to alter the concept of a totally independent newspaper in favor of one attractive to outside investors on the condition that editorial policy remain relatively independent) eventually led to a split among the editors. This made possible the appearance of the newspaper *Segodnya*, founded in 1993. Modeled on the London *Times*, and under the direction of the former deputy chief editor of *NG*, Dmitry Ostalsky, *Segodnya* was produced with the participation of such journalists as Mikhail Leontyev, Sergey Parkhomenko, Mikhail Lantsman, Tatyana Malkina, and the other "golden pens" of *NG*. The new publication cost *NG* almost half its readers.

As the political analyst Boris Kagarlitsky correctly noted, the disagreements between Tretyakov and the above-mentioned journalists were not so much commercial as ideological. If we define the views of the young journalists as radical-liberal (or as Kagarlitsky describes them, "cannibalistic"), then the journalists could not be denied the right to be consistent. A conflict with Tretyakov, whose views had evolved quickly in line with recent political history and the newspaper's deepening economic problems, was thus inevitable.

A Second Wind: A Newspaper of Opinions

Even after the split, however, *NG* was still considered one of the best-informed newspapers in Russia, and enjoyed enormous influence within the country's political elite. Tretyakov soon managed to restore the newspaper's reputation without renouncing his ideal, despite making certain compromises without which *NG* would not have lasted a single day.

In practice, the newspaper made up the difference between its expenses and revenues (from subscribers, retail sales, and advertising) through private contributions. Discussing *NG*'s sources of finance, Tretyakov often mentioned that the newspaper had numerous friends (he did not name names) who provided it with assistance. The fact was that the political clash of 1993 and the massive intrigues that followed set off a veritable gusher of politicized capital, which poured into the central press. This influx of money was felt everywhere and was employed for every purpose, from "assisting" newspapers to bribing individual journalists. In an interview with the journal *Lyudi*, Tretyakov later declared that the total sum of private donations had exceeded a billion rubles.

Such a situation might have seemed destined to be short-lived. But at this point in its existence, *NG* experienced something like a second wind. The newspaper's popularity underwent a particular rise following the parliamentary crisis of October 1993 (which ended with the Supreme Soviet being shelled from tanks, and with the adoption of a pro-presidential constitution). During the crisis, *NG* succeeded in maintaining a demonstratively neutral position, and became one of five publications that appeared with white patches where materials had been excised by the censors. After this, the newspaper remained constantly at the center of political exposés and sensations. It was often quoted on television and in the foreign press, and in general, continued publishing controversial analytical articles of an oppositional cast to such effect that its weight in the political world increased rather than diminished.

Delicate diplomacy in its relations with sponsors allowed *NG* to retain its independence, while at the same time taking part in "palace" (that is, presidential) and "cabinet" scheming and plotting at all levels (it was this involvement that allowed the newspaper to attract "investors"). *NG*'s participation in these intrigues gave it unprecedented access to first-hand information, although another effect was to keep the newspaper remote from the needs of ordinary readers.

NG had nevertheless degenerated from the point of view of the original concept according to which the newspaper, for all its independence, was regarded as a quality news publication. The second incarnation of *NG* was as a combination of an independent analytical bulletin with traditional Russian personal journalism. *NG* became a newspaper of opinion. The majority of its writers preferred expressing their point of view to carrying out the task of informing the reader. The materials were aimed exclusively at an educated, politicized elite.

Prior to 1993, the only people to write for *NG* in this fashion had been Tretyakov and a few others. This was fully in line with the proportion of personal journalism in a quality newspaper, including *NG*'s competitors. *Kommersant-Daily*, for example, had the columns of Maksim Sokolov, and *Segodnya* those of Mikhail Leontyev. In *Moskovsky Komsomolets*, more than half of the journalists wrote in this fashion, but only Aleksandr Minkin did so successfully.

From time to time, however, real scoops appeared in *NG*. The newspaper was then quoted widely on television and radio and deservedly confirmed its reputation as the daily Russian language publication most cited abroad. *NG* had definitely found its place in the market, but it had not managed to become profitable, or even to cover its costs.

Political Stabilization, Financial Disaster

Nezavisimaya spent the years 1994 and 1995 in a state of unrelieved financial catastrophe. Like most publications in the Russian capital, the newspaper ran at a loss, and few now remembered the fabulous wages it had once paid its journalists. Most of *NG*'s correspondents held other jobs, earning their daily bread working for other media institutions (most often Radio Liberty and foreign newspapers and news agencies).

The prestige of being published in *NG*, however, served as a reliable stimulus for the devotion of creative workers. Meanwhile, the low wages forced the liberal Tretyakov, at times sacrificing the newspaper's quality, to give middle-level management, that is, heads of departments, a degree of creative freedom that had probably never been enjoyed by newspaper section editors in the entire history of Russian journalism. Not only editors, but journalists as well, benefited from this situation.

On the other hand, the low wages paid by *NG* could not fail to ensure a host of articles written to order for people outside the newspaper (it is said that *NG* was distinguished by its unusually low prices in this regard as well). These materials dealt a blow from within to *NG*'s credibility and harmed the newspaper's reputation.

The thunderclap struck on December 10, 1994. Readers received copies of *NG* that were half the previous length—four pages instead of eight. In a front-page column on December 21, 1994, written for the fourth anniversary of *NG*'s first appearance and published in the now "thinned-down" newspaper, Tretyakov made an emotional assessment of the path *NG* had traveled. In his commentary-style piece, this was closely intertwined with a critique of the political situation in Russia:

> Over the course of four years, we aimed to do a great deal and planned to live much better. In the first of these aims we have had a considerable degree of success, but as for the second, almost none. Nevertheless, we have kept our name—"Independent." No one can be called the owner of this newspaper, even among those who would very much like this status. *Nezavisimaya* exists; an owner does not. Colleagues on other newspapers silently admit this to themselves: there is no owner. We condemn whom we choose, and praise whom we like. We like people who do not lie, or at least, who try not to lie.

Even after *NG* had been forced to cut its size in half, in its four-page format, it maintained the level of its commentary. To a large extent this was due to the efforts of the chief editor. The newspaper also found new forms, which to a degree helped it to replace quantity with quality. These innovations included, for example, the "Misanthropy" column, which became *NG*'s calling card and served as the basis for the book by "Titus Sovetologov," *Their Struggle: Essays on the Idiocy of Russian Politics*, which appeared under the imprint of the *NG* publishing house in 1995. In essence, the "Misanthropy" column was a viciously sarcastic daily commentary, written by the newspaper's journalists who used pseudonyms, and who often changed the names of the column's subjects in order to avoid prosecution.

As in the past, *NG* carried highly important news summaries, published commentaries, printed analytical articles, and, together with Boris Grushin's public opinion research service, continued running its "100 Politicians" ratings list. This became an important barometer of influence within Russia's political elite.

The last regular issue of *Nezavisimaya Gazeta* appeared on May 23, 1995. The editorial staff was on leave. Subsequently, two special issues of the newspaper appeared; one of these took the form of an insert in *Obshchaya Gazeta*, while the other, on June 21, was devoted to the idea of forming a joint-stock company like *NG*. Debts to printers, according to various sources, amounted to somewhere between 500 million and one billion rubles.

Russian prime minister Viktor Chernomyrdin, who during a personal meeting with Tretyakov had promised support to *NG*, did not fulfill his pledge, at least through government channels—Tretyakov does not deny that it could have been the premier who suggested the idea of buying the newspaper to Boris Berezovsky.

Tretyakov's attempt to organize a joint-stock company with capital of four million dollars was not successful. At a time when there was a catastrophic shortage of capital investment in Russia, finding people prepared to invest in the joint financing of a newspaper—even one currently being published—was extremely difficult. For *NG*, no longer appearing regularly, burdened with debt, and barely able to scrape together the money for a special issue, the task was next to impossible.

The intelligentsia, from whom Tretyakov had collected money for the first issues of the newspaper, had mostly been ruined by the reforms. The intellectuals who had achieved a certain financial success were virtually indifferent to an "ideological" project, except for a few bankers and other company executives, none of whom, however, could grant the project more than half a million dollars. The total sum offered would not have covered the newspaper's printing debts, let alone finance its production, since it had operated at a loss.

From the standpoint of the political climate, this period was unlike both 1992, with its "shock therapy," and the turbulent year of 1993. From the spring of 1994 until the autumn of 1995, Russian political life was relatively quiet. This brought a significant drift of capital out of politics and a cooling of enthusiasm on the part of the sponsors on whom *NG* had been so dependent.

A Deceptive Balance and a Careless Optimism

Competition between press organs had done its work; now journalists could enjoy the fruits, finding a publication that was ready, on the basis of its own interests, to publish their writings. Society, it appeared, no longer had a need for absolutely or even formally independent mass media in order to ensure that the most important issues were covered.

The standoff in the political arena was reflected (naturally in a somewhat different form) in the mass media, which now served as the mouthpiece for various social groups. The dominant view among professionals was a cautious optimism concerning freedom of the press in Russia. In time, it seemed, everything would change for the better; things would be made right, that is, they would come to resemble what existed in "civilized countries." I should confess that, working at the time as *NG*'s economic editor, I shared these illusions. No one at that time could imagine either the course of the 1996 elections or the battles over Svyazinvest.

It seemed as though a certain balance had been established. The authorities were able to influence public opinion through state television and the state newspapers. Large-scale capital was now able to present its position through the new media outlets: NTV and the newspapers *Segodnya* and *Kommersant*. The opposition still had its publications, whose role in the 1990s was marginal, but who unquestionably had their readers. In addition, *Izvestia* and *Komsomolskaya Pravda* in practice remained independent, though this did not stop the first of these newspapers from showing extreme partisanship and the second from drifting toward yellow journalism.

Under these conditions, the struggle waged by *Nezavisimaya Gazeta* seemed to lose its relevance. Independence was no longer a commodity in demand from readers; the thinned-down newspaper was competing with publications from another weight division who were offering sub-scribers a high-quality product. *NG* was the newspaper of a very narrow circle of politicized readers, as it offered its audience neither wide-ranging news nor entertainment. It was only natural that among *NG*'s journal-ists, a powerful opposition to Tretyakov would arise. This opposition was headed by deputy chief editor Aleksandr Gagua.

The Takeover

All "takeovers" of newspapers in Russia have been more or less similar, and it can be said with confidence that the seizure of any property in Russia in the 1990s followed approximately the same pattern. To de-scribe in detail how this happened in the case of *NG* is to provide a key to understanding how it occurred in principle.

At the time of the split in the early *NG* and the departure of most of the editors and journalists, Gagua remained faithful to the newspaper, and his influence rose significantly as a result. Controlling the "Repub-lic" section (this was a provincial chronicle that continued defending the interests of the Russian regions in the tradition of the early *NG*), he set out to maximize his resources and contacts, forging links and win-ning the support of most of the editorial collective, with a view to chang-ing *NG*'s policies and finding a strategic investor for the newspaper.

As Gagua set out to achieve this goal, one of the greatest advantages he enjoyed was an alliance with Yury Skokov, leader of the Congress of Russian Communities (KRO). Sociologists were predicting that in the 1995 parliamentary elections the KRO would win 15 percent of the votes due to its alliance with General Aleksandr Lebed and its nationalist ori-entation. Throughout 1994 and 1995, moreover, Skokov had been con-sidered one of the likeliest candidates for the prime ministership if Chernomyrdin were to resign, and he had been doing everything in his power to ensure that this resignation took place. Skokov and his allies in the KRO, unlike the party in power, the democratic opposition, the com-munists, and the nationalists, did not have their own mass media.

As well as pursuing a political career, Skokov, a former secretary of Yeltsin's Security Council and a close presidential associate who long aspired to the prime ministership, evidently worked as a political influence-broker. It was probably Skokov who in the summer of 1995 recommended Gagua to OneksimBank, which had been trying to show its interest in buying *NG*.

Lacking power, and in spite of Tretyakov's obvious reluctance to revive the newspaper given the new circumstances, Gagua managed to push through a meeting of the *NG* editorial staff a resolution naming representatives for negotiations with would-be investors. In addition to OneksimBank, these potential investors included the Aeroflot Bank and several less well-known financial structures that had earlier offered to put sums of $500,000 into the *Nezavisimaya Gazeta* joint-stock company, but that were not making any claims to control the newspaper.

After these talks had collapsed, and in accordance with NG statutes, Gagua on August 30 managed to put the question of confidence in the chief editor up for a vote at a meeting of the newspaper's work collective. It was proposed that commercial director Igor Kuzmin be appointed temporarily as acting chief editor to hold talks with investors. The voting turned out to be very difficult; the choice was between the newspaper's commercial management, which appeared more realistic, and Tretyakov's creative, idealistic policies, which for many of the staff were the main reason for working at *NG*. However, the fact that the newspaper had not paid wages for two months had an effect. Not many of the newspaper's employees had the opportunity to work "on the side." Tretyakov remained true to the idea of *NG*'s independence to the very end. When he finally recognized that the newspaper had collapsed as an independent publication, he personally urged that it be shut down.

Only a few people voted for closure, that is, against the resolution moved by Gagua. A week after the vote, the work collective was paid its back wages. The new chief editor managed to find 14 million rubles to put out an issue of the newspaper, and on September 8 this issue was sent to the printer. However, the paper still failed to appear; for some reason—perhaps pressure from Tretyakov or Berezovsky—the *Izvestia* print shop did not print it.

The defeat of Tretyakov's ideas, however, was not fated to become a personal defeat for Tretyakov. While in seclusion thinking over his creative plans, he was sought out by Boris Berezovsky, who made him an offer he couldn't refuse. Then, legend has it, he was flown to Moscow from Greece in Berezovsky's personal plane on September 12. With the help of a private security firm, he made his return to the *NG* editorial offices at 13 Myasnitskaya Street.[7]

Meanwhile, Tretyakov's lawyers found a contradiction in the newspaper's statutes, and based on this, the vote by the work collective was declared invalid. At the decisive moment, Kuzmin handed over the newspaper's official seal to Tretyakov, and *NG*'s history of coups was at an end.

Gagua and Kuzmin then gave several press conferences, and Tretyakov spoke out as well. The newspaper's employees were once again paid their wages, with an additional 200 percent bonus "for the results of work performed in August." Gagua, Kuzmin, and several other members of the *NG* staff quit their jobs.[8] On October 3, 1995, the newspaper resumed publication.

NG *Under Berezovsky*

The takeover of *Nezavisimaya Gazeta* by OneksimBank three months before the parliamentary elections, aided probably by the leader of an opposition movement with a highly regarded presidential candidate, Aleksandr Lebed, would have posed a threat to the existing powers and to the business entrepreneurs close to them. This was especially true considering *NG*'s power and influence, which existed despite its low circulation. It may be that Berezovsky's blitzkrieg represented a sort of defensive reaction on the part of officials, since in 1995 Berezovsky also launched other mass media projects that were in the interests of the Kremlin. All these projects had a single goal: to take control of the media system in preparation for the propaganda campaigns that marked the 1996 presidential elections.

On the other hand, it is hard to deny that the purchase of *NG* ensured Berezovsky important political and even commercial dividends, since this move on the eve of the elections would be valued very highly by the regime and its supporters. Berezovsky now had at his disposal the organ of the Russian political and intellectual elite and a tool for shaping public opinion that was highly individual, but which, if used skillfully, could be very effective.

Just as the defeat of Tretyakov's conception of *Nezavisimaya Gazeta* did not become a fiasco for him personally as chief editor and commentator (at least until he resigned in 2001), *NG* to a degree retained its niche in the mass media and influence markets, despite having lost its idealism. Thanks to the infusion of investment capital, the newspaper immediately regained its former size, and then effectively doubled it through supplements (*NG-Regions*, *People and Characters*, *NG Religion*, the literary supplement *Ex Libris*, and others). Thanks to

Berezovsky's support, the newspaper was even able to establish its own literary prize, the Anti-Booker.

There is no question that the investor influenced the newspaper's contents. This was most apparent during major political media campaigns. For example, during the information war that followed the auctioning of Svyazinvest, the newspaper unleashed a campaign against the government and competitors. Often, the fact that *NG* belonged to Berezovsky was noticeable in one article or another.

It appeared that Tretyakov managed to convince the owner of the newspaper that only maintaining an autonomous editorial policy would allow *NG* to keep its role as a forum for political studies and commentary, that is, as a "newspaper of opinions." Despite the tendentiousness of some articles, *NG* thus continued to provide a platform for politicians and intellectuals of the most diverse views. Although it switched to color, its circulation continued to fall, but it managed to attract a significant readership on the Internet. With its press run at 37,000 copies per day, in the winter of 2002 the newspaper's Web site attracted 13,000 readers daily from Russia and abroad.

The Lessons of *NG*, and the "Forgotten" Market in Influence

Initially, the concept embodied in *NG* was neither utopian nor unrealizable. If the Russian authorities had not limited themselves to rhetoric and had really pursued a course of market and democratic reforms, regulating the activity of the monopolists and helping to strengthen the institution of a genuinely democratic press, *NG* might have continued to play a leading role. Operating under different conditions (outside the framework of Berezovsky's shady holding company and as an independent publishing house with a large number of small investors), it might have shown the world that a quality independent press could exist in Russia.

Given the actual circumstances, *NG* was unable to fulfill even one of the four goals that its chief editor set for it in the first issue—complete information, the presentation of all points of view, the avoidance of editorializing, and independence not just from the government but also from the opposition. In the course of *NG*'s struggle for independence, each of these aims was, to some extent, compromised.

In the euphoria of the political struggle of the early 1990s, it was enough to reject censorship in order to obtain and publish complete information. Later, this required a definite level of investment; information, it turned out, came at a price. This price had to be paid not only to sources and news agencies but also to newspaper employees; failure to pay wages led to corruption and to a degraded quality of the articles.

Since *NG* had no money, the information in the newspaper was gathered accordingly. The "backbone" staff worked out of commitment, but this applied only to the most important topics dealt with by *NG*'s most professional journalists who earned their living elsewhere and had their work published in the newspaper for the sake of their reputations and influence.

The same applies to the representation of all points of view in the one newspaper. Even if we accept that doing this in full was impossible by definition, it must be acknowledged that the attempt failed. Working for a pittance, the newspaper's employees preferred to express their own points of view and to lobby for the interests of the forces with which, for one reason or another, they were associated. It was only in the area of political and economic commentary that the necessary pluralism was observed in the newspaper.

After swearing off editorializing in news articles, Tretyakov later returned to this genre, but in the form of articles in the proper sense. These, however, had all the attributes of editorials; that is, they were printed in bold type on the front page. In this way, it emerged that the newspaper had a position—but no one had any influence on this position except Tretyakov. Setting aside the articles by the chief editor, an editorial column nevertheless appeared in the newspaper, in the form of the politician-hating "Misanthropy" section. This was established on orders from Tretyakov, and non-staff writers and independent journalists were banned from writing for it. In the four-page *NG*, this column played an important role; it was the clearest and most sarcastic witness to the newspaper's independence, since, like the television program *Kukly* (Puppets), it spared no one. It was the newspaper's front line, doing battle with the state of society.

Finally, as far as independence from the opposition was concerned, the newspaper's failure was total. Through the efforts of Aleksandr Gagua and in the course of its natural search for its own readership in 1994–95, *NG* became in practice the organ of the Congress of Russian Communities. Of course, there could be no question of the newspaper formally renouncing its independence; but in fact it came increasingly to voice the positions of this movement, captive to particular political sympathies. This might well have ended in an alliance with OneksimBank—had Berezovsky not shown an interest in *NG*.

Tretyakov's struggle for the independence of his newspaper was unique. Almost to the end, it was a fight with dragons, a selfless fight, but a personal one for personal ideals. It was not merely a struggle against objective economic circumstances (conditioned in the first instance by the antidemocratic and essentially antimarket policies followed by the executive branch in relation to the mass media), but also a struggle within the editorial offices to affirm a conception whose existence only a few people, the chief editor among them, even remembered. Why did others not remember it? For the reason that toward the end, only Tretyakov was fully aware of the link between the original concept of an independent quality newspaper and the bulletin of political argument and commentary that the newspaper had become. If Tretyakov had been a little more demagogic, a little less idealistic, a little more self-interested, and not so stubborn—that is, if he had been less of a journalist, and more of a capitalist—the drama of *NG* might have ended differently.

Here is how Tretyakov himself characterized the ending of the utopia of the independent press and the subsequent status of *NG*, in "A Letter Not to B.N. Yeltsin," on the occasion of the seizure of *Komsomolskaya Pravda* and *Izvestia* by OneksimBank:

> The legal status of *NG* today is as simple as the tears of an old woman coming into a branch savings bank after the Gaidar reforms. *NG* is now a joint stock company of the closed type, with a controlling packet of shares held by Obedinenny Bank. I am the chief editor and also the general director of this joint stock company. The owner of the controlling shares can sack me from my job practically at any moment. At my request, this has been made clear to the staff. I will not resist this, since it was purely circumstances, and not in any way Obedinenny Bank, that forced me to place my signature on the joint stock company's charter documents.
>
> Has the consequence of this been the death of the free *Nezavisimaya Gazeta* or of the free press? The free *NG* and the free press of the years from 1990 to 1992 have indeed perished. But on the whole, the answer is no. Not a single monopoly in Russia (if only because of the size of the country) can be absolute, least of all in the mass media. This is not the gas complex and not even the MPS [Ministry of the Railway System]. Ever since 1993 our marketeers have been extending their grasp over the whole

democratic press, in the broad sense that includes the electronic mass media, and are now gravitating with particular speed toward ideological and financial monopolism. They themselves, along with millions of ordinary readers, will turn to reading left-wing, communist newspapers. *Pravda*, *Sovetskaya Rossiya*, and others will finish up with an unprecedented revival of their popularity and a colossal rise in their circulation. In order for this not to happen, it will be necessary simply to install a dictatorship. An attempt to do this is not ruled out, but there are no obvious signs that it would be successful—or more precisely, it will not be a real prospect for a long time to come.[9]

Another important lesson of *NG* from the point of view of "transformational utopia" and market ideology is that by the very fact of its existence, the newspaper showed the narrowness and inadequacy of these theories.

The newspaper in fact failed as a commercial enterprise; that is, it suffered defeat in the market for news and advertising. At the same time, it continued to appear and to have a substantial influence on the political life of Russia, while also remaining one of the country's best-informed publications.

From the point of view of market ideology, this situation can be explained if to the "traditional" markets for news and advertising (which in the view of the reformers should have had a decisive influence on the formation of the Russian media system) one adds the market for political influence. In some cases this market can also be described as the market in public opinion, although in the next chapter we shall see that during the period we are examining, work with public opinion at large was conducted primarily through television, and that as a result the zone of intensive influence of the Moscow media (except for the presidential elections, of course) was reduced to the economic and political elites of the capital.

From the point of view of the market ideologues, the market for political influence was perhaps a "bad" market, and should not decide the fate of newspapers. But if we borrow a dash of their cynicism, is this really important? Influence, after all, is bought and sold, and a multitude of publications (as well as television companies) compete with one another to exert the greatest possible influence on groups of readers on demand. We can also draw a parallel with the advertising market; behind the mechanisms used for financing the commercial mass media, a deal is struck for the sale of an audience to an advertiser. Where is the difference? Only in that the first case involves the political preferences of the mass audience, and the second case, their economic preferences.

It was the success that *Nezavisimaya Gazeta* enjoyed in the market for political influence that made it so attractive an object for the investment of private capital. Even in the epoch of television, newspapers to a degree retain their role as incubators of political discourse and factories of argumentation, which is later used in the electronic media. Forging another link in the chain of generalization, we may add that it was the market for political influence that was responsible for the formation of the Russian mass media system in the 1990s.

3

The "Mediatization" of Politics

It cannot be said that the authorities had the unconditional support of the "democratic" mass media, even during the events of 1993. Despite the existence of subsidies, relations between the regime and the press at the dawn of the Second Republic did not amount to the purchase of support, but to partnership. This partnership was defined above all by the fact that the directors of the "democratic" publications felt a sense of participation in the formulating of the policy of democratic market reforms, and hence actively supported these reforms and propagandized in their favor. Fear of revenge from the former owners no doubt facilitated the adoption of firm anti-communist positions. The press was obliged to the new political regime for its very existence as an independent institution, as well as for its popularity and influence, not to mention the privatization of the publications.

Nevertheless, the press in the early 1990s genuinely perceived itself as a "fourth estate," that is, as one of the governing institutions wielding enormous influence in society. This meant that the chief editors and journalists felt a sense of responsibility toward society and thought that the press could and should criticize the authorities when the latter allowed mistakes to be made.

Until the outbreak of the war in Chechnya, the president of Russia was forced to heed the views of the press, especially when these views were expressed in unison. Chief editors, it appeared, could not be removed from their posts. For example, decrees dismissing the general director of Russian State Television, Oleg Poptsov, known for his obstinate character, were signed repeatedly—but generally without any result.[1]

The alliance between the press and the regime fell apart after Boris Yeltsin launched the war in Chechnya. From the point of view of the "democratic" publications that had earlier supported the president, the "democratic" television, and the commercial mass media, not to mention the opposition press (apart from national-patriotic publications such as the newspaper *Zavtra*), the war in Chechnya was a totally inept and senseless adventure. Wars in general can only rarely be justified in rational terms. The degree of rationality behind the Chechen war was neither more nor less than in the case of Operation Desert Storm, and the list of casualties was considerably longer. In addition, journalists did not neglect to mention that it was the Chechen war that put an ace in the hand of the supporters of NATO expansion.

The War in Chechnya: The Media Versus the Regime

However mythological the value system of the "democratic" press might have been, in the case of Chechnya these publications could not have been accused of showing a lack of principles. The ideals of the Second Republic, the journalists considered, were not compatible with war, especially civil war. Properly speaking, one of the main tasks of democracy is to prevent the outbreak of wars by developing democratic procedures. The Afghan war was fresh in everyone's memory, and the Chechen campaign was launched in just as mystifying a fashion. Its causes were not explained, and the need for it was not demonstrated. The press and the public could only guess that in this case oil had conjoined with the desire for an easy victory that would strengthen the authority of the president. Moreover, the war would provide a possible pretext for introducing a state of emergency and canceling the presidential elections. At least these explanations were popular. The real reason perhaps was a clash of ambitions and misunderstandings between Boris Yeltsin and Chechen president Dzhokhar Dudaev.

When the united position that the Russian press and television adopted failed to bring any changes to the government's policy, the press was faced with a serious dilemma. The choice before it was either to recognize the supreme authority of the president, verging on dictatorship—and by so doing, to accept that this dictatorship had been established through the efforts of the "democratic" press and television—or to show the authorities who was boss, that is, to prove that as before the "democratic" press had a real influence on the policies of the regime and that the dictatorship had turned out at least to be enlightened.

The upshot was that *Izvestia, Komsomolskaya Pravda, Argumenty i Fakty, Moskovsky Komsomolets,* and also NTV and the Russian State

Television channel RTR changed their loyal attitude to the president to one of sharp opposition. Only the first channel Ostankino (soon to be transformed into ORT) and the state-run *Rossiyskaya Gazeta* remained faithful.

Such was the beginning of a conflict between the press and the government that lasted for almost two years. Despite doing serious damage to the regime, the "fourth estate" ultimately emerged from this conflict in defeat, though to onlookers it might have seemed that the outcome was a draw.

In the literature on the history of the mass media in Russia, two diametrically opposed views are presented on the development of the war in Chechnya and on the way the conflict was reported in the mass media. This is how the authoritative historian of the Soviet press Rafail Ovsepyan describes the events in Chechnya:

> Society perceived what happened in Chechnya in a contradictory fashion. The official sources were silent on the heavy losses suffered by the Russian army and the Interior Ministry forces in military engagements with Chechen armed formations. The mass media used their right of free expression to the fullest. They were the first to start discussing what was being concealed from the population. Television and radio reports, as well as many newspaper articles, told the truth about fierce battles and about the death of poorly trained soldiers, who had been drafted into the army only shortly before.
>
> From the first days of armed operations in Chechnya, the citizens of Russia voiced their protest at the bloodshed, at first muttered under their breath here and there, then more and more loudly and persistently. In 1996, this protest grew significantly stronger. Early in the year a letter to Boris Yeltsin was published in which a hundred well-known members of the Russian scientific and creative intelligentsia called for a halt to the war. Reports appeared in all the media of a genuine mass action led by the governor of Nizhny Novgorod, Boris Nemtsov, who delivered to the Russian president the signatures of a million Nizhny Novgorod residents demanding an end to the war in Chechnya. Many regions of the country supported this action. The press had every reason to declare that the war was highly unpopular in Russia, that the country had no need of bloodshed, and that Russian citizens did not want to expose themselves to the bullets of Chechen fighters. This meant it was time to stop the war.[2]

Another view of how events in Chechnya were reported is presented in a book by A.A.Grabelnikov, one chapter of which bears the title "The

Confrontation with the Mass Media." In a paragraph headed "The De-stabilizing Character of the Present-Day Mass Media," Grabelnikov describes this historic episode as "one of the rare cases in the history of journalism when the national mass media spoke out on the side of the enemy at a time of war."[3]

> The Chechen crisis showed that the "fourth estate" can be executive in its functions as well as legislative and judicial. Instead of reflecting public opinion, some media organs set about shaping it.[4]

Grabelnikov saw the war in Chechnya as a way of preserving the integrity of the Russian state against attack by the rapacious countries of the West. Although his views would not have been out of place in the age of Bismarck, some of his observations were quite apt. Grabelnikov listed the instances of what he described as "destabilizing" action by the central mass media:

> *Obshchaya Gazeta*, published by Yegor Yakovlev, thus reported the pro-ceedings of a "trial" of the president and, alluding to the sentence, printed his portrait with a black border. . . . The television channel NTV and [the RTR news program] "Vesti"[5] stepped up their coverage of demonstra-tions in support of Chechnya,[6] even if only a few dozen people were taking part. . . . A speech delivered at one of the demonstrations by Valeriya Novodvorskaya, who called on Moscow residents to collect money to arm the Chechen militants and who maintained that to desert was a sa-cred duty of any self-respecting Russian citizen, was shown every hour for a whole day by the news program on Channel 2x2.[7]

Grabelnikov also quotes from an article by a *Rossiyskaya Gazeta* correspondent who could not conceal his indignation, describing Novodvorskaya's speech as "treason":

> Television plays on what is most sacred: human sympathy. Television broad-casts are full of mothers' tears and of their cries at the loss in battle of their soldier sons. Television behaves just like the Chechen bandits who put women and old people in front of the columns of fighters and who shoot at the Russian soldiers from behind the backs of this living shield.[8]

Valeriya Novodvorskaya is one of those marginal political figures whose radicalism threatens to compromise any ideas they express. It is curious, however, that during the first war in Chechnya, *Rossiyskaya Gazeta*, whose "patriotism" would seem so appropriate to the wartime press, found itself in the same position.

> The Chechen conflict brought substantial changes to the disposition of forces within the mass media. Democratic publications, forgetting about such former adversaries as the newspapers *Zavtra* and *Sovetskaya Rossiya*, found a new target for their massed firepower in the government-run *Rossiyskaya Gazeta*. This happened because *Rossiyskaya Gazeta*, unlike other newspapers, including the patriotic and Communist ones, supported the actions of the president and of the federal forces sent to smash Dudaev's fighters. *Moskovsky Komsomolets* declared that the entire nation unconditionally condemned the "Chechen adventure," while only *RG* was resisting the whole country. A.N. Yakovlev, in an interview with Radio Liberty, described *RG* as a "pro-fascist publication and the most untruthful newspaper in the country."[9]
>
> Genrikh Borovik, who as a foreign correspondent used to condemn American imperialism in his pamphlets, now turned with the same fury on his own government. Breaking into the network broadcast, he went on the air, interrupting the children's television program "Good Night, Little Ones!" In his characteristically sarcastic manner, he approved the decision by the Russian authorities to bomb the bandit gangs in Chechnya and suggested that a request be made to NATO to bomb Moscow, since there were also large numbers of bandits there. It is interesting that after this speech went on the air, the recording was destroyed on the orders of A.N. Yakovlev.[10]

According to Grabelnikov, the reports by newspaper and television war correspondents were subjected to extensive editing in Moscow editorial offices.

> The massive reworking of public opinion by the mass media became so obvious and so intolerable to the army that the officers of a combined group of forces in the Chechen Republic addressed a declaration to the president, to the head of the government, to the chairman of the State Duma, to the defense minister, and to the head of the Russian General Staff describing their difficult situation. They stressed that in essence, they were surrounded. In front of them were bands of professional killers, recruited from throughout the world, while from the rear they were being attacked by opponents of the strengthening of Russian statehood. These opponents had been planted in a series of media organs, and in the

membership of particular pseudo-patriotic Russian political movements and social organizations. Shielded by the support of unprincipled politicians, consciously juggling facts, quoting out of context particular words and expressions from speeches by army commanders, and openly falsifying events, many Russian media outlets were misinforming the population, deliberately heightening political tensions in the country, and undermining the authority of Russia in the international arena.[11]

After quoting at length from this document, which most likely was prepared by army propaganda experts, Grabelnikov spends another five pages unmasking a propaganda campaign in the mass media.

According to Gleb Pavlovsky, the president of the Foundation for Effective Politics and a prominent Kremlin political consultant who figured among the campaign ideologues of the 1996 elections, the campaign in the mass media cost Yeltsin the 20 percent support he had retained throughout his political career, "and which might always have been turned into 50 percent." Properly speaking, this also led to the situation in which, according to surveys by Russia's largest polling organizations, the president's rating early in 1996 stood in the region of 6 to 10 percent, the lowest at any time up to the 1996 elections.

In Pavlovsky's view, the image of the president suffered particularly from the lifting, during the Chechen war and the antiwar press campaign, of the earlier taboo on the themes of "the president and alcohol" and "the president's health." During this period, at least two scandalous incidents broke through into the newsprint and the television screens. As Aleksandr Korzhakov records in his memoirs, the first of these occurred after the president, having partaken liberally of white wine, collapsed on board his aircraft:

We were returning to Russia from America via Shannon. Our aircraft was scheduled to remain at the Irish airport for about an hour, and a forty-minute meeting had been planned for Yeltsin with the Irish prime minister. The meeting, however, did not take place. Instead of Boris Nikolaevich, it was first deputy prime minister Oleg Soskovets who came down the stairs and who, without giving the dumbfounded Albert Reynolds a chance to collect his composure, launched into the [standard] diplomatic protocols. The press "exploded" the next day. Russian and foreign journalists proposed dozens of versions, each more unlikely than the last, of why Boris Nikolaevich had not emerged from the aircraft. No one believed the official report issued by the presidential press service, to the effect that Boris Nikolaevich had been so tired that he had simply slept through the meeting at Shannon. Many people obviously realized that something quite out of the ordinary had happened on board the aircraft, and that the curtain of secrecy was concealing something more than ordinary diplomatic embarrassment.[12]

The story of "sleeping at Shannon," which caused a sensation in the newspapers and on television, raised the issues of alcohol and of the president's health. In the next incident, as Korzhakov writes, the Russian president drank to excess in the heat and then tried to conduct an orchestra during a visit to Berlin. This time his action was treated simply as the boorish prank of an alcoholic and a disgrace to the nation.

Showing the same zeal with which it had earlier defended the course of the reforms, the press now debunked the image of the president as a national leader, reporting in detail the ham-fisted campaign in Chechnya and the numerous casualties among army personnel. The position of the media community was not unanimous, since a number of journalists expressed views that were less straightforward and less decidedly anti-war. The liberal journalists Mikhail Leontyev and Maksim Sokolov, for example, turned out to be "great-power chauvinists." In the new situation, the government acquired new allies; these included the father of the new Russian nationalism, the journalist Aleksandr Nevzorov, who as a film director was responsible for the documentary *Our People* about the Vilnius events and the 1998 feature film *Purgatory*. During the 1996 election campaign, Nevzorov hosted a special program on the first channel of Russian TV for jingoist patriots, helping to split the Communist Party's National-Patriotic Union.

Nevertheless, it would take several more years, another war (this time in Yugoslavia), and serious development of the techniques for manipulating public opinion before Russian officials learned to use the mass media for their own interests with the same virtuosity as the NATO countries. During the period preceding the elections of 1999 and 2000, the war in Chechnya flared up with new force, but instead of becoming a hindrance to the election battle, the bloodshed in the Caucasus would serve as a favorable background to the whole campaign, a basis for molding the image of the candidate for the party of the authorities, Vladimir Putin, and a foundation on which the nation could be unified. The unsuccessful war in Afghanistan had filled journalists with confidence in their strength and signaled that change was in the offing, and on the eve of the 1996 elections the first Chechen war showed the decline in the influence of the mass media in society and the vulnerability of the regime. Now, the second Chechen war would bring about a rebirth of the image of Great Russia. At the cost of human tragedies and bloody sacrifices, the war in the Caucasus would thus play a role in the political drama after all—a few years later than planned, but nevertheless to striking success.

The Presidential Elections of 1996: The Triumph of the Spectacle

On the eve of the presidential elections of 1996, the situation was such that a victory for Yeltsin seemed to be ruled out. While leaders of the democratic forces searched for a new candidate, many people in political circles were convinced that Aleksandr Korzhakov was planning a coup d'état. Yeltsin himself was sunk in depression, and the war in Chechnya was continuing as before. Armed Chechen bands were staging terrorist attacks one after another, proving the inability of Russian troops to control the situation.

Given the circumstances, some analysts panicked and suggested to the government that they reach a compromise with the opposition and cancel the elections.

> Few people are taking into consideration the real Russia or the contradictions tearing it apart. The political elite is preoccupied solely with the question of how to get the country as quickly as possible through the presidential elections, which would free it (that is, the elite) from the need to make responsible political decisions and to work out constructive policies. On the eve of these supposedly "fateful" elections, public consciousness has no real image of the Russia, cut down while still alive, that has remained since the disintegration of the USSR, nor of the serious discussion about the lessons of the past, about the real prospects and possibilities for the development of the new Russian state.[13]

In his notorious article "The Presidential Elections in Russia Must Be Canceled" (excerpted above), Aleksandr Tsipko proceeded from correct premises to absolutely incorrect conclusions. If Russia was to be saved, he maintained, democracy would have to be rejected. Against the background of the war in Chechnya, his conviction that a dialogue of the elites could change the situation in the country for the better appeared extremely naive, and the article was regarded by many people as a provocation.

The situation was complicated not only by the fact that the press had gotten out of control, but also by the scandalous results of the 1995 parliamentary elections, during which the party in power, despite having the support of the regional press, lost to the Communists and to Vladimir Zhirinovsky's Liberal Democratic Party of Russia (LDPR), which had been denied access to the central mass media.

The new media system was structured differently from its predecessor. The press was divided among regional markets; in the provinces, the central mass media served an insignificant proportion of the population compared to the regional publications. Television had become the key to the all-Russian information space. On the eve of the presidential elections, television was already controlled substantially by a coalition around the party in power. ORT was managed by Berezovsky, and at RTR the obstinate Poptsov had been replaced by Eduard Sagalaev (the details of how the media assets were distributed will be explored in Chapter 6). In addition, Berezovsky had succeeded in drawing Gusinsky into the election campaign. Throughout the war in Chechnya, Gusinsky's NTV had done perceptible harm to the image of the Russian president and, as a consequence, had built up an enormous store of trust.

Mere control over the mass media was clearly not enough to ensure victory. The success of the Communists and of Zhirinovsky's party in the parliamentary elections, conducted as always under the intense pressure of the mass media, made this quite obvious. In this dark hour a group of bankers assembled by Berezovsky managed to convince Yeltsin (who had thought seriously about canceling the elections) that it was possible to change everything by using modern electoral techniques.

Prior to the 1996 elections, the owners of the mass media, despite wielding formal or effective control, had not known how to manage their media organs. Modern information techniques proved to be the missing link that made it possible during the elections to revive the mass media as the propaganda apparatus of the party in power and to secure victory at the polls—or, as some observers argued, to provide an alibi good enough to allow the results to be falsified.

The essence of the new techniques consisted of making skillful use of the methods of "information dramaturgy" in order to seize the initiative from the opposition and create a new image for the president. First of all however, the people in favor of holding the elections had to convince the president that if the new techniques were applied and use was made of the mass media that were at the disposal of the state and of politicized capital, victory in the elections could be guaranteed to a candidate with a minuscule rating.

The Election Campaign Ideologues

To cope with this daunting task, the Foundation for Effective Politics (FEP) spent the period from January 26 until March 10, 1996, drawing up a strategic report on the methods needed to secure victory.[14] At some point during this time, an analytical memorandum entitled "The President's Victory: Our Approach" was handed to members of the administration and the election campaign team. This document, not kept secret but little known, deserves to be quoted.

> The strength of the president's adversaries does not lie in real mass support or in alternatives to the president's policies—there are no such alternatives, as everyone knows. The strength of the president's opponents lies in their ability to make a communicative impact on the image-system, feelings, and predilections of the ordinary person, who has been traumatized and "abandoned" by the state and who does not trust anyone in authority. The strength of the opposition is in informal, horizontal structures. . . .
>
> The weakness of the authorities lies in their elitist contempt for the views of the "backward populace." Taking root during the perestroika period and becoming transformed into a bureaucratic prejudice, this attitude has provided real channels of communication at the local, grassroots level for the tyranny of left-wing activists and other leaders of "public opinion." . . .
>
> With Russian society profoundly divided, consensus is impossible on virtually any question. The uncoordinated activity of a number of official and semiofficial structures is now helping to bring about a situation in which the president is "losing democratically." For this reason, achieving results through an ordinary election campaign of whatever variety is impossible. The likelihood is becoming greater and greater that in the spring of 1996 there will be a wholesale flight of entire sectors of the administrative and economic elite to the side of the imagined "inevitable victor." . . .
>
> A consolidation of the Russian political elite on the territory of all-national development is possible and, given time, inevitable. But it is unattainable within the framework of the present elections; the prerequisite for it must be the victory of the president and the banishing of the

prospect of a "second revolution." Society has to cross over to the side of the president even before the corresponding economic and political preconditions make their appearance. Before election day, the president will have to be victorious both in the mass consciousness and among the elites; the advantage he enjoys must become obvious to everyone, and have an overwhelming effect on the political propaganda of the opposition. . . . [15]

After analyzing the electoral blocs and the opposition's vulnerable points, the report reviews various scenarios for the campaign and the campaign strategy (*emphasis added*):

> If the president is to conquer the information space, he needs a new distinctiveness in the eyes of the electors. For this, new channels of communication are needed, channels that are not those of the government. Propaganda and counter-propaganda have the aim of opening a window on the level of *real contact with the masses*, the level of mass communications. The outcome of the struggle for victory will not be decided by administrative control over the mass media, but by dominance at the grassroots level of mass communication—at the level of family conversations and "popular chatter."
>
> At the basis of all the failures at the start of Yeltsin's campaign has been a delusion about the campaign team's real resources in the areas of organization and coordination and the manageability of the candidate. This delusion arose as a result of previous successes. All the candidate's previous successes rested on the creation of an image, that is, the symbolic image of a reality that was necessary, but effectively unrealizable in a brief timespan. There are no miracles, so the problems remain, and after the elections they have to be solved by the usual methods. If a chance of victory is to be retained, it is essential to create an image along the lines that "the solving of all the problems has begun." In other words, we are *putting on the stage something we have neither the time nor the ability to create*. . . .
>
> As soon as the President regains the central place on the all-Russian scene, he must once again become the "ruler of popular feelings," the "people's hero." Today's scenarios, however, are being written by his enemies. In our view, the key to victory lies in the *informational dramaturgy of the campaign*. . . .
>
> The present, growing chorus of eulogies, which the mass media are transmitting throughout the country, is having the opposite result. People never repeat to one another the official formulas and the obsequious hymns of the government. In their own circles, people tell one another what they think important and interesting.

The mass media are significant only to the degree that they supply the content, ideology, and pretexts for the real mass political discussion, occurring at the grassroots level, which in Russia never ceases. Political situations and initiatives are able to be translated onto the grassroots level (the level of mass communication) to the degree to which they are *dramatic* or *dramatized*, that is, the degree to which they have been transformed into topics which people find interesting and accessible (anecdotes, scenarios, and myths are all varieties of sociopolitical dramaturgy). The mass media are also needed in the campaign in order to carve a direct channel "between the Russian capital and the Russian land."[16]

The McLuhan Galaxy and the Public Sphere

By 1996, the print media could no longer compete with television in the market for political influence and advertising. The antiwar campaign had shown that the importance of television had increased to the point where, for the authorities to leave state television in the hands of Oleg Poptsov—a journalist of the first democratic generation who thought of himself as a representative of the "fourth estate"—was impossible in the true sense of the word.

In fact, after the street battles of October 1993, when the Russian parliament was destroyed and the new constitution confirmed the supremacy of the executive power, the political process shifted onto the symbolic space of the mass media, linked to radio and television. The competition between the media images of politicians differed strikingly from the "battle of ideas," or competition between parties, seen during the period of early perestroika, the era of the print publications. The new state of affairs, however, should not be confused with the "public sphere" about which independent commentators dreamed in the early 1990s.

By the mid-1990s Russia had become part of the global "McLuhan galaxy" described by Manuel Castells.[17] In this sense development of the Russian media system has become synchronized with the global process of transformation. Here is what Castells says about television:

The television image has a low level of resolution, so that the viewers themselves have to fill in the gaps in the picture, and this means that people perceive the image more emotionally. . . . This involved perception does not in any way contradict the hypothesis of the least effort, since television relies on associative-lyrical thinking, and there is no expectation that mental energies will be expended on understanding and analysing information. . . . Neil Postman, a serious scholar of the media, thus considers that the advent of television marks a historic break with the past, with the style of thinking that developed under the influence of the printed word. . . . In order for the distinction to become clear, I shall cite his own words:

"Of all the well-known media, the print media have the strongest bent toward elucidation. In the print media, refined methods of conceptual, deductive and consistent thinking are demanded, and explanation of the causes and sequence of what is occurring is considered essential. The printed word brings discrepancies to the surface, and admits of a striving for detachment and objectivity; as well as this, the print media foster patience, teaching people not to expect immediate enlightenment. . . . the main ideology of television discourse is entertainment. It does not matter what is shown on the screen, or from what point of view; the implication is that this must serve to satisfy our curiosity or to provide us with pleasure."[18]

These conclusions provide grounds for doubt that television is guilty of spreading any coherent ideology, especially when compared to the Soviet propaganda machine, whose principal means of exerting influence was the printed text. To dwell on this conclusion, however, would be to simplify the topic, and since we are concerned with the printed word, we shall try to delve into the very essence of things.

For a particular ideology to hold a dominant position is possible only when there is a single center of power. In the post-Soviet state, meanwhile, a multitude of such centers have arisen and continue to appear to this day. Television creates an open symbolic space, a field of battle, and dictates the rules of combat. However, almost everyone without exception has access to this field:

Television has become the cultural epicenter of our society. The television mode of communication has become a radically new means of transmitting information, whose characteristics can be defined as follows: attractiveness; the sensual simulation of reality; and ease of perception, requiring a minimum of psychological effort.[19]

What cannot be communicated to the audience on the level of reasoned argument can be implanted in the consciousness of the viewer with the help of combinations of pictures that are easily remembered and comprehended on the level of myth. In this respect, television approximates the function of newspaper pictures, caricatures, or illustrated leaflets. On the television screen, heroes, heroines, enemies, and mystical forces come together in a dramatic public spectacle. The conflicts between them, and the results, are presented as if on a public stage that takes the place of the ideal of the "public sphere," an ideal that is attractive, but which in tele-reality is unattainable. Television does not appeal to reason, but to faith.

To manipulate the audience, it is thus necessary to use the rules of drama and the logic of myth. If the director of the public spectacle is sufficiently resourceful and persistent and has substantial financial resources, the disbelief of the viewer will be overcome, and the message will find its addressee.

This was the hypothesis that was tried out successfully during the Russian elections of 1996. Instead of "supporting" Boris Yeltsin (as can be seen from campaign documents, the mere support by television was considered inadequate), television, and in particular news broadcasts, became a fundamental campaign tool.

There is a contrary view that, compared to the "public sphere," the "public stage" is exceedingly narrow. A number of discussions on this topic have shown that the "public stage" is not considered a means of communication at all, but is regarded as a sort of dead end. This view, in my opinion, is held by scholars and intellectuals who value the principles of scholarly thought too highly to draw a distinction between the culture of the printed word and television.

At conferences, some speakers read from prepared texts, while others prefer to improvise. Scholarly knowledge is structured according to the laws of the book, and as a result documents are often too complex for the speakers to be able to repeat their logic from memory. Not everyone has the gift of oratory, and not everyone likes appearing before the public. It would be logical to suppose that such speakers would find the concept of the "public sphere" attractive. Meanwhile, it is hard to deny that it is more interesting to listen to speakers who depart from the written logic of the presentation, and who set forward their own points of view according to the laws of the spoken word, without forgetting to crack jokes, cross swords with opponents, and ply the audience with rhetorical questions or ready-made paradoxes. Such orators find it easier to grab the attention of the audience and, as a rule, what they have to say is better understood, though often in simplified form, and not without mistakes. All the same, what is apparent in this case is a game played according to the rules of the "public stage."

This is a felicitous example, since it embraces all the peculiarities, virtues, and shortcomings of these concepts. The "public sphere," the programmed presentation of material, puts to sleep everyone who lacks a command of the specialized terminology, who cannot follow the development of the ideas, or who is uninterested in the questions dealt with in the report. The audience maintains a polite silence and starts nodding off.

A good orator, by contrast, attracts and holds the attention of the whole audience. The emotiveness of the spoken word, graphic examples, and jokes make the presentation more accessible, and of interest not only to specialists, but to the whole audience. The listeners revive, and (unless they are Finnish students) react emotionally to what is being said. Such a presentation is often followed by numerous questions, often quite foolish, since many of the people present are simply unfamiliar with the topic or have incorrectly interpreted some of the arguments in the report.

Those who disagree start arguing heatedly, and at times the arguments are stronger than those of the speaker; but if the latter manages to keep his or her nerve, the audience usually ends up convinced that he or she is right—or at least, those members of the audience who have little idea what the discussion is about or who understand only the speaker's side of it. There are also cases in which the audience agrees both with the speaker and with someone who takes issue with the speech. As a rule, a good orator evokes sympathy. If in the course of a speech the orator "goes over the top" or does something unbecoming, he or she may arouse antipathy. But whatever the case, some kind of emotional reaction, either positive or negative, is more likely than a neutral reaction—that is, the mode of apprehension with which a reciter, reading out information about his or her findings in a patient monotone, would be satisfied.

As a rule, a mass audience has only a poor understanding of the questions being examined. In the classical case of a newspaper from the elite bourgeois press of the eighteenth century—the press that Jurgen Habermas uses as his basis for constructing a model of the "public sphere"—it is still possible to imagine the victory of rational, precise argumentation, with a detailed positing of the essence of the question, over a superficial opinion of a journalist or opponent. In a contemporary mass-circulation newspaper, however, this is hard to count on. The only people able to believe in such a phenomenon were those in the early 1990s coming out of the ideocratic Soviet system. As for television, the only people able to believe in the victory of reason on the airwaves are those who think the law prevails every time in court.

Importing Political Technology

Besides the Foundation for Effective Politics, there are other claimants to the role of ideologues of the election campaign. They did not leave behind them any known documents in the Russian language. To this day, nothing has been heard in the Russian press about the participation of these people. *Time*, however, published an article by the journalist Michael Kramer—an article difficult to regard as anything other than a promotion piece—under the title "Rescuing Boris: The Secret Story of How Four U.S. Advisers Used Polls, Focus Groups, Negative Ads and All the Other Techniques of American Campaigning to Help Boris Yeltsin Win."[20]

Feliks Braynin, who emigrated to the United States in the 1970s, acted as a consultant to U.S. investors, and had contacts in the Council of Ministers. The article in *Time* credits him with recruiting American election campaign specialists. The idea of inviting the Americans came to Braynin while he was observing the tallying of the count in the Duma elections of 1995. Everyone in the government and the presidential administration was certain that in some magical fashion Yeltsin would win the elections, but Braynin was not so sure. Securing a commission from Oleg Soskovets, who early in 1996 was heading the campaign staff, and working through San Francisco lawyer Fred Lowell and Lowell's Republican friends, Braynin met with Joe Shumat and George Gorton, key advisers to California Governor Pete Wilson, who had at some point aspired to the U.S. presidency.

Shumat and Gorton in turn drew in Richard Dresner, a political consultant from New York who had taken part in many of Pete Wilson's campaigns. Dresner's importance, however, lay elsewhere; he had ties to Dick Morris, who had helped to organize Bill Clinton's campaigns for governor of Arkansas in the late 1970s and early 1980s.

Dick Morris was considered Clinton's "political guru." His brilliant career had been cut short during the Democratic Convention, when the newspapers discovered his involvement with a prostitute with whom he was alleged to have shared information about intrigues in the White House. Nevertheless, he retained his influence, and during Boris Yeltsin's election campaign acted as a channel through which the American consultants agreed on measures in the international arena that would increase the rating of the Russian president. At times, working through Clinton, they also resolved other problems of the election campaign; for example, this is how they managed to persuade Yeltsin to have himself filmed in a campaign clip for central television.

On February 27, Dresner met with Soskovets. The latter hired the Americans, who instructed the campaign staff in modern electoral techniques. The Americans were also entrusted with another task. A month before the elections they were to report whether Yeltsin had any chance of winning. If there were no chance, the elections would have to be canceled. Over the course of four months, the Americans were to receive $250,000, plus all their expenses, and an unlimited budget for the needs of the campaign.

At their disposal was a two-room office, along with rooms in the President Hotel, a car with a former KGB agent as driver, and two bodyguards. Recruiting two more young people, Braynin's son Alan and Alex Moore, a public relations specialist from Washington, the American team set to work. The group worked in complete secrecy, with the cover that they represented the producers of flat-screen American television sets and were researching the market.

The consultants, however, did not work for long under Soskovets. Real control over the campaign soon passed into the hands of the president's daughter Tatyana Dyachenko, the only person who could get to see the president on a daily basis. In the President Hotel, Dyachenko's office was located opposite the office of the Americans. Thanks to their close contact with Dyachenko, the American consultants found that their role grew immeasurably in importance to the point where it became decisive. Their first task was to instruct Dyachenko in the basics of election campaign techniques.

Another task of the Americans was to do battle with the prejudices of the president's entourage. The failure in the Duma elections of movements that had spent vast sums on television campaign advertising had convinced Yeltsin's associates that the mass media were of little effectiveness. Meanwhile, the scant use they made of voter surveys was preventing them from working out the necessary strategy. In the Americans' view, the clips used in the Duma elections were well conceived in creative terms and competently produced, but they could not have been described as appropriately aimed.

One of the first analytical memoranda produced by the group bore the title "Why Bush Lost the Election." The parallels were obvious. As in the case of Bush, Yeltsin's associates thought the economy was recovering, though only a minority of the population were feeling the effects of this. Like Bush, Yeltsin refused as a matter of principle to believe that his opponent could be elected. As with Bush, the organizing of Yeltsin's election campaign witnessed power struggles between diverse groups, and the content of the campaign amounted to a mix of ill-assorted ideas, assembled without a unifying strategy or even the recognition that a strategy was needed.

Identifying delays in wage payments as the most important problem that the president faced, the American consultants insisted on a change from promises to the demonstrative payment of the back wage. The president was to put the blame for the increase in wage arrears on his subordinates, publicly rebuking them for not using funds as directed. Yeltsin adopted this recommendation with relish.

Another idea of the American consultants, however, was not destined to succeed. This was their recommendation that the election campaign should begin with a fifteen-minute speech by the president, that next to him should be Moscow mayor Yury Luzhkov and other authoritative figures, and that the president should came out onto the platform through a crowd of supporters. The president spoke for a whole hour in front of a grey-suited audience. To show they had been right, the Americans organized a preview of the speech during which members of the audience could use a special apparatus to express their reactions, turning a dial to numbers on the right or left depending on their impressions of what they were seeing. The results shocked Yeltsin's advisers. The president could not promise anything, since people did not believe him in the least.

The president's low rating, and the population's lack of trust in him, convinced the Americans that there was only one possible strategy for the election campaign. First, it was necessary to convince the population that Yeltsin was the only alternative to the Communists. Second, people had to be convinced that the Communists had to be stopped at all costs. Obvious though this decision might have seemed, the fight to make anti-communism the sole issue in the campaign continued throughout March.

Having chosen a strategy, it was essential to find tactics as well. Aleksey Levinson, who had been hired by the Americans to coordinate the work with focus groups, was to decide what there was about the Communists that frightened the population most. Long queues, food shortages, and nationalization of businesses were often mentioned, but the most widespread fear was of civil war. *Time* magazine quoted Richard Dresner as saying:

> This was why Yeltsin, his aides, and all our advertising stressed the possibility of disorder if Yeltsin lost. Many people were nostalgic for Soviet times, and no one liked the president, but they liked the possibility of revolts and class war even less. Vote for Yeltsin, and at least everything will be calm—that was the line we wanted to put across. So the drumbeat about the possibility of disorder rang out right to the end of the campaign, and all the final advertising was devoted to the repressions carried out by the Soviet regime.[21]

During the first stage of the campaign, Yeltsin had problems with television. Even in March 1996, the president was mercilessly criticized on state television about the war in Chechnya. "It is ludicrous to control two channels and not make them submit to your will," Dresner concluded.

> "When measures are undertaken," the memorandum from the advisers states, "it is essential to let the state television and radio outlets know the aim of these measures, their importance, and how they should be depicted." Beginning in April, the Russian television became a virtual arm of the Yeltsin campaign. This was not hard to achieve. When it became clear from voter surveys that other democratic candidates would not attract the required number of votes, most Russian journalists began to view Yeltsin as the only rival to the Communists, and hence the best guarantee of their careers.[22]

The Americans hoped that the removal of Soskovets would render null and void the task he had been assigned of deciding the outcome of the elections in advance. On May 5, however, Aleksandr Korzhakov urged that the elections be postponed. It was at this time that the group first drew up a memorandum stating that Yeltsin's victory in the elections was assured. Yeltsin publicly rebuked Korzhakov but declared that there were also other people who believed that a victory for Communist candidate Gennady Zyuganov would lead to civil war. Many people regarded this declaration as a hint that Yeltsin might later return to

Korzhakov's suggestion. In fact, Dresner states, the declaration was in the spirit of the campaign strategy of showing that electing Yeltsin was the best way to avoid chaos.

> The Americans were "vitally necessary," says Mikhail Margolev, the co-ordinator of the campaign at Video International. Margolev spent five years working in two American advertising agencies but openly admits that his approach is based as before on the experience he received as a propaganda journalist at TASS. . . . "The Americans helped us to learn Western political techniques," Margolev says, "and most importantly, they created the demand for our work, because they were close to Tatyana. . . . It was an extremely clever move by Yeltsin to appoint his daughter in order to be sure that everything would be done properly, but she definitely relied on the Americans."[23]

Virtual Reality

In one way or another, major television stations and most of the mass media cooperated with the government, providing the election campaign team with a field for "information dramaturgy." The only media outlets to take a demonstratively neutral position were *Obshchaya Gazeta*, *Novaya Yezhednevnaya Gazeta*, and a few regional publications that either were not caught up in the candidates' political advertising network, or that based their editorial policy on resisting the nonalternative approach thrust upon them by the Yeltsin team.

The campaign was a success. First, all the candidates apart from Yeltsin and Zyuganov were easily marginalized. This was the fate of Gorbachev, Zhirinovsky, Yavlinsky, and even Lebed—although later, after Lebed had agreed to work with Yeltsin, some of the resources of the presidential team were put behind Lebed's campaign.

The main resource at the disposal of the party of the government was the mass media, mobilized not only by politicized capital (whose role was unquestionably decisive), but also on an ideological basis, thanks to cleverly organized public revelations of revanchism and extremism in the ranks of the Communist Party, trends that posed a clear threat to freedom of expression, to the institution of the mass media, and to the new status enjoyed by journalists. It should not be forgotten that similar views were held by many people, who for various reasons did not want a return of the Communists (this was described as "a return to the past," in the language of the election campaign), but this was the card the president's team played, and ultimately, it was what ensured Yeltsin a second term in office.

NTV chief Igor Malashenko, whose channel represented the greatest danger to the president, was given responsibility for the propaganda aspects of the campaign and for molding the image of the president. The success with which the president's team coped with the task that in the FEP report had been formulated as "putting on the stage what we have neither the time nor the ability to create" appears in an article by the well-known St. Petersburg journalist Viktor Toporov, published after the elections in the journal *Svobodnaya Mysl* under the headline "The Virtual Reality of the Elections":

> Independently of the personal, group, clan, or idealist motives of each particular actor, the electronic and mass circulation media in toto, supposedly the expression and guarantee of the interests of society, acted in a fundamentally different manner during the election campaign, ensuring that the powers of the present head of state would be prolonged. To this end, the media, using both traditional and alternative methods, went so far as to create and to instill in the mass consciousness a virtual (that is, a fictitious and false) reality . . . in which, and only in which, the positive changes that would remove or at least minimize the general dissatisfaction with the president proved to be possible. For six months this virtual reality took the place of actual reality. Within this virtual reality, a decisive choice was made. By virtue of this, naturally, the choice could not fail to be illusory. . . .
>
> The mass media, which only recently had prided themselves on their independence and their oppositional stance with regard to Chechnya, "swallowed" this shameful peace, "swallowed" the inevitable new victims, "swallowed" and acclaimed the president's peacemaking initiatives . . . the visit to Chechnya (to a virtual Chechnya, we would note), and the rest. . . . And so, a virtual peace was achieved in Chechnya. And similarly, a virtual peace was concluded with the mass media on the Chechnya issue.[24]

In the same fashion, Toporov lists other virtual achievements of the presidential campaign—the payment of back wages, economic stabilization, "virtual" entry into the "Big Seven" club, handouts from a nonexistent "presidential fund," and miraculous cures for all sorts of illnesses. The president "sometimes spoke hoarsely, but this was neither the result of a hangover, nor evidence that he was in his death throes."

Journalists no longer had any illusions during the election campaign, but this did not prevent them from spreading misinformation. Since we are now familiar with the contents of the FEP report and with the work of the group of American advisers, we know that this was the task that was assigned to them by the campaign staff.

It would be hard to come up with a more accurate description of the effect of the election campaign than the following by Leonid Ionin in *Nezavisimaya Gazeta*:

> A powerful new weapon of political struggle has appeared in the hands of Russian politicians—so-called modern political techniques. These, of course, already existed and were applied earlier. Only the current presidential elections, however, have demonstrated the power and potential of these techniques to the fullest, since it is modern political techniques applied by professionals that have ensured victory for Boris Yeltsin.[25]

The significance of the presidential elections for the Russian political system and the mass media lay in the fact that the 1996 presidential elections saw the rise of a new class of media managers, who in the course of the campaign had been schooled in the manipulation of public opinion. It should be noted that the number of new "cadres" who appeared as a result of the elections was not limited to the "star team" described earlier. The total concentration of the resources of the state structures, advertising agencies, banks, and large private financial-industrial groups meant that large numbers of "specialists" received an education in the field of manipulating the mass media. To these people should also be added those who worked to support other candidates, and those who simply watched what was happening with interest.

Thanks to the embedding of modern techniques for manipulating public opinion, the place of the "public sphere" utopia, a place left vacant following the collapse of independent journalism, was taken by the public stage. From then on, the symbolic space of the mass media came to be regarded as a theatrical expanse on which virtual heroes (the images of politicians and business entrepreneurs and of industrial and financial structures) staged various performances whose meaning was not articulated but was conveyed on a symbolic (that is, mythological) level.

The period of hegemony of the liberal-democratic utopia that had filled the vacuum of social reality during the hard times of the "transition period" was vanishing into history along with the high circulations of the "democratic" newspapers. The epoch of the spectacle, brought by television, began its reign in Russia at the time of the elections.

More than once in this chapter, emphasis has been placed on the resemblance between the political process and theatrical dramaturgy. But in discussing the presidential elections—and the Russian politics of the 1990s in general—one key difference must be stressed. The social function of the spectacle as a particular form of practice lies in the legitimation of social norms. Sometimes, of course, "good guys" get killed, if tragedy is involved. But in the most popular theatrical form of our era, the Hollywood movie, the good guys always win. This means that politics becomes a field for the construction of moral judgments, which are embodied in political leaders.

> The idea of leadership renders intelligible the complex and mainly unstudied world of the socium. . . . In imperceptible changes to the economic conjuncture, in the dramas of events and ideologies, it is easy not just for ordinary voters to get confused, but also for scholars and historians. Faith in the benevolent or evil power of political leaders offers an easy and readily available means of simplifying the situation. . . . Leaders become the embodiment of whatever alarms or gladdens the observer of the political scene, since it is easy to identify oneself with leaders, to support, oppose, love, or hate them. There are also passions of other kinds. People who feel overwhelmed by the possibility of making choices in their own lives hand over this right to a leader; in the words of Erich Fromm, they "escape from freedom."[26]

The society of the spectacle comes increasingly into conflict with the monotheist principles of the binary opposition of "good" and "bad." The image of the political as opposed to the spiritual leader (in Russia this latter role has traditionally belonged to writers)[27] no longer has any relation to fundamental values. Beneath the image of the successful politician in 1990s Russia we are more likely to find archaic and mythological elements, such as archetypes or fantastic motifs.[28] Moreover, it turns out that in political TV-reality even a politician who embodies harshness, boorishness, and high-handedness combined with nationalist ardor and theatricality (Vladimir Zhirinovsky) can count on a secure place on the political Olympus.

It is paradoxical but true that democracy in Russia has become possible only because modern techniques for the manipulation of public opinion have allowed the party of those in power to pass through the legitimizing process of elections with the help of the media, that is, without resorting to force.

Information Wars

Public relations, political consultants, advertising agencies, and experts in the use of the media existed in Russia even before the presidential elections of 1996. There were also scandalous instances in which public opinion was manipulated using the press and the electronic media; it is sufficient to mention the affair of Sergey Mavrodi, whose financial empire (a pyramid scheme) conducted its main operations through state television and the pages of the all-Russian newspapers. Until the presidential elections, however, "virtual reality" was a local rather than a universal phenomenon; the instances of it that appeared were islands in a sea of common sense, or in the seas of the open political partisanship of the publications—a partisanship that determined their circle of readers. Apart from this, there were no developed techniques for directing and manipulating the mass media even by their owners. As the report by the Foundation for Effective Politics notes, a managerial signal from an editor in chief would be transmitted to a department head, and from the department head to a journalist, gradually losing its force. Right up until the 1996 elections, in fact, the techniques that had persisted since Soviet times could ensure only silence (in the case of censorship) or crude provocation. For practical purposes, the sacking of chief editors was impossible, and any attempts by the owners of the media to use their publications to publish leaks or information compromising to competitors made them stand out sharply in the general information field, and hence aroused mistrust.

What, in sum, was the influence of the elections on the mass media of this period?

- An alliance was concluded between the owners of the mass media and the media experts, that is, the professional manipulators of public opinion.
- A modus operandi was established individually with each information entity, by which the information entities could be used as tools for "information dramaturgy."
- The reputation of all the press entities fell to such a low point that there was no longer any reason to be afraid of competition on the basis of ethics.

Prior to the elections no one had known how to manage the mass media, but now everyone who had worked on the campaign staff—and this included an important segment of the Russian political and economic elite, along with virtually everyone who specialized in the techniques of political manipulation—knew this the way a Christian knows the Lord's Prayer. In addition, such new information methods as "character assassination,"[29] tried out on Gennady Zyuganov in the course of the campaign, had proven their effectiveness.

From the time of the 1996 election campaign, politicians and media owners came away with the conviction that politics made sense and politicians had a future only to the extent that this was reflected in the mass media.

On the basis of the experience of the election campaign, various organizations worked out methods and guiding principles for analyzing the political process on the basis of the content of the mass media and for using the intrinsic laws of the media for implementing one or another information policy.

Finally, immediately after the elections, the politicians and the media magnates, who had united in the name of a common goal, fell to arguing among themselves, and thus acquired targets at which to aim their information weapons. Hence, after a certain interval following the counting of the national vote, a new epoch began in the history of the Russian media, an epoch of compromising reports and incessant information campaigning.

As noted earlier, the widespread use of negative political techniques was a distinctive feature of the 1996 election campaign. Yevgeny Krasnikov, writing for the newspaper *Moskovskie Novosti*, cites these examples:

> One of the first "anti-Zyuganov" actions mounted by the FEP was the sabotaging of a press conference which the Communist Party (KPRF) leader had called immediately after the meeting between the "Big Seven" leaders and Boris Yeltsin. As Gleb Pavlovsky relates, "We knew that Zyuganov was trying to lessen the impact of what had taken place, and we therefore decided to change the topic of the press conference." Using its channels, the foundation floated a report to the effect that Zyuganov was expected to declare a campaign alliance with Zhirinovsky. "As a result, the journalists peppered Zyuganov with questions on this subject; he was forced to justify himself, and the original plan for the press conference came undone."

Just as successful was an action timed to coincide with the arrival of the KPRF leader in St. Petersburg. In the words of one FEP employee, "We managed to substantially increase the confusion that surrounded the organizing of this visit. As a result, the journalists turned up for the meeting with Zyuganov either two hours early, or two hours late. . . . "

During the election campaign, FEP experts painstakingly followed the Communist and nationalist newspapers, even the most marginal ones, and through their own channels passed on the most obnoxious articles to the mainstream press.

At times, what seemed like totally incredible information was released by the mass media. For example, it was reported that if Zyuganov won, he would cancel all the television serials. Or that the reason Zyuganov hated Yeltsin was a hoard of "CPSU gold" said to have been found by Yury Luzhkov during the reconstruction of Manezh Square. "But we never invented anything," Pavlovsky declares. "We simply focused attention on particular facts. Anpilov really did declare that the 'soap operas' would be canceled, and the story about the 'CPSU gold' was published in a newspaper in the Altai territory. The main thing is that thanks to us, this information was reprinted numerous times in the regional press."

Employees of the FEP also acknowledged their complicity in calling sensational press conferences at which several organizations declared that they were pulling out of the coalition of popular and patriotic forces: "We simply located people who had founded these organizations, but had later dropped out, and suggested that they speak."

Among its services, the FEP also lists the frequent appearance on television of such radicals as Anpilov and Terekhov. It may be that these politicians saw their access to the airwaves as being able to 'break through the information blockade.' Nevertheless, their chance to make such speeches, the topics, and the length had been discussed in advance by Gleb Pavlovsky, Igor Malashenko, and the hosts of the television programs.[30]

In elections, especially those that are "fateful" and involve a "choice between two evils," such tricks are commonplace. The same events appear quite different in "peacetime," especially when everyone expects, if not a complete, then at least a relative, rehabilitation of the reputation of the press after the election campaigning has concluded.

The final months of 1996 and all of 1997 were marked by the use of compromising information—*kompromat*. The first shot in the new information war was fired by *Moskovsky Komsomolets (MK)* journalist

Aleksandr Khinshteyn, when the newspaper published a transcript of a conversation between Anatoly Chubais, Viktor Ilyushin, and an unidentified third person (it is now widely believed that this third person was Sergey Zverev) in Yeltsin's campaign headquarters in the President Hotel. The participants discussed the problem that had arisen with the arrest by the president's security service of two high-ranking "fundraisers" as they left the Russian White House with $500,000 in "shady cash." Carrying the famous photocopy-paper box had been the media magnate Sergey Lisovsky, and accompanying him had been Chubais aide Arkady Yevstafyev. Thanks to the publication of the transcript in *MK*, Chubais ended up as one of the accused in the "cardboard box affair,"[31] which, as it turns out, never came to trial.

The first person to sacrifice his reputation in the name of the information war was, however, Yevgeny Kisilev, the host of the NTV television program "Itogi." It was Kiselev who throughout the night of June 19 and into the early hours of June 20, 1996, went on the air with reports of a "coup d'état." His broadcasts could not have deceived anyone except the most ardent democrats, who hated presidential security chief Aleksandr Korzhakov as a matter of principle, and the presidential family, who according to Korzhakov spent the whole night trying to persuade General Mikhail Barsukov to release the detainees.[32] Unlike the American muckrakers of the early twentieth century, their Russian counterparts in most cases were not oriented toward the interests of the public. Their main goal was to influence the politicized elite. Herein, to some degree, lies the secret behind the fact that the political influence of the low-circulation *Nezavisimaya Gazeta* and that of *Moskovsky Komsomolets*, with its press-run of a million copies, was virtually identical.

The main line of confrontation in the information space and in most of the propaganda and counterpropaganda operations in the Russian media in 1997 and 1998 ran between two competing groups: on one side Vladimir Potanin's Interros group backed up by George Soros, and on the other, an alliance between Vladimir Gusinsky's Media-Most and Boris Berezovsky. The beginning of the new epoch of information conflict, which replaced occasional bursts of *kompromat*, can be dated to July 25, 1997—the day on which an auction was held. Properly speaking, the campaign of revenge by the defeated side, and the counter-campaign mounted by OneksimBank, became the first information war between the oligarchs.

The Battle for Svyazinvest

Yeltsin's victory in the 1996 elections was largely a service rendered to the president by Berezovsky and Gusinsky, and after the elections they remained especially close to the government. This was evidenced by their support for government initiatives on the one hand and the priority access to the privatization process they enjoyed on the other. Not surprisingly, Berezovsky and Gusinsky were counting on certain favors in the case of the privatization of Svyazinvest. The days of "auctions" where no money changed hands were of course past, and the government, which now included members of the so-called team of young reformers (Nemtsov, Kokh, Chubais, and others), desperately needed money to pay pensions and wage arrears. The oligarchs were not against paying—but they did not want to pay too much. Also, for obvious reasons, they found it convenient to agree in advance on who was to win the auctions. There was nothing unusual about such an arrangement, which corresponded to the traditional way in which property had been distributed during privatization. Under the established rules of the game, in fact, the partners had every reason to count on their undertaking being successful.

For Berezovsky and Gusinsky, Svyazinvest was a very important investment target. Founded especially in order to be sold off, the holding company included controlling packets of shares in seventy-six regional telephone enterprises, five city telephone companies, four telegraph centers, and three international communications operations. For Berezovsky and Gusinsky, who owned extensive mass media properties, access to the telecommunications sector was tantamount to admission to the twenty-first century; it would allow them not only immediately to stake out strong positions in the rapidly developing markets for local telephone and mobile communications, Internet access, and so on, but also eventually to integrate their telecommunications channels with the content supplied by their print-media holding companies.

It is more than likely that Svyazinvest would have gone to Berezovsky and Gusinsky had Vladimir Potanin not shown an interest in it. Potanin had also played a role in the 1996 election campaign, but unlike Berezovsky and Gusinsky, he managed subsequently to capitalize on his success by penetrating the government apparatus; after the elections, he became first deputy prime minister. One of the results of his work was the system of mortgage auctions, in which controlling packets of shares in enterprises were mortgaged against investment credits. This scheme provided easy access to privatized property for business entrepreneurs close to the government, and so helped to cement the "oligarchy" in place. With the help of a mortgage auction, Potanin himself won control over Norilsk Nickel, one of the world's largest producers of nickel and other metals, for a few hundred million dollars.

The victory scored by George Soros and Vladimir Potanin at the auction on July 25, 1997, cost the partners $2 billion (this was $600 million more than the bid entered by Berezovsky, Gusinsky, and their partners). For a long time thereafter, rumors circulated in business circles to the effect that the sum bid had not been paid, but it was impossible to determine the truthfulness of these rumors. In any case, the holding company was acquired by Potanin and Soros.

This defeat threw cold water on the hopes of Berezovsky and Gusinsky to enter the top league of players in the telecommunications market. The two partners felt deceived and left out. Their desire to show their strength and gain revenge was mixed with dim hopes that the outcome of the auction might be reconsidered. The result was the most powerful information campaign ever launched against business competitors and the government in the 1990s. The techniques developed during the elections were employed by well-coordinated teams of specialists, with the media resources of both holding companies at their disposal, to deal the government a crushing blow. In response, the government and the Potanin media began an active countercampaign.[33]

The first shots in this information war rang out on Saturday July 26, the day after the auction. An article by A. Soldatov[34] in the newspaper *Segodnya* (which belonged to Gusinsky) expressed doubt about the legality of the auction; the way the bids were compared behind closed doors, and the drawn-out procedure for opening the envelopes led the author of the article to suspect foul play or a behind-the-scenes deal.

On the current affairs program "Vremya" that same evening, Sergey Dorenko (from ORT, the channel controlled by Berezovsky) accused the top executives of OneksimBank of misappropriating several tens of millions of dollars belonging to the Cherepovets chemical combine Azot. Summing up the results of the auction, Dorenko put special emphasis on the fact that the shares in Svyazinvest had been won by foreign investors with dubious reputations, as was confirmed on the spot by accusations against them.

On Sunday, Dorenko gave an interview on the radio station Ekho

Moskvy (controlled by Gusinsky) and repeated all his charges. On Monday, the newspaper *Segodnya* came out with a lead article by A. Zvyagilsky entitled "The Money Stank." In the article, partners of OneksimBank were accused of plundering budget funds; the implication was that OneksimBank was at odds with the law. A list was presented of breaches of the law said to have occurred during the auctioning of Svyazinvest, the implication being that the auction should have been declared illegal. The article also pointed to the "close and warm" friendship between Potanin and Kokh, who were said "not to hide their sympathy for one another"; this meant that the government was favoring OneksimBank.

In the same issue, *Segodnya* broached another topic: ORT. According to information that the writer of the article claimed to have, the government was planning an attack on the "independent channel," and ORT was most likely doomed to suffer the same fate as *Izvestia* and *Komsomolskaya Pravda*.[35] Why did OneksimBank need media organs, the author of the article asked. More than likely, to mask the stench from its own vile operations.

On Tuesday, four more articles carried on the campaign in one way or another. The newspaper *Kommersant-Daily* published an interview with Sergey Dorenko; there were two more articles recounting and "analyzing" the content of the "Vremya" program on which Dorenko had appeared.[36] *Nezavisimaya Gazeta* also carried an article by Rustam Narzikulov and Tatyana Koshkareva entitled "Will Potanin Become President of Russia?" In the view of the authors, Potanin needed media outlets, money, and influence in order to be elected as the country's president.

Every day, articles were published that fit into the framework of the campaign by Berezovsky and Gusinsky. At the same time, all sorts of press conferences were held and declarations issued; these acted as pretexts for covering the relevant topics in television news broadcasts. Articles in different newspapers owned by the holding companies were often written by the same people.

Ever-new accusations surfaced, aimed at Potanin, OneksimBank, and the members of the government. The campaign kept growing in intensity throughout the first week of August, culminating in a press conference featuring LDPR leader Vladimir Zhirinovsky and Nizhny Novgorod business entrepreneur Sergey Klimentyev. At this press conference, Boris Nemtsov was accused of corruption and bribe-taking, as well as of trying to organize the murder of Zhirinovsky. This declaration received a huge amount of coverage on television and in the newspapers of the media holding companies.

Naturally, a series of counterattacks was launched on the part of OneksimBank. Unlike Berezovsky and Gusinsky, however, Oneksim-Bank did not have its own television channels and radio stations, and this significantly limited its media-influencing ability. In essence, the government and Potanin had to make use of state television (the RTR channel) and the newspapers *Izvestia* and *Komsomolskaya Pravda*, controlled by OneksimBank. The fact that the government and OneksimBank were unprepared for a media war explains why their response was slow in coming.

Nevertheless, an interview with Boris Nemtsov appeared on July 29, on the front page of *Komsomolskaya Pravda*. In this interview, the first deputy prime minister appealed for an end to the building of "bandit capitalism."[37] Defending the government's position, Nemtsov argued that the auction had been the first to be conducted honestly. On the same day, Anatoly Chubais declared to the press that the bankers had tried to reach agreement on the outcome of the auction, but that the government had refused to tolerate a breach of the rules. As a result of the auction, the first deputy prime minister stated, the wages owed to military personnel would be paid. Chubais went on to voice the cabinet's final position: there would be no review of the outcome of the auction. On the next day, another article was added to those that had been published in *Komsomolskaya Pravda* and *Izvestia*.[38] Appearing in the popular Moscow newspaper *Moskovsky Komsomolets*, the article bore the title "Investment or Incest?" and described the efforts of Berezovsky and Gusinsky to reach agreement with the government on the purchase of Svyazinvest. The media war was explained as resulting from the wish of the "oligarchs" to avenge themselves.[39] Finally, on the same day a press conference was held in Moscow by former Security Council head Aleksandr Lebed, who accused Berezovsky of making a fortune out of the war in Chechnya.

The countercampaign, like the "onslaught," went on for several more weeks, culminating in the publication of excerpts from the autobiography of former presidential bodyguard Aleksandr Korzhakov. In these excerpts, Korzhakov testified that Berezovsky had asked him to "liquidate" Vladimir Gusinsky, Moscow Mayor Yury Luzhkov, and Luzhkov's business partner, the entrepreneur (and Soviet-era pop star) Iosif Kobzon.[40]

The Svyazinvest episode marked the beginning of a series of information campaigns in which those in power were the victims of the media holding companies. The second half of 1997 and the first half of 1998 were marked by opposition to the federal government on the part of ORT, NTV, *Segodnya, Nezavisimaya Gazeta,* and *Moskovsky Komsomolets*—opposition motivated strictly by the interests of a few media owners.

A peculiarity of the battle for Svyazinvest was the fact that for the first time since the 1996 elections, the government and the media owners were on different sides of the barricades. As noted earlier, instead of putting media outlets at the disposal of the government, the owners started using them in their own interests, including against the regime, particularly in cases where conflicts of interest had arisen. From that point on, the struggle of the contending economic groups among themselves or with the federal government dominated the mass media and was behind numerous propaganda initiatives.

The press campaigns were so numerous that an entire book would be needed to describe them. We shall therefore restrict ourselves to listing the most notorious of them. These unquestionably include the "cardboard box affair,"[41] the two "writer affairs," when Aleksandr Minkin in *Novaya Gazeta* first published an intercepted conversation between Boris Nemtsov and his publisher about royalties for Nemtsov's recently published book *The Provincial,* and later, a much more scandalous report that members of the "Chubais team" had received a hundred thousand dollars each for providing a chapter of a book, in this case not yet published, on the history of privatization in Russia.

Finally, in the newspaper *Sovershenno Sekretno,* the journalist Larisa Kislinskaya published photographs of Justice Minister Valentin Kovalev in the company of nude women in a bathhouse, a move that led to Kovalev's resignation.

Other Campaigns

Nemtsov, who was viewed as one of the most promising potential candidates for the presidency in the year 2000, came under attack from the Luzhkov group. Along with the head of the presidential administration Pavel Borodin, media organs friendly to the Moscow government unleashed a vicious campaign against Nemtsov's efforts to get state functionaries out of foreign-made cars and put them in Volgas. *Moskovsky*

Komsomolets brazenly misrepresented the facts to put the price of a Volga at $50,000, while the real price was the equivalent of $10,000–15,000 depending on equipment. In addition, Nemtsov was accused repeatedly in the magazine *Lyudi* and the newspaper *Sovershenno Sekretno* of having ordered the murder of political opponents, of being unfaithful to his wife, and of simple depravity. The latter charge was made by Sergey Dorenko, deservedly regarded as the most biased journalist in post-Soviet Russia, referring to testimonies by striptease artists whom Nemtsov was supposed to have "smacked on the bottom" while at the OneksimBank sanatorium. Dorenko assigned the topic of Nemtsov's "depraved" behavior more time than any other on his program. Dorenko later admitted that there was no proof, but he made this admission only in order to pass on to the next accusation against Nemtsov.

Many commercial publications that were able to take a more or less independent approach to their news reporting used the conflict between OneksimBank, Gusinsky, and Berezovsky for their own purposes—to show the difference between their own editorial policies and the behavior of the publications that had been divided by politicized capital. The first publications to react to the campaign were *Moskovsky Komsomolets*, which published a table of the media holding companies; the newspaper *Kommersant-Daily*, which reported on the actions of the contending media groups in the form of dispatches from the information war; and the magazine *Novoe Vremya*.

Novoe Vremya placed on its cover the heading, "Newspaper-war novel / Information wars: until the first blood is drawn?" In this issue, the journalists tried to sort things out. As Andrey Kolesnikov wrote:

> Free speech has died in the newspapers without even managing to be born. In theory, the newspapers could have become respectable and independent. But without discovering any other form of existence apart from selling themselves to financial bosses who lay claim to political influence and economic rents (which flow directly from this influence), and who understand nothing about how to manage a publication, the newspapers have acquired their own little personal agitprop. A whole generation of journalists has grown up who have trouble imagining (or have already managed to forget) what "pure" journalism, without a basis in any "social requirement," might be. A new journalistic professionalism has appeared, one not exclusively related to newspapers, magazines, or television, but one relating to PR—the professionalism of specialists in advertising and in pushing information (or misinformation) in the marketplace.

Newspaper type has become the weapon of the banker and the politician; the journalist has been transformed into a mouthpiece. I am not quite sure why we denounce the party journalism of the time of stagnation. After all, the journalism of that time was also carried on in a professional fashion, and according to the canons of verbal mastery.[42]

In her commentary on "past services," the temperamental Valeriya Novodvorskaya does not forgive the pioneers of *kompromat*:

It is appalling to see how NTV pushes out onto the stage the jack-of-all-trades Minkin, who, like the person who has not read Pasternak but condemns him anyway, crawls into the affair surrounding the publishing house, royalties for Alfred Kokh, and Chubais's interview on this topic—an affair which he does not understand in the least. Minkin, because of his total incompetence and lack of information (the relevant organs had not yet come up with the films involved) could only say that no one should believe Chubais, since Chubais is a liar, and the father of lying. Minkin does not believe him, but why should we believe Minkin, who in Gaidar's virtual dacha found a virtual publicly owned divan?[43]

Following the scandal over the latest "writer affair," which culminated in a string of resignations from the Cabinet of Ministers, the magazine *Kommersant-Vlast* (formerly *Kommersant-Weekly*) came out with the ironic cover headline "Persecuted by Journalists." Beneath this headline were pictures of Sergey Dorenko, Aleksandr Minkin, and Yevgeny Kiselev. *Kompromat* was the theme of the issue. The magazine featured a detailed investigation of the campaign around the "writer affair," from Minkin's on air outburst on Ekho Moskvy radio (when he admittedly did not have even documents at his disposal) to the "unraveling" of the topic on the channels ORT and NTV by the "professional propagandists" Dorenko and Kiselev.[44]

One of the articles from the wide selection carried in this issue of the weekly gave a detailed description of the stages through which the information campaign passed. According to *Kommersant-Vlast*, the campaign consisted of "three echelons." In the first stage, the basic item of information was put into circulation, and more information was then added, through one of the low-circulation but influential newspapers. To this, an analysis scripted in advance and put in the mouths of analysts or newsmakers would be added if possible.

In the second stage, television would be used to "cement" the theme.

The main burden of the campaign would lie on the weekly analytical broadcasts of the current affairs programs. In the usual news summaries the topic could receive only "less coverage," since a single topic could not take up a whole broadcast; meanwhile Dorenko, for example, devoted one of his analytical programs exclusively to the "writers' affair." Then, discussion of the topic would take place, or would be relayed. However, "no one was interested any longer in the reality, in the legal side of the matter. The image, the opinions and attitudes, had been shaped. The goal had been achieved." The third stage, according to the article, saw the mounting of a defense and its overcoming by the attacking forces—and also, the real consequences of the campaign in the form of resignations and appointments. It is possible to disagree with the author as to whether the third stage was obligatory, at any rate for all the participants in the campaign, though this outcome was unquestionably what they were aiming at. At the end of the article, the author comes to the following conclusion:

> I would compare the campaign against Chubais with the presidential campaign. On that occasion a negative image of the Communists was created, and now a particular functionary has been discredited. The sole difference is that in the case of Chubais only the Moscow media were brought into play. There was no organized campaign in the provinces. This means that from the very first everything was oriented toward the political elite. Toward the president.[45]

The same selection of articles also contains a curious observation concerning the motives of one of the journalists taking part in the information campaign:

> It is enough to be even slightly familiar with Minkin, with his attitude to the young reformers, his reputation as a scandalmonger, and his vanity, inherent in our profession, about being first. It is enough to hint to a journalist that today only you have this information, and that tomorrow it will run out of control, for him not to wait a week until the next issue of his publication appears.[46]

In late May 1998, Maksim Sokolov was among the first to turn his attention to the tendentiousness with which ORT and NTV were reporting the miners' strikes.[47] Later, this point of view became extremely widespread. It is striking that those who agreed on this question included

President Boris Yeltsin, who held a special meeting with the heads of the state television channels, and Professor Sergey Muratov of the journalism faculty at Moscow State University, who recognized that the work of the television companies during the strike had been "unprofessional." When reporting from the blocked rail lines, the television channels ran interviews only with passengers who expressed approval of the strikers' actions. The topics relating to abuses in the mines and the problems of the coal mining sector appeared in television news broadcasts only after a deputy prime minister began speaking about these matters.

Even if the owners of the television channels were guilty of ill intent, this intent fitted squarely within the framework of the usual practice of the press and television—that is, following passively the best newsmaker. In this case, the miners were able to use television in their interests, and the government was not. On this basis, the way the media acted at the beginning of the "rail war" can at any rate be justified.

As the political crisis deepened, however, more and more people came to support the view that tensions were being whipped up deliberately. Writing in *Izvestia* (which, it is true, belonged to OneksimBank, like *Russky Telegraf*), the chief editor of the journal *Iskusstvo Kino*, Daniil Dondurei, laid responsibility for the events of the spring and summer of 1998 directly on the oligarchs, that is, on the owners of the large financial-industrial groups that controlled the mass media:

> The most deplorable subjects were covered exclusively, in detailed reports and in special political clips. At the height of the rail conflict, ORT and NTV at times presented no fewer than ten horrifying subjects out of thirteen to fifteen in each evening broadcast.
>
> The information campaign reached its culmination with the events around Gazprom. For example, no less an expert on energy and tax problems than Gennady Zyuganov was invited to appear on the program "Hero of the Day." Zyuganov explained that the attack on Russia's greatest monopolist meant that the government was trying to "dismember the country." The program "Parliamentary Hour" spelled out in full the parliament's indictment resolution listing the crimes of the president, while on the sixth channel, the program "Reviewer" presented the details of the conspiracy against General Rokhlin. . . .
>
> . . . a few years ago the government made us all hostages to the oligarchs' conviction that they had caught by the tail the golden bird of public opinion. In 1996 they elected the current president; now they earn a little extra thanks to the social hysteria they have whipped up. They

have brought down the ruble, and tomorrow they will cope readily with the chaos after they have elected, in the name of the people, the parliamentary membership and the system of power that will preserve the market, the Russian-style market that they find so attractive.[48]

The wave of *kompromat* that rolled over the press was generated not only by the demands of the media owners but also by the journalists themselves. An unquestionable characteristic of the new information technologies is the possibility of using journalists "blindly." Credible falsehoods, transcripts of telephone conversations obtained by eavesdropping, and versions of events prepared especially by propagandists are thrown to the press in the guise of "information," especially since journalists under the law are not obliged to reveal their sources except as ordered by a court.

There are also other propositions, for example, Pal Tamas's "rat theory." When the number of journalists becomes too many, they stop observing professional ethics and start devouring one another. Wages fall, and journalists are forced to seek new sources of income, including articles written to order.[49]

The phenomenon of corruption in journalism deserves separate treatment. In Russian publications, corruption is encountered in the most diverse forms, starting with a provincial review written to order for a thousand dollars, and extending to reports of new discounts for cellular phone operators paid for through advertising departments. "Black PR," or in the slang of Russian journalists, "dzhinsa" (jeans), is a serious problem for any editorial office.

Nevertheless, articles written to order represent perhaps the last harmful type of bias in journalism. For anyone who dreamed of a free press, one of the unpleasant discoveries of the late 1990s was that journalists rarely formed and defended their own positions, but preferred to support the position of the owner of the publication. A characteristic of Soviet psychology was identification with the interests of the collective, the institution, the production unit, the enterprise, the party, the country, and so forth—that is, the very spirit of corporatism. Overall, the privileged position of journalists in the publications of the large politicized holding companies did a good deal to mold this feature of the Soviet, or to be more precise, corporatist mentality.

In the commercial media, the level of wages can make for social bias of a somewhat different kind, a bias that is natural for media oriented toward one or another homogeneous group of consumers. This is particularly evident when a conflict of values arises. For a business publication, this might be a conflict between economic success and freedom. It is worth recalling the almost propagandist interview with Pinochet in the journal *Kommersant-Vlast*; here the former Chilean dictator set out for his grateful listener (the well-known journalist Natalya Gevorkyan) his precepts for the struggle against communism, and the advantages of dictatorial regimes from the point of view of economic success. As luck would have it, the interview was published not long before Pinochet was arrested in Great Britain. If this had not been the case, the article would have been perceived exactly as it was written, as an apology for authoritarian rule, using economic growth as a justification for suppressing communists.

Consequences of the Information Wars for the System of Mass Information and for Mass Consciousness

An interesting characterization of the new type of information war was proposed by G. Vinokurov in an article entitled "In the Trenches of the Information War," which appeared in the Internet publication *Russky Zhurnal*:

> Here we are present at a struggle between political and financial titans, a struggle waged through "respectable" mass media organs that are roughly equivalent in terms of their place in the media establishment and comparable in terms of their influence on public opinion and the political elite. This means not just that the methods of waging military actions are more complicated but, most importantly, that there is a shift from using information as a weapon of war—even a decisive weapon, but subsidiary in relation to the main aim of the war—to the use of techniques for the manipulative alteration of meanings as a goal in itself. From now on the battle will be waged in the form of clashes, on a single information field, of meanings and interpretations of equal strength but different polarity, and this will call to life new, more sophisticated forms of propagandist influence, which will act not in an applied but in an independent sense.
>
> In order for public opinion to function as an active element of the political system, it is essential for a start that it should at least exist as a phenomenon in social relations—as an articulated expression of the will of social groups constituted in a particular fashion. Instead of this we have at best a passive and inert "mass mood," and at worst, a largely unintelligible "collective unconsciousness."[50]

In Vinokurov's view, public opinion can nevertheless constitute an important force, but only "as a symbol of itself, and it is in precisely such a role that it is employed by the warring sides." Public opinion was not a factor in the information wars of the late 1990s; that is, it did not become a reality, and manifested itself only as a threat, as a possibility that no one had time—or, in the final accounting, a reason—to call into being.

> The argument that the manipulators present as evidence of their own might to the arbiter on whom the making of decisions depends is not the strength of public opinion, but precisely and solely the interpretation of this strength, and the imparting of an exaggerated significance to its form. In fact, instead of painstakingly nurturing civil society and shaping real public opinion (even if this is manipulated and fundamentally biased), in order later on to use it as a means of putting real political pressure on the centers of official power, the media magnates find it much more convenient to take another approach. They set out to convince these centers that they, that is, the centers, are isolated and in a state of panic-stricken dependence on "the voice of the popular masses," something that the media magnates have cooked up without any mediation whatever. In this way, the magnates act directly on the "person making the decisions," using as a threat the bogeyman of public opinion.
>
> As a result, there is not much significance in the fact that no one has yet learned how to adequately determine the effectiveness of the propaganda impact of the mass media, or whether such an impact exists at all—that is, the power of the mass media as a means for shaping public opinion. . . . It is the very precedent of unleashing a propaganda campaign, and the degree of its intensity (or more exactly, brazenness), and not the question of its results, that has significance. What prevails is, so to speak, a method of gauging effectiveness on the basis of expenditure; since there is a great deal of noise on television and in the newspapers, the consequences are supposedly evident.[51]

This does not mean that the information wars occurred without any consequences whatever. On the contrary, in circumstances where the mass media embrace all of society, such "sorties" can give rise to a mass of consequences that have not been planned by anyone, including the ringleaders themselves.

> As a result, the rational interpretation of events, which from the very beginning has been turned to the purpose of propagandist reporting, becomes mythologized, transforming itself into nihilist mass concepts that are irrational in their essence and sensual-emotional in their form. . . .

In order to perceive the actions of the main performers in the "bank wars" show, actions that do not correspond to the usual system of values or to the models of behavior, and that with the help of the mass media have been brought to the absurd and illogical, the recipient extracts from the depths of his or her consciousness a different, archaic logic, and starts interpreting what is happening not with the help of the categories of juridical and political analysis or even of common sense, but through image-symbols based on the archetypes of the collective unconscious.[52]

In the view of the experts at the Foundation for Effective Politics, who were advising the government during this period, the reasons for the broad incidence of information campaigns lay in government abuse of information techniques. Once these techniques had shown their effectiveness during the election campaign, they came to be seen as the answer to every question, as the formula for success in modern-day politics. Instead of a developed political strategy, and the formulating, adopting, and implementing of various political decisions, the government resorted to the techniques of crisis image-management, and to what the FEP defined as "grey" methods—that is, leaks and similar tactics. As a result, all of the performers in the information arena received a further education in the new media techniques, without any qualitative changes in the political situation or any real impact on the state of affairs.

Although the experts at the FEP studiously refrained from investigating the reasons for this state of affairs, it is obvious that these reasons lay in the prestige of the team that had managed to win Yeltsin a second term as president. The key figure involved was Valentin Yumashev, journalist and presidential biographer, who after the appointment of Anatoly Chubais as first deputy prime minister became head of the presidential administration. It was to Yumashev that Boris Berezovsky reported in his role as adviser on public matters, and this fact alone speaks of the influence this functionary wielded. It need hardly be said that the FEP was part of the same circle.

In the document "'Managed Crises' as an Uncontrolled Weapon," the foundation's experts summed up the changes to the information system that had resulted from all the players being schooled in the new information techniques, and came to the conclusion that the government had lost its monopoly on crisis and image management:

In the first place, lower-level actors—mayors, governors, trade unions, rectors, and others—now know how to create "crisis packages" with participation by the masses; the masses have learned to manipulate journalists and to mount plausible informational-political spectacles. Second, the government, who in the view of society is divided, has lost the right to dominance. . . .[53]

For the federal government, losing the monopoly on the initiation of media campaigns meant not just the loss of one of its levers for managing situations but also the appearance of a powerful new weapon in the hands of anyone who wanted to use it. When everyone uses the "crisis weapon," the total effect is multiplied many times over. The result of its use is not the strengthening of any single player, but the strengthening of the main element—that is, the crisis component—in the information field.

> The controlling of mass consciousness through crises has given rise to a chain of unmanageable crises and has been transformed into the expectation of crisis. Since the time of the "1997 bank war" [the battle for Svyazinvest], the consciousness and behavior of the masses are losing their nerve. The positive results of this activity, even where they exist, have been unstable, fragile, and uncertain where long-term consequences for the prestige of the authorities is concerned.

This is not the sole effect and not the most dangerous one. Because this document was written at the height of the coal miners' "rail war" and during a resurgence of the economic crisis, the attention of FEP analysts was riveted to new events in the symbolic space of the media, events that indicated the formation of something close to a pre-revolutionary situation:

> Amid the crisis expectations, a new type of *crisis subject* has taken shape. In the lexicon of the mass media, it is called *the people* and represents mass disobedience in support of one of the demands approved by the media, under the patronage of this or that media-approved newsmaker. . . .
> Specific features of the image include its *positive* character, the virtual impossibility of making any meaningful criticism of its manifestations, and the ready manipulation of these manifestations by the mass media and shadowy pressure groups. A new political potential of colossal significance is being postulated here, and among the contending forces a fierce struggle has broken out over the role of *principal mouthpiece of the interests of the people*. For the winner, success in this struggle will mean a uniquely favorable position, and unquestionable electoral prospects.

The fact that the mass media operate within a context of information wars is bringing about a situation in which the mass media are ceasing to support communication in society, to provide an adequate idea of reality, or to distinguish the primary from the secondary, the immaterial from the significant.

FEP president Gleb Pavlovsky has linked this trend to the formation of a class of media bureaucrats with a stake in the continuation of feuds within the regime, since every war is a source of super-profits for the chief editors and journalists.[54] The weaponry of the media magnates has started to function in automatic mode, blocking any possibility for the elites to manage society on the level of more or less rational, long-term policies.

> As a result, the mass media have effectively lost their role as intermediaries between society and the government and as catalysts of social change, while their ability to serve as a means for dialogue between social groups has been weakened significantly. Russian society has often come to perceive the media as a continuation of politics by the "dirty means" of *kompromat*, as a tool for the squaring of accounts in the struggle between the powerful of the world, people who are indifferent to the everyday needs and cares of ordinary readers. An atmosphere has arisen in the mass media that does not reflect public interests at all, but only private interests that are divorced from the real feelings, moods, and preferences of the overwhelming majority of the country's population.[55]

With the help of the mass media, the political and financial elites engage in self-intoxication, at the same time as the sphere of "real mass communications" (as defined by the FEP) shifts gradually into opposition not only to the government, but to the mass media as well.

It would be wrong to conclude the discussion of the information campaigns with a one-sided assessment. The new information techniques are not a temporary phenomenon but an inevitable consequence of the transformation of information systems throughout the world. Special mention should thus be made of the media campaigns that can conditionally be described as positive, that is, they help to legitimize the existing political system and its institutionalization, or to put it differently, using the terminology of the people who mounted these campaigns: the formation of civil society. This scenario was part of the campaign by the "team of young reformers" to make a strong start to their reforms—the campaign whose inglorious ending was described earlier.

It began after the presidential elections of 1996 with the creation of a permanent mechanism for consultations between representatives of the executive branch and the experts responsible for public relations. During the election campaign, these meetings and discussions usually took place on Fridays; and after the victory it was decided that these "Friday consultations" would continue. Representatives of the president and government who had taken part in the election campaign received the opportunity to add information techniques to their array of traditional political instruments.

This interaction resulted in a campaign to shape the image of the "team of young reformers," beginning a month after the appointment of Boris Nemtsov as first deputy prime minister. Nemtsov's appointment was a key factor in molding the public image of the government; at the time, according to data from the Public Opinion Foundation, Nemtsov had a record public confidence rating of more than 40 percent.

The task of the media campaign was to build on previous successes by creating the image of "a united team of reformers capable of making a breakthrough in economic policy," and also to ensure the implementation of the unpopular measures to which the Chernomyrdin-Chubais-Nemtsov government would have to resort. Key elements in the policies of the new cabinet were cuts to budget spending and benefits; as a result, the cabinet encountered bitter resistance in the State Duma, where left-wing factions held the majority.

During the campaign, the question was raised of how to prepare public opinion for explanations of the need to cut the budget and for a review of the system of public benefits inherited from Soviet times. Also during the campaign, an application to the Constitutional Court was organized, seeking the abolition of the 5 percent barrier for election to the Federal Assembly on the grounds that this discriminated against public organizations. The importance of this application lay above all in the fact that if the left-wing opposition decided to force a vote of no-confidence in the government, at subsequent elections the large parliamentary fractions could be eroded by small parties and groupings. In 1995, many of these political groups had failed to win 5 percent of the votes, attracting only 2 to 4.5 percent, but these groups remained active. It was no secret that the protests were financed from the Kremlin, and that in elections these small groups could expect to receive serious attention from the media controlled from the Kremlin and its allies; the threat was thus twofold.

Properly speaking, the positive aspects of the "campaign of the team of young reformers" were the "civil society" and "positive challenge" projects. In particular, the "civil society" project proposed the transformation of political discourse through the inclusion in the public arena of numerous small social groups and organizations that were not represented in the parliament. The idea behind this project was that civil society already existed in Russia in the form of numerous nonstate, noncommercial organizations that at times played an important role in public life. These included the Committee of Soldiers' Mothers, environmental organizations, feminists, and the Women of Russia Party, youth and antimilitarist groups, and "greens." Together these groups represented a new system of self-organization of society that was coming into being; if certain costs were borne and conditions were met, they might constitute a new base of support for the Russian government, who had lost the support of the intelligentsia and the middle class.

The "positive challenge" involved the organizing of positive regional initiatives in response to the publishing of the government's program. These initiatives were not, however, to come from the governors, but from public organizations, on the principle that "you in the center have made decisions, but the communists are sitting on us and nothing is happening, so try to change the situation."

The campaign of the "team of young reformers" culminated with the issuing of a government program in the form of "seven actions by the Cabinet of Ministers." Thanks to this packaging, the government managed to have its program widely reported in relatively undistorted form, bypassing the obstructions of the decrepit reformist discourse, which in the public consciousness had not only ceased to resound clearly but had lost all meaning.

The campaign was abandoned when its financing was cut off early in the summer of 1997. In all likelihood, the reason behind the rejection of the "civil society" and the "positive challenge" was fear of the potential unpredictability of independent organizations, and the open hypocrisy of the "positive challenge." The "team of young reformers," however, had no other projects of the kind. Consequently, although the government at first managed a tactical advantage, the executive branch lost the initiative. As a result of several powerful campaigns, beginning with Svyazinvest and ending with the "writers' affair," the "team of young reformers" was crushed by its opponents.

Could anything have saved the Chernomyrdin-Chubais-Nemtsov government? It needs to be recognized that on the whole, the Council of Ministers in 1997 and 1998 was pursuing a risky and largely pointless course of maintaining an extremely high ruble exchange rate and covering its expenses through the use of a pyramid of short-term state bonds, privatizations, delays in wage payments, and cuts in social benefits. The result of these policies was conflict with the parliament, a series of political crises including the "rail war," and the extreme vulnerability of the economy on the eve of a global crisis. The reason behind this policy was to enable investment in production by importing the equipment at reasonable price. However, the high exchange rate meant that the production sector could not compete even on the domestic market, so it had no capital to invest. The Foundation for Effective Politics had done everything for the government that it could, but in essence the government was already doomed.

The positive elements in the program of the young reformers—above all, the abolition of the system of authorized banks, the introduction of a competitive system of bidding for state contracts, honest privatization auctions, and limitation of the power of monopolies—were in essence the first attempt at realizing the constructive part of the liberal project of the Second Republic. This attempt was made, however, at a time when it no longer enjoyed real political support either in society or in parliament, and still less among the media owners who had achieved success thanks to their ties to the government and who were not about to renounce their accustomed strategy for multiplying their capital. By contrast, the program of struggle against crime and the social and industrial policies initiated by the subsequent government of Yevgeny Primakov immediately found support both in society and among the political establishment. When such support was assured, it became clear that the interests of the large media owners could be disregarded. Under Primakov, for example, the prosecutor's office started investigating the activity of Boris Berezovsky. In the course of the year when Primakov was prime minister, his government, which established itself in office following the crisis of August 1998, became a real center of power. Often, it proved capable of resisting pressure from the direction of the Kremlin, which in the eyes of society had become transformed into a sort of analogue of the CPSU, but with a liberal-democratic ideology. Not surprisingly, this government was subjected to incessant attacks from the media outlets of the large media holding companies, but by the time of the parliamentary and presidential elections Primakov had nevertheless attained the status almost of a popular hero.

To prevent the bloc of Luzhkov and Primakov from winning the parliamentary and presidential elections of 1999–2000 required all the power of the Kremlin-aligned media, along with all the provocateur's talents at the disposal of Sergey Dorenko, who each week throughout the entire political season in the autumn of 1999 unmasked Primakov and Luzhkov during prime time on the first channel of Russian "public" television. Other ingredients were the alternative election campaign bloc "Unity"; the ex-KGB agent Putin; the second Chechen war; and the resignation of Yeltsin, not to mention an intricate filigree of rituals and cultural codes. Vinokurov was right when he wrote that in a situation marked by powerful and aggressive noise coming from the information system, mass consciousness begins to interpret events on the level of the archaic logic of myth.

In a certain sense, Primakov could be overcome only by another Primakov. The task of securing victory over the ex-premier thus boiled down to fostering a symbolic double for him, while adding a few winning facets to this image. For example, if Primakov was old, the new hero should be young. If Primakov was sluggish, the new hero should be lively and dynamic. If Primakov bore the genetic traits of the Brezhnev cultural code, the new hero should mimic a no less strong and popular cultural tradition. If Primakov, for all the demonstrative toughness of his policies, was peace-loving and inclined to negotiations, he could be defeated only by a military hero.

The Media-Political System and the Rules of the Political Spectacle

Every expert in the field of public relations knows that you do not have to own the press in order to manipulate it. Ownership of the mass media makes access to it considerably easier, and bestows the right to a deciding vote in case of conflicts—that is, under Russian conditions, the right of censorship. At the same time, if this right is not exercised, and the information does not contradict the interests of the owner, the laws of operation of the mass media come into force. It is on these laws that modern-day information techniques are constructed.

Along with other scholars, Hermann Main notes the phenomenon of the "mediaization of politics." Citing Heinrich Oberreuter, he

speaks of the subordination of politics to the internal laws of functioning of the mass media. Main also quotes Reinhard Hoeppner, the
head of the German Social Democratic Party faction in the Landtag
of the state of Saxony:

> The place that used to be called politics, the place of discussion, of the
> shaping of public opinion, and of political decision making, is increas-
> ingly being occupied by symbolic actions. Symbolic politics makes its
> appearance where politics cannot change anything, where the expecta-
> tions that have been aroused cannot be satisfied. We hear, read, and at
> times also see pseudo-events that occur only to the degree to which we
> are told about them. These pseudo-events close off the path to socially
> important events and to critical thinking. Accordingly, the competitive
> struggle for circulation and viewer ratings more and more often forces
> journalists to artificially create the important out of the inconsequential,
> to remark on singularity where nothing is unusual, and to seek out sham
> sensations or even to create them.[56]

So far we have spoken about manipulation of the mass media, about
the influence of one or another ideology on journalists and publications.
This, however, is only one side of the question. We have bypassed the
influence of the technological laws of the mass media on the political
process in society. Meanwhile, if we define the term "mediaization of
politics," then we shall see that it is the process through which political
life is transferred to the symbolic space of the mass media. However, in
order to understand how the regime of operation of the media became a
crucially important (though also unwritten) law of public policy, we
need to dwell on this in more detail.

It is very difficult to organize and carry on a discussion about concepts and political platforms for an untrained mass audience. In these
circumstances, political struggle is transformed into a succession of information campaigns, the meaning of which is often reduced to personal attacks on individuals who at best embody particular sets of views
in the symbolic field of the media, and who at worst are simply members of the opposing team (in chess it is sometimes important to capture
a pawn). Many very obvious things have been noted earlier: for example, the huge influence of television, which first manifested itself in
the USSR in the time of Gorbachev and which since then has only increased. The influence of television leads to the personification of the
political process, to its assimilation in a way that is emotional and to a

large degree irrational. In Russia, the mediatization of politics has led
to the triumph of *kompromat*, to a sort of competition between media
experts and journalists to achieve the most striking identification of
one or another group of business entrepreneurs or political figures as
good or evil.

This is the most obvious example of the influence of the mass media
on the political process, but it is far from being the only one. The Foundation for Effective Politics, which worked intensively at fulfilling orders from the government during the second half of the 1990s, devoted
a good deal of attention to analyzing the techniques for selecting and
interpreting information used within the mass media. The report "The
Information Practice of the Mass Media in Relation to the Government"[57]
provides a detailed analysis of "the stereotyped, repetitive reactions of
the mass media to the development of subjects, which allows the media
to select subjects and manage them. This represents a sort of fixed 'rules
of the game,' established in the information field during 1996 and 1997."[58]
In other words, these are the algorithms according to which the media
function and which politicians are compelled to take into account.

Although the aim of this applied research was to study how the media
report the political process, there is nothing to stop us from understanding it in a broader sense, that is, as a sample of the techniques that journalists use as they try to make sense of what is happening in the world,
forming a picture of reality and displaying it to a mass audience. It is
worth noting that a feature of this research is that it excludes the factor
of interference by the media owners, and this makes the findings by the
foundation's analysts especially valuable.

According to the authors of the report, a basic characteristic of the media is the way it selects the center of the information agenda; this is determined by the media themselves, at times independently of the actions and
news made by the government. This process is expressed in the attracting
of attention and in the gathering together of all peripheral themes and subjects in an idea-forming center, thus providing a context and evaluations.

> It is because of this that the media always express dissatisfaction when
> the president "fails to react" or "pays no attention" to an occurrence that
> in the mass media has been elevated to the rank of a "major event."[59]

An initiative by one or another political figure (that is, a newsmaker)
aimed at drawing together the semantic and informational threads in
"center field" can for a time make him or her the "owner" (or core) of

the information agenda; then the media gather other figures and topics in the symbolic field around this "owner." The program through which such an initiative is prepared links its meaning with other themes of the information agenda that exist at that particular moment, so that this initiative may be "extinguished" by other themes without having been recorded in the existing information field. The campaign that surrounds the preparing of an initiative gives rise to a wave of expectations. Even a successful propaganda campaign for the preparing of such a field can play a negative role, if the launching of the initiative itself is unsuccessful or is not perceived as successful; one example of this was the campaign around the "team of young reformers."

The successful launching of an initiative calls forth a wave of positive expectations in the media. The slightest failure, however, is enough to reduce this wave to nothing. The unrealized expectations of the mass media start to form a negative information agenda field into which other themes are drawn. In this way, a crisis of expectations arises. It is curious that a crisis of expectations arises not only when a government initiative cannot be successfully implemented, but also when the government has ignored "advice" and "prompting," transmitted by the mass media, which are elevated by the journalists to the status of "universal national demands." This latter situation, of course, is readily explained; the press never has its own opinion on the subject of government initiatives anyway, so the promptings and advice that it transmits reflect not only the opinion of the opposition or commentators but also the only understanding of the situation that is available to journalists. Consequently, when the actions of the government do not coincide with this vision, journalists feel that the government is doing something wrong.

Finally, if there are unexpected events for which an information agenda has not been prepared, and if a complex of expectations has not taken shape, the media suffer from information stress. The report states that such stress arose, for example, after the sacking of Prime Minister Viktor Chernomyrdin on March 23, 1998:

> In such a situation the mass media start looking for links that can explain what has happened; when these links are not found, the media lose their self-confidence. Hence significant events that happened in the information field the day before (in this case, an interview given by Berezovsky or the activities of Nemtsov) come to serve as such links. As soon as certainty appears, the previous events lose their ability to "keep people in suspense," and the mass media being a search for other "genuinely important events."[60]

As was shown by the cancellation of Primakov's visit to the United States after the start of the bombing of Yugoslavia (Primakov had the airplane turn back while over the Atlantic), events do not always develop so badly for the government; at times an unexpected gesture can help transform the information agenda to the advantage of a newsmaker. But for this to happen, some weighty proof of the correctness of such a step is required (in this case, the proof was supplied by the allotting of an IMF credit).

The appearance on the scene of an integral model for the behavior of the mass media is explained by the common standards of the mass media both in Russia and throughout the world—the standards of the commercial media, which in the late twentieth century, according to Denis McQuail, were beginning to be seen as the global culture of the mass media.[61] Even state television and the information organs of the politicized holding companies, which are locked in unavoidable competition for the attention of the audience, accept these standards. If we are to use the definition advanced by Manuel Castells,[62] this is how the laws of the informational "McLuhan galaxy" come into being.

In this context, our observations coincide in principle with the so-called market theory of the press that was advanced in the early 1990s by Russian scholars, in particular Yelena Androunas, who before turning into a "marketeer" was critically studying American information monopolies.[63]

For Androunas, the formation of a new media system on the basis of the post-Soviet print publications and television was impossible without a fundamental change in the attitude of journalists to their work. Instead of serving the authorities, journalists had to satisfy the information demands of consumers. Even at the dawn of the 1990s, a "market" theory could exist only if it took a critical attitude to the surrounding reality.

> It appears that journalists, on the whole, do not see this problem. They confuse freedom from control by the communist *nomenklatura* with freedom itself. In the majority of cases, however, everything concludes with a change of bosses: from the old boss who everyone is tired of, to a new boss who seems liberal and understanding.[64]

"Only economically independent structures, private ownership of the information media, the sale of information for the sake of profit rather than in pursuit of ideological goals, and the effective use of information as a commodity will allow the creation of a real market in the mass media,"[65] Androunas wrote, predicting the rapid bankruptcy of all the conservative post-Soviet publications.

As can be seen from these quotations, market idealism has not justified the hopes of its supporters. We who gave our backing to "market theory" were forced there and then to reject its idealist premises, since all the battles surrounding the media have been associated precisely with efforts by particular social forces and centers of power to "correct" the mass media's market strategy. In Great Britain, such efforts resulted in the formation of the BBC and strict regulating of the operations of commercial television, as well as the formation of the Press Council, a public committee reviewing complaints about the mass media. It is widely considered that these moves have raised the ethical and professional standards of the mass media significantly in both state and commercial television. As we know from country studies, maintaining the standards of the commercial mass media at a high level and ensuring the opportunity for free expression (often despite the demands of the market) are the tasks of state and television and radio companies in the countries of Northern Europe as well.

"Free communication under conditions of democracy, especially representative democracy," writes Yelena Vartanova, "presupposes discussion of contradictory questions from various points of view, which has the function of preserving and expanding the basis for political participation by citizens. In the view of the Finnish commission on the media, the role of the press, principally the national press, remains central."[66]

If we are to proceed from the history of the Russian media, however, we need to turn our attention first and foremost to the strategies of the financial-industrial groups and the political clans whose goal has been to exert the maximum influence on the symbolic space of the mass media through the formation of large media holding companies.

For interested parties, venturing into the "ideal" market of ideas represents an excessive and unjustified risk. In this situation, even the right to censor information, and especially the chance to influence the editorial policies of the mass media, become especially attractive to political investors. For large companies, the purchase both of controlling blocks and of relatively small shareholdings in large media concerns often represents a vitally important guarantee of stability, a means of defending their own interests (both in politics and in business) and influencing public consciousness. This happens throughout the world, but in Russia in the nineties it took on a particularly clear and expressive character. In the absence of established political institutions in Russia in the 1990s, the large politicized media holding companies played the role in essence of ersatz parties, providing media backing and links to the electorate, the mobilization of resources, and lobbying for one decision or another. By 1997 it was therefore possible to speak of the formation of a media-political system.

The Structure of the Media System

The media-political system is a structure of the institutionalization of power (or more precisely, of its various centers) that can be distinguished within the Russian mass media. The media-political system is unquestionably narrower than the information system and even the system of the mass media, since in isolating it we have used as our main indicator the presence of politicized investments. As well as the ownership of the information outlets, we have also been interested in the character of the influence on their editorial policy.[67]

The Russian information system has a three-level structure. The first and most important level consists of the all-Russian electronic mass media, which make up a single Russian information space. As a rule, the mass media on this first level are controlled by politicized capital or are state property. This group includes the central television channels, which can be picked up in most of the country, and the quality Moscow press publications, many of which are controlled by politicized capital. Their significance is not as great as that of the all-Russian electronic mass media, but for the politicized media holding companies they are an essential additional tool, which is extremely effective in narrowly directed political campaigns, especially when combined with television. In essence, the "influence newspapers" supply television with an indispensable argumentative base on key questions of the day, shaping the information environment from which the television news services take information for distribution to their mass audiences.

The second level, involving print and electronic mass media of all-Russian, interregional and regional scope, is made up of commercial publications and television and radio companies. To this group can be assigned all the business periodicals and the commercial television and radio stations that broadcast to the regions, but which do not have all-national audiences. These are less attractive to politicized capital, but up until the crisis of 1998 and during the second half of 1999 they were in big demand by advertisers. In theory, the commercial mass media are not part of the media-political system, but in a number of cases they are integrated into it either structurally, through politicized investments (a trend to which the elections of 1999–2000 and the low level of development of the credit market contributed a good deal), or functionally under the conditions of particular information campaigns.

For the media-political system, the commercial mass media form an environment that can either help to dampen information campaigns (the "cushion" effect) or act as a sounding-board for them, multiplying their effectiveness. Theoretically, the professionalism of journalists should help to isolate the information wars and *kompromat* and ensure that these events are reported in the sorted-out and reinterpreted form. However, the weakness of television and radio stations and mass-circulation publications for the scandals and sensations that help boost ratings and readerships can yield the opposite outcome, producing, to use the term coined by Yassen Zassoursky, an "echo effect." One of the tasks of media experts is to create the sort of scenarios for information campaigns that mean that the commercial mass media are drawn into these campaigns of their own accord, adopting the position of one side or another.

The third level of the system, the regional electronic and print media, has generally been under the control of local administrations or, much more rarely, of large regional corporations. This reflects not only the relationship between the press and the authorities that is traditional for Russia and that has proven more durable in the conservative provinces than in the capital, but also the difficult economic situation whose effects have been particularly noticeable in the regional information systems. Also of importance has been the real distribution of power in the provinces, where the system of rule has often been more autocratic than in the Russian political system as a whole. In this last respect the regional information system is taking on an extremely closed character.

There is also, it is true, a fourth level of the information system, the Internet. In essence, the global communications medium represents a vast set of communications channels, which also can be used by the media-political system. They can be used, for example, to issue *kompromat*, which can later be taken up at any level of the information system, and if the information on the Internet interests the public, the items involved can be circulated endlessly in the commercial and politicized media. But they are also, and more extensively used as an independent information network that brings quality journalism to the provinces and the vast Russian-speaking diaspora abroad.

The development of the Internet in Russia has stemmed not just from the enthusiasm of ordinary users but also from large investments by political figures and hi-tech entrepreneurs. Since 1999, capital has poured into the Internet—and the Internet is being transformed into one of the most commercialized sectors of the communications system. The development of the Internet in Russia will be examined in more detail in Chapter 5.

To complete the picture, mention also should be made of what Iosif Dzyaloshinsky has described as the extrasystemic media—the Russian-language Radio Liberty and the Russian services of the BBC and Deutsche Welle. Although in terms of their sources of financing and the potential size of their audiences they should be assigned to the first level of the information system, in terms of the professional standards of their broadcasting they are closer to the media outlets of the second group, that is, the commercial mass media. Their role in the information system during the 1990s was not especially great, except for peaks in their popularity at the beginning and end of the decade. At the dawn of the Second Republic, it was Radio Liberty and the BBC Russian Service that served as the standard that to a large degree helped to instill a factual approach in journalism and acted as the bearer of global media culture. At the end of the 1990s, the "voices" returned to their accustomed and popular role as the democratic opposition to the propagandist mass media. The case in which Radio Liberty correspondent Babitsky was arrested in Chechnya, and criminal charges were later brought against him, bears witness to this.

By the late 1990s, there existed in Russia about ten large politicized and commercial media holding companies, although only four of them could boast of a powerful presence in the media-political system, that is, the ability to pursue an independent information policy.

These four were the state holding company (VGTRK), the mass media controlled by Boris Berezovsky, Vladimir Gusinsky's Media-Most Group, and also the media group controlled by Yury Luzhkov and by companies close to the Moscow City government. The next chapter will analyze in detail the structure of the media system in Russia as it developed and of most of the large holding companies; here we shall simply note that their advantage compared to the other concentrations of media ownership lay in their control over the first-level mass media, and above all, of the all-Russian television channels. It is true that Luzhkov's TV-Center was unable to begin broadcasting throughout Russia prior to the elections of 1999–2000 (a fact that helped doom the bloc of Luzhkov and Primakov to defeat), while Boris Berezovsky later lost his hold on ORT due to the strengthening of the state, but these questions will be examined in more detail in the following chapters. Here we are interested in how the politicization of the media holding companies has manifested itself. The signs of this politicization are clear, since the information policies of the mass media that the companies control have changed in line with the way the forces they support have positioned themselves in the political arena.

This should not distract us from our main observation concerning the media-political system: whatever changes have occurred in their information policies, at the basis of each holding company we find an alignment to one or another audience, an orientation expressed in the company's sociocultural orientation, in its adherence to particular systems of views and cultural paradigms. However these systems were formed, as a result of the direct influence of political patrons (in the case of TV-Center), or as a consequence of the historically based commonality of views of the last generation of the Soviet intelligentsia (in the case of the Media-Most group), the angle from which the media have perceived reality has been maintained with a certain constancy once it has been chosen.

The definition of the media holding companies in Russia during the second half of the 1990s as political parties sui generis rests primarily on this, and only secondarily on their technical role in the political system. Except for the Russian Communist Party (KPRF) and to a degree, Zhirinovsky's Liberal Democratic Party of Russia, the political parties that identified themselves as such possessed neither structures nor activists. They were fragile formations established not long before elections by players on the political scene who each time regrouped themselves into new combinations in order to win seats in parliament. All the parties except for the KPRF thus played the role of political brands, promoted through the active participation of their leaders in the political spectacle.

Just as historically the political parties and other civic associations aided the articulation of particular interests, and consequently, the consolidation of one or another picture of reality, the media holding companies played an analogous role, without requiring any activity or membership dues in return. The sole condition for participation was socialization through the information and entertainment products of these media monopolies, inasmuch as the sense of reality was bestowed by the strategies of behavior and identification lying at the basis of the political choice.

Luzhkov's holding company, whose politics followed a modern version of the formula coined by the tsarist education minister Count S.S. Uvarov[68] (the latter's "orthodoxy, autocracy, and nationality" became "orthodoxy, *derzhavnost*, and nationality," where *derzhavnost* means basically taking refuge and pride in the larger identity of the empire), was characterized by glorification of authority, a moderate oppositional stance with relation to the federal government, and patriotism. Luzhkov's mass media were also notable for their closeness to the Orthodox church. If an outside observer were to have judged the realities of Russia in the late 1990s on the basis of the programs of TV-Center, he or she would inevitably have drawn the conclusion that orthodoxy was the established religion of the Great Russian State.

The organs of the Media-Most holding company adhered to the democratic and liberal positions of the "first wave" of the early nineties. The radio station Ekho Moskvy became arguably the most straightforward liberal media outlet in Russia.[69] As with NTV, its most favored political figures were Grigory Yavlinsky and the leaders of the Union of Right Forces, although prior to the elections of 1999 it was capable of changing its sympathies and of supporting Primakov and Luzhkov—though without forgetting to cover relentlessly the activities of Yavlinsky's "Yabloko" bloc and the Union of Right Forces of Sergey Kirienko, Boris Nemtsov, and Irina Khakamada.

It was characteristic of the Media-Most journalists that they emphasized professionalism as the most important quality ("News is our profession") and social value. From the point of view of information politics and the reporting of the political spectacle, what was typical was a stress on objectivity and detachment, combined with an orientation toward the entertainment component. In principle, the latter is not surprising for television, but if TV-Center might ignore an interesting "picture" for ideological reasons, this is hard to imagine in the case of NTV.

The position of the Berezovsky group changed with each new alliance and with each episode in the competitive struggle. At the same time, the amplitude of its oscillations was not particularly wide; on the scale of political positions it was situated between the chauvinist-democratic and national-patriotic poles, inclining to the latter during election campaigns and to the former in times of political calm. Of all the media groups, Berezovsky's media were the most "mass" in the sense that they were propagandist information organs, oriented toward entertainment in the Hollywood style, toward a sensationalism behind which, more often than not, there lay concealed the labyrinthine intrigues of Berezovsky and his enemies.

Until the very end of the 1990s, things were somewhat more complex in the case of the state-owned mass media. The lack of a consolidated position on the part of the executive branch, the tensions in the relationship between the government and the president, and also the machinations of former intermediaries like Berezovsky, who still controlled ORT, all made their effects felt. The first channel, in which formally speaking 51 percent always belonged to the state, became a major problem for Yevgeny Primakov during his prime ministership. Trying to revive something resembling a unified state information policy, the premier came into conflict with Berezovsky—and lost, since in this confrontation Berezovsky managed to bring the presidential administration, concerned at the strengthening of the prime minister's position, over to his side.

Despite its official status—or because of it—the state channel RTR did not exert substantial influence on the political processes in the 1990s. The ideology of RTR always coincided with the position of the government (except in the case of the first war in Chechnya), varying from radical-democratic at the beginning of the nineties to moderately democratic, so to speak, at the dawn of the Yeltsin epoch, and to "triumph of the will" in 1999. Then, after the appointment of Putin as prime minister and the beginning of the second Chechen war, one of the founders of NTV, Oleg Dobrodeev, came over to RTR and instituted a serious reconstruction of the channel.

The result of Dobrodeev's efforts was the appearance of a powerful state broadcasting apparatus, which made an enormous contribution to the heyday of misled patriotism surrounding the war in Chechnya. In general, the military theme helped the channel to define and project its keynote; in the same way as the Uvarov formula for TV-Center, liberal values for NTV, and mass entertainment programs for ORT, the keynote of RTR turned out to be tough propagandist broadcasting, embodied in straight talk by the presenter and highly wrought drama in the reporting, with soldiers' burials, minutes of silence, and military news that later softened in style, but not in substance.

Just as the military role of prime minister became a key element in the image of presidential candidate Vladimir Putin, RTR became a sort of assembly shop for the symbolic reality of Russia in 1999, a prototype for the "Great Russia" that the commentators, the politicians, the army and the government finally succeeded in building at the end of a decade of chaos and power struggles.

4

Reconstructing Russia

The Succession

Once Boris Yeltsin had made his move to the Kremlin, no political force could seriously hope to evict him. However, Yeltsin's second term as president expired in 2000, and he could not lay claim to a third term without destroying the most important legacy of his rule—the constitution. Although speculation that the elections would be cancelled appeared in the press just as it had in 1995, none of the serious players on the political scene, including the president himself, had any doubts that this time the script for the political drama would be different. The figure of a successor thus appeared in the wings of the political stage. The spectre of this presidential heir was to haunt the country for some time. Various politicians were considered as possible candidates for the role, and several of the most likely claimants to the throne of Russia's elective monarchy very nearly paid for this with their political careers.

One example was Boris Nemtsov, who in 1997 had quit his post as elected governor of the region of Nizhny Novgorod for the job of first deputy prime minister of Russia. Nemtsov seemed on his arrival in Moscow to be the ideal presidential candidate, with as many as half the inhabitants of Russia expressing confidence in him. Appearing in the capital three years before the elections, however, Nemtsov became easy prey for political enemies whose existence he had not even suspected. In fact, he had not even had enemies until he moved to the capital. Neither Luzhkov nor the mass media he controlled, nor the media outlets of Gusinsky and Berezovsky, who joined up with Luzhkov in the course of the struggle for Svyazinvest, were enemies of the throne; nevertheless, they sniped at likely presidential successors. As the saying goes, there was nothing personal about it. After two years in the government, years thick with accusations of incompetence, corruption, and visits to brothels—none of which were ever confirmed—Nemtsov found that his rating had fallen so low that he no longer posed a threat to any future presidential candidates. This allowed him to breathe freely at last and to emerge from the hail of criticism. Fortunately, the remains of his political popularity and his standing in business circles were enough to allow him later to take the number two position on the electoral slate of the Union of Right Forces, and then to renew his career by taking the post of deputy speaker in the lower house of the Russian parliament, eventually to become the leader of the Union of Right Forces faction in the Duma.

The fall of the Kirienko[1] government as a result of the crisis of August 1998 saw both Kirienko and Nemtsov out on the street and ushered in the political crisis that led eventually to the appointment of Yevgeny Primakov as prime minister of Russia. Primakov had been chosen as premier on the recommendation of parliament, and throughout the entire period his cabinet was in office, relations between the prime minister and the president were strained. The center of decision making shifted from the Kremlin to the White House, and as a result, the role of the presidential administration diminished significantly. Although Primakov had worked in the state apparatus throughout the 1990s, heading the Foreign Ministry and the Foreign Intelligence Service, Yeltsin and, maybe even more so, his administration, did not trust his prime minister. Primakov's increasingly close relations with Moscow mayor Yury Luzhkov, known for his longstanding hostility to Boris Berezovsky and for his statements on the need for a partial review of the results of privatization, merely added fuel to the flames. So too did the growth of industrial production that began as a result of the fall of the ruble exchange rate. Primakov, who was never viewed by Yeltsin as a possible successor, proved to be a consummate politician. His popularity grew, and he enjoyed support in the "power ministries." He did not suffer confrontations with the parliament, since first deputy prime minister Yury Maslyukov had been a Communist deputy before his appointment, and thereafter was able to ensure the government the loyal support of the Communist Party (KPRF). Primakov thus became the first prime minister who managed to consolidate his power.

Moreover, despite Yeltsin's comically outrageous actions while abroad, Primakov managed to establish the image of Great Russia, especially on the international scene. Primakov embodied that image. With his imperious bearing, unhurried manner, unimaginably dull speeches, *nomenklatura* modesty, and old-fashioned vocabulary, he evoked in people who were weary of change a feeling of stability, a recollection of times when there was no need to watch what was happening with the authorities because everything there signaled that time had finally stopped, and the feeling was powerful enough to project this calm into the future.

Although Primakov held the post of prime minister for only a year, it seemed as though a whole epoch had passed. By ordering his aircraft to turn back while over the Atlantic after learning that Yugoslavia was being bombed by NATO forces without Russia's approval, he instantly restored Russia's international prestige—at least in the eyes of Russians. By insisting on Russia's particular view of the Balkan crisis, he restored the country's status as an independent player in the international arena. Perhaps it was a player only on a par with China, but as a result of Primakov's action, the sense of Russia's importance increased. Finally, Russian units on the night of June 11, 1999, made a forced and unexpected march across Yugoslavia and took control of the airport at Pristina. Against a backdrop of a decade of powerlessness, this seemed a triumph, even though journalists credited the decision to Boris Yeltsin. As the political analyst Boris Kagarlitsky put it:

> The war in the Balkans revealed the scale of anti-American feelings in Russian society, especially among the younger generation, which Western journalists out of habit were continuing to describe as a support base for the liberal reforms. . . . The rotten eggs and paint bombs that were thrown at the building of the American Embassy signified that a psychological turning point had been reached in the country. People had grown tired of being ashamed of themselves. They wanted to act, to achieve something they could be proud of. The failures by the Americans in the Balkans became the subject of jokes; earlier, Russians had only joked about their own government. Russian hackers, the youth press reported sympathetically, had launched systematic attacks on official sites in the United States.[2]

Primakov's dismissal on May 12 was largely provoked by the impeachment process that was launched by the KPRF, more from vengefulness than with any hope of removing the president from office. Primakov asked the deputies to refrain from voting on impeachment or to shift the vote to a different date, as had happened once already. However, the deputies and especially the KPRF faction decided that to retreat was impossible; otherwise they would simply look ridiculous. Moreover, a section of the Communist Party leadership had no qualms about putting Primakov's cabinet in the firing line. It was not only the Kremlin that found the premier's rapidly growing popularity irritating, but also many leaders of the opposition.[3]

Nevertheless, the sacking of Primakov was a surprise. Data from a survey conducted by the agency Finmarket the day after the dismissal showed that 72 percent of those polled expressed regret at the development, while only 20 percent supported Yeltsin's decision.[4] In the spring and summer of 1999, Primakov's status as the leading candidate for president of Russia was unquestionable. If parliamentary and presidential elections had been held that summer, the polls all indicated, the Fatherland movement that he chaired would have won a majority, and Yevgeny Primakov would have been elected president.[5] The government formed by Sergey Stepashin proved to be transitional. Although the population responded positively to the actions of his cabinet, Stepashin was clearly unsuccessful in coping with Primakov's popularity. Stepashin did not become the successor, and perhaps, was never intended to be one.

On August 9, 1999, immediately after Stepashin was dismissed, Vladimir Putin was installed as acting premier, and on August 16, after his candidacy had been approved by the State Duma, as prime minister of Russia. The pretext for Stepashin's dismissal was supplied by an incursion of Chechen fighters into Dagestan on August 7. As Kagarlitsky states:

> The war in Dagestan was also superimposed on the conflict of interests in the Russian oil business. On the one hand, the firm Sibneft, belonging to Boris Berezovsky, had an interest in ensuring that Azerbaijani oil reached Europe as late as possible and that its cost was high. By any accounting, the cost of extracting oil was far more in the north than in the south, and the flow of oil from Azerbaijan would depress market prices. Meanwhile the company Transneft, which was involved in the building and exploitation of pipelines, had an interest in Azerbaijani oil, on the condition of course that it was Transneft that gained the relevant contract. Significantly, the fighting in Dagestan coincided with an increasingly fierce struggle for control of Transneft. Here the contending sides also resorted to force. Transneft president Dmitry Savelyev was removed, and the firm's central office was seized by a detachment of riot police. According to reports that leaked to the press, Berezovsky financed Basaev's campaign in Dagestan together with Saudi sponsors who were also anxious to block the flow of oil from the Caspian. If these reports were true, it might be said that in Dagestan Sibneft was fighting Transneft, the former using Chechen fighters, and the latter Russia's regular army.[6]

It is hard to say how accurate this account and conclusion may be. Nevertheless, oil played a definite role in the development of the Chechen conflict, perhaps no *less* a role than the 1999–2000 election campaign. In other words, the Chechen war appeared to solve both the economic and political problems of the Moscow elite.

The Distribution of Political Forces

Two parallel parties of the government had taken shape by the time of the 1999 elections. One of these parties—herein referred to as Fatherland–All Russia—had among its members the popular politician Yevgeny Primakov, the entire Luzhkov media holding company and the publications controlled by it, and a number of influential governors, whose authority, along with the regional media, provided an additional cause to hope for victory. Media-Most owner Vladimir Gusinsky participated in the "great game" on the side of this bloc, while maintaining his loyalty to such second-rank players as Yabloko and the Union of Right Forces—in the latter case, even though this formation was part of a hostile grouping. Burdened by debts he had acquired while investing in his media holding company, Gusinsky was forced to actively take part in the political game, on the calculation that his partners would give him financial assistance. The other party of the government, that of the Kremlin, had at its disposal all the resources of the power hierarchy, as well as the capital of the oligarchs who were close to the regime and who feared a redivision of property if Primakov were to win. Apart from state television—strengthened with the advent of Oleg Dobrodeev, but still extremely weak—the Kremlin had on its side Boris Berezovsky's ORT, a large section of the national periodical press, and those governors who were not part of the Fatherland–All Russia bloc.

Although from the point of view of its media weapons the Kremlin was unquestionably in a winning position, in terms of the electability of its candidate, Fatherland–All Russia led by a considerable margin, and it was the presidential elections that represented the real field of battle for both groupings. The parliamentary election campaign was viewed by observers as no more than a rehearsal for the general contest; for this reason, no one paid attention any longer to the Communists, who had a stable electoral following, but whose resources were clearly inadequate for participation in the presidential race. In this "great game," no one apart from the Kremlin and Fatherland–All Russia played an

Table 4.1

Distribution of Forces on the Eve of the 1999 Elections

	Kremlin bloc	Regional bloc
Presidential candidate	Vladimir Putin	Yevgeny Primakov
Political trademarks	Unity, Union of Right Forces	Fatherland–All Russia
National television channels (controlled)	ORT, RTR, TV6	NTV, TNT, TV-Center
Media holdings (supporting)	State media, Berezovsky's media, regional media	Media-Most, Moscow and regional media
Strategy	All-out assault carried out with great precision, personal attacks on Luzhkov and Primakov	Defense with counter-attacks, concentration on "traditional" politics, personal attacks on Yeltsin
Shared beliefs	Great Russia	Great Russia

independent role; other players could hope at most to receive financing in exchange for collaborating with one side or the other.

It was in this context that materials on corruption in Russia were published for the first time, as details surfaced of the affair involving the Bank of New York and the Swiss company Mabetex. The latter company was accused of having paid bribes to presidential administration chief Pavel Borodin[7] in exchange for large-scale building contracts. For the Kremlin, it would have been hard to imagine a worse gift.

In August 1999, the *New York Times*, *Corriere della Sera*, and other Western newspapers began publishing articles on massive corruption in the Kremlin, money-laundering through Western banks, and related stories. The Russian press began quoting the accusations. For the Russian reader there was virtually nothing new in all this. In the Kremlin, however, the articles appearing in the West were interpreted as a political signal. The change of mood in the West was perceived in the Kremlin as treachery.[8]

It should be noted that, unlike outside observers and the entire political establishment, the Kremlin was not inclined to regard the parliamentary elections as a mere warm-up. On the contrary, it was precisely during this period that a turning point would be reached in the country's political life. Vladimir Putin would not simply appear on the political scene, but would immediately seize a dominant position. Fatherland–All Russia would not simply be denied victory in the parliamentary polls, but would suffer a catastrophic loss, and this defeat would be so crushing that it would not even occur to the losers to put up their own candidate in the presidential elections. This was because the question of victory or defeat in these elections, perhaps for the last or next-to-last time in Russian history, implied a full-scale reapportioning of property and of spheres of influence.

> Luzhkov's assault on the Kremlin could not fail to meet with resistance from Berezovsky. Preparing for an information war, the latter bought a controlling interest in the newspaper *Kommersant* and replaced its chief editor. Joining in the campaign alongside Berezovsky were the state media organs controlled by the presidential administration. Against the enemy they used unorthodox methods such as extraordinary tax audits (in Russia, these are tantamount to natural disasters). . . . The Ministry of the Press, Television, and Mass Communications Media, headed by Mikhail Lesin, this time also actively participated in the information war. What could be done with the help of sympathetic bureaucrats was shown by the events of September 2, when the ministry simply switched off the St. Petersburg television channel, which had dared to mock the election campaigning of the right forces.[9]

By this time, the many scandals and media wars had revealed to viewers the mechanisms being used to influence the public consciousness. This theme is central to the plot of writer Viktor Pelevin's bestseller *Generation P*, published in English with the title *Homo Zapiens*. Pelevin's protagonist makes a spectacular rise as an advertising copywriter for Western consumer products, until he lands at a top firm that—he comes to realize—is actually generating a virtual political reality, including a digitally enhanced Boris Yeltsin. This fantastical plot quite accurately reflected the skeptical attitude of urban viewers: that what appeared on television was not necessarily true. This feeling led many people to keep their distance from the TV-reality, creating additional problems for political managers. To secure victory in the elections, it was necessary to think up something new. The Kremlin's political experts thus came up with two major ploys. The first was to create an opposition to the Moscow mayor, who was also a leader of the Fatherland bloc, on a par with Primakov. Luzhkov was seeking a second term as mayor and faced no

serious competitors. Under an agreement with the presidential administration, the Union of Right Forces leader Sergey Kirienko announced
his candidacy for mayor of the Russian capital. In the process, he opened
a "second front" against the Fatherland bloc, secured a new source of
funding for the union's election campaign, and acquired new allies in
the shape of the pro-Kremlin state media and Berezovsky's media.

The second ploy was to clone the Fatherland bloc, using the same
scheme of reliance on governors. This was how the "Unity" bloc, whose
leadership was entrusted to the Minister of Emergency Situations Sergey
Shoygu, came to be established. The idea behind "Unity" and "Fatherland" was indeed the same: to capitalize on the public's craving for "law
and order" and its willingness to rally behind state power to overcome
the popular identity crisis. It is unclear what the outcome of this campaign might have been had Shoygu, accompanied by groups of television journalists, not flown so often to Chechnya, where war was raging.
One could hardly think of a more dramatic setting.

Drama-99: The Second War in Chechnya

The incursion into Dagestan by Chechen fighters was suicidal. Instead
of the local support they might have expected to receive due to shared
religious traditions, the Chechens were met by the popular militia and
troops of the regular army. The public reaction to the incursion was
instantaneous and categorical. Of 1,600 Russian citizens polled by the
public-opinion research organization VCIOM, 52 percent called for the
fighters to be wiped out in one way or another, although only 10 percent
insisted on the destruction of the fighters' bases in Chechnya. In all, 24
percent of those interviewed supported talks with the leaders of the fighters or with the official Chechen government.[10]

On August 11, 1999, four days after the incursion by fighters under
the command of Shamil Basayev and the Saudi jihadist Khattab and two
days after Vladimir Putin had been appointed acting prime minister,
federal forces began an operation to liberate the occupied territory. On
August 26 Putin announced the completion of the first stage of the operation in Dagestan. On August 31 came the first explosion in Moscow,
in the Okhotny Ryad commercial complex. Forty people were wounded.
(In a comic note, a leaflet of the Union of Revolutionary Writers, written by Dmitry Pimenov, was found at the site of the blast. After the
leaflet surfaced in the press, the Internet provider shut down the writer's

Web site. Pimenov was unable to bear the burden of his instant notoriety and possible criminal prosecution, and thought it better to set off for Prague and his friend, Avdey Ter-Oganyan, a radical artist in exile who is being prosecuted by the Orthodox Church over the destruction of Orthodox icons at the Art-Manezh exhibition.)

The conclusion that Chechens were implicated in the explosion did not become the main one, so this blast was followed by others. On September 4, in Buynaksk, a five-story apartment building was bombed; its residents included the families of five servicemen from the 136th Brigade of the Defense Ministry; 64 people were killed and 120 were injured. Thereafter:

> On the night of September 8 a building on Guryanova Street in Moscow was bombed; around 90 were killed. . . .
>
> On September 13, the day of mourning for the victims of the explosions in Buynaksk and Moscow, a residential building on Kashirskoe Boulevard was blown up; more than 120 people were killed.
>
> On September 15 Defense Minister Igor Sergeyev reported to Vladimir Putin that the territory of Dagestan had been completely purged of fighters.
>
> On September 17 an apartment building in the city of Volgodonsk, in Saratov Province, was bombed. Seventeen people were killed, and about 150 were injured.
>
> On September 20 the creation of a "safe zone" around Chechnya was begun.
>
> On September 24, at a press conference in Astana, the capital of Kazakhstan, Vladimir Putin declared: "Russian aircraft are launching and will continue to launch strikes in Chechnya exclusively against terrorist bases. We'll pursue the terrorists everywhere. If we catch them taking a crap, we'll waste them right there in the shithouse."[11]

Whether the conflict in Chechnya was planned as an accompaniment to the campaign or whether the Kremlin was simply lucky, the war provided the "turn of the screw" that not only destroyed the political configuration that had existed in the late summer of 1999, but that also installed, or helped install, a new political hierarchy. Putin and Shoygu, while directing the military and the relief operations in Chechnya, respectively, were able to show themselves to be "men of action," capable of protecting people in time of war.

Of all media events, wars and terrorist acts are unquestionably the most powerful. A war, especially if it is being fought a few thousand kilometers off, becomes a spellbinding drama that millions of viewers, huge armies of fans—far more than with any conceivable football or hockey tournament—can watch with a variety of emotions. When combined with acts of terrorism, the impact of this drama is enhanced, because fear instantly penetrates everywhere and people can no longer shut themselves off from it.

In Moscow the epidemic of fear resulted in an immediate break-up of the urban space and the tightening of the pass system for access to all areas, including the stairwells of apartment buildings. Traffic jams increased due to lengthy inspections at entry points to the city. Residents installed coded locks and kept watch around the clock, until as a result of natural selection these posts were transferred to concierges and alcoholics, who wielded their new authority with a delight that recalled the noir aspects of Soviet life.

Most importantly, however, the image of the enemy became firmly fixed in society. The Identikit pictures of suspects shown on television were devoid of individual features; all that could be seen in them was a type—an "individual of Caucasus nationality," a specific construct that emerged in the Russian press during the 1990s to describe people from the southern republics of the former USSR. In everyday speech these people were known as "blacks." This time, however, the image of the enemy was more concrete and distinctive. The government immediately blamed the Chechens. Not a single one of the accusations was proved, and no one seriously tried to prove them. A veritable racist hysteria came to grip the mass media. Expressing these moods most openly was the well-known liberal commentator Mikhail Leontyev (a former *Nezavisimaya Gazeta* columnist), who declared that "the Chechens want only one kind of independence—independence from the Criminal Code."

From the point of view of the propagandists, the entire Chechen people should have been made to pay for the actions of field commanders Basayev and Khattab in Dagestan and the bombs detonated by unknown people in Moscow. "To defeat the enemy, you have to hate them—such is the law of war in the late twentieth century," journalists for *Moskovsky Komsomolets* argued cynically. "The only thing that is different about such a war is that it is preceded by a barrage from the media artillery." Without the slightest criticism, they related how "the image of the enemy was swiftly established." Journalists had been given strict guidelines, which had not existed in 1994 and 1995. At the head of this movement stood the newly created Ministry of the Press, which effectively introduced partial censorship to the airwaves.[12]

A war, preferably abroad or in remote provinces, whose existence is perceived mainly through reports from the scene of the battles and the terrorist acts, provides the ideal dramatic background for establishing and reinforcing the image of a political leader, while the image of the enemy helps to direct the dissatisfaction of the masses into a "safe" channel. As Murray Edelman states:

> It is not important whether this substitution is just or not; it is indispensable, since it makes it possible to direct discontent against an object that cannot answer back. . . . Creating the image of a foreign enemy in order to weaken internal opposition and distract the attention of the public from domestic problems has become a typical political gambit for the reason that more often than not it is successful. . . . The choice of substitutes for the object of indignation usually falls on "typical" enemies—ones who always arouse the suspicion and aggression of the population. The discontent intensifies and links up, providing a basis for the establishing of political coalitions. The characteristic of the enemy that is employed most often is that he or she is of a different nationality, one that is considered in society to be less "human" compared to the nationality with which the majority associate themselves, for example, "American," "Englishman," or "Swede." Some peoples are easy to present as enemies; Russians, Salvadorans, or Vietnamese are given the features of a stereotype, which aids in the condensing and transferring of a negative attitude onto them from other objects of hatred.[13]

After the incursion into Dagestan and the terrorist acts in Moscow, the war in Chechnya and the embodiment of the enemy in the Chechens were in fact accepted by society, one could even say received with enthusiasm. Just as Yevgeny Primakov made his reputation with the Balkan crisis and the low exchange rate of the ruble. Under the circumstances, Putin had no alternative but to seize his chance and demonstrate his character using the case of Chechnya, providing leadership in a "just war." If he had not done this, the course of events would have swept him from the political scene just as pitilessly as they did his predecessor Sergey Stepashin.

One of the peculiarities of modern-day election campaigns is the obvious contradiction between the natural need on the one hand to state one's intentions plainly in an election program, and on the other, to retain the maximum flexibility and diffuseness in one's political platform in order to avoid frightening part of the electorate. The only way to avoid this dilemma is to fix public attention on immediate events, on crises or a war.

When claimants to the leadership win power, doubts concerning their views vanish, and along with these doubts, their popularity usually diminishes as well. Now they have to attract and hold attention, using as their lever specific, immediate situations. A domestic or foreign crisis may serve to keep interest on the leader, even if his or her policies are completely clear, as we saw in the case of Roosevelt and his long term in office, or as history again showed with the Falkland Islands during the time of Margaret Thatcher.[14]

The abundance of limited regional wars in the modern world forces us to look seriously at the hypothesis according to which war has become one of the structurally indispensable elements of modern media-based democracy. One is tempted to agree with Edelman's conclusions: squeezed within the inevitable limitations of the political system and the bureaucratic apparatus, political leaders are rarely able to display the qualities that allow them to win elections: firmness and the ability to act quickly and achieve rapid results. The practical activity of politicians, of course, also brings results, but never with such speed, or so visibly. Who is going to observe the political routine with the same intense attention people use in following a war?

Coverage of the Election Campaign

With the media-political system in place as a systematically structured, predictable information environment, the task of political experts and scriptwriters of the political spectacle became working out the kind of drama and the kind of moves that would cancel out the expectations of the audience and awaken in it an interest in what was occurring. Only then would the political leaders—the actors in this political drama— receive the attention they required and have the chance to play their role to a full house.

At the same time as Sergey Kirienko and Pavel Borodin stood as candidates for Mayor of Moscow, Berezovsky's television channel ORT was starting to make harsh attacks on Fatherland leaders Yury Luzhkov and Yevgeny Primakov. The Saturday public affairs program "Vremya" became a focus for revelations and criticisms. Noisy television campaigns were aired, alleging that corruption was occurring in the mayor's office with the complicity of Luzhkov's wife, a businesswoman. The "analytical" shows on television have shocked even Russian viewers who thought they had seen it all. Their screens have shown General Prosecutor Yury Skuratov, who had fallen out of favor with the Kremlin, making love to two prostitutes; Chechen fighters beheading a prisoner; and even a surgical operation similar to the one that was performed on Primakov in Switzerland.

Evidently, television had a serious influence on people's political preferences, since it was television that provided the main channel for information on what was happening in the world. The most important broadcasts were the news programs; to judge from the ratings, according to Laura Belin, the free time provided to candidates and the political advertisements played an insignificant role. Here, too, odd collisions took place from time to time. For example, when Primakov prepared a clip in which he made a strong statement to the effect that people in the Kremlin were afraid of serious corruption investigations, what happened next "was, perhaps, the most effective 'dirty trick' in the whole election campaign. ORT and RTR ran this clip only in conjunction with a hurriedly made bogus advertisement that seriously diminished the force of Primakov's words."[15]

As it was aired, jammed between the speeches of the other two candidates, dressed in similar suits and sitting at identical tables, Primakov's address appeared comic. Similar methods of political montage, based on the experience of 1996, were used in the information broadcasts of ORT and RTR throughout the election campaign.

As well as being determined by the political orientation of the owners of the print publications and television stations, the reporting of the election campaign was governed by legislation on elections for the State Duma and the presidency that had been adopted by the parliament. A new law limited the right of journalists to make commentaries while covering the campaign. It is thus curious to learn of the results of a study, performed by the European Media Institute, which set out to calculate the number of times the various candidates in the presidential race were mentioned in the news broadcasts of the main television channels. These data show that one candidate clearly dominated the coverage. They also reveal a close correspondence between the results of the voting and the number of times candidates appeared on television screens—that is, the presence of one or another political actor in TV-reality.

Table 4.2

Television Coverage of Candidates and Results of the Elections, %

Candidate	All TV channels	ORT	RTR	NTV	Election results
Vladimir Putin	48.3	43.8	53.3	45.0	52.9
Gennady Zyuganov	11.4	10.2	10.7	16.9	29.2
Grigory Yavlinsky	8.0	8.0	7.4	9.5	5.8
Aman Tuleev	2.7	2.5	4.2	2.6	2.9
Vladimir Zhirinovsky	11.8	11.3	8.7	16.9	2.7
Konstantin Titov	4.5	5.6	5.5	3.7	1.5
Ella Pamfilova	2.8	4.3	2.8	2.1	1.0
Stanislav Govorukhin	2.6	3.1	1.2	2.9	0.4
Yury Skuratov	1.9	3.1	2.4	1.8	0.4
Aleksey Podberezkin	1.8	2.8	1.9	1.4	0.1
Umar Dzhabrailov	2.0	3.9	0.6	1.4	0.1
Yevgeny Savostyanov	2.1	1.5	1.4	1.1	0.0

Source: Study by the European Media Institute, March 3–21, 2000.Quoted in the paper by Andrey Raskin "The Russian Presidential Election Campaign-2000 and National Television" at the ICCEES conference in Tampere, Finland, August 2000.

This table is of course a collection of dry figures; it provides no idea of the drama the political actors were enacting. As revealed by an analysis of the campaign coverage in sixteen newspapers that was also included in the study, the drama was both rather tedious—due to the lack of a worthy rival to Putin—and inconsequential, since it did not spark public discussion. Passing up his free television time and refusing to take part in television debates, the presidential candidate remained "above the fray." Moreover, he no longer held the post of prime minister, but was now acting president of Russia.

As indicated by the results of the above-mentioned study, the campaign coverage had the overall effect of centralizing power. Dialogue between different regions was absent, along with any effort by the media to engage in a dialogue with the audience. The sole exception noted by one of the people heading the study, Lyudmila Resnyanskaya, was the hard-line Communist opposition newspaper *Sovetskaya Rossiya*, whose journalists proved quite incorruptible. Something resembling a dialogue could also be observed in *Nezavisimaya Gazeta*, which tried to serve as a forum of discussion for the intellectual elite; however, the interests of the newspaper's owner, Boris Berezovsky, weighed heavily on the results of its analysis.

Resnyanskaya, meanwhile, points out the impossibility of coming up with a precise definition of the role of the mass media in deciding the political choices made by voters, especially compared with so-called "administrative resources," that is, the authority of regional leaders and enterprise chiefs. When expressed plainly and backed up, the positions taken by these bosses and governors could have a decisive impact on the preferences shown by local audiences.[16]

The New Year

Boris Yeltsin's resignation was the most momentous move in the history of election campaigns in Russia so far. One might even go further. The fact that Yeltsin announced his resignation on New Year's Eve, December 31, and let a tear fall as he asked Russians to forgive him for his failure to achieve the results he had promised, in many ways predetermined the outcome of the campaign. In the process, it demoralized once and for all the country's political elite, which had been savoring the prospect of a full-blown season of juicy intrigues as Putin clashed with Primakov.

Following the traditional strategy of penetrating the mass consciousness, political specialists discovered once again the huge significance of rituals and celebrations as a means of political communication. The process of a "resignation-appointment" killed two birds with one stone. First and foremost, the presenting of Vladimir Putin in a new capacity took place in front of the largest possible viewing audience. New Year's is the only celebration in the calendar of the new Russia that has survived from Soviet times. In fact its significance has increased since those times. This is a celebration with ritual television shows and family dinners. According to an old Soviet tradition champagne bottles are opened with the striking of the chimes (12 times) in the Spassky Tower of the Kremlin, accompanied by a congratulatory announcement in a deep male voice. All day, politicians and stars of every caliber congratulate one another on television, appearing in a precise hierarchy of importance and influence. The closer the speech to the New Year, the more people watch it, the more prestigious it is, and the higher the standing of the speaker.

A few minutes before year's end, the speech by the president of the Russian Federation is transmitted. This is watched by many, if not all the people; it is shown simultaneously on all the main channels.

According to data from the television monitoring organization NISPI, even on a single channel (ORT) the president's New Year greeting was the most popular television program of December 1999, attracting 1,851,000 viewers in Moscow alone. The same top-10 rating of the most popular political broadcasts during December also included the transmissions of the president's greeting on the other television channels, RTR and NTV. These reached 885,000 and 797,000 viewers, respectively.[17] This indicates a total of 3,533,000 in Moscow alone—record for 1999, especially since the figures, in my view, are a bit low. This speech also served as the occasion for Russia to acquire a new president and to hold an informal inauguration. Moreover, after recording his New Year's greeting to Russians, Putin set off for Chechnya in order to celebrate the holiday with the soldiers. Everyone was aware of this as well, since the sacred drama of bidding farewell to the old year and seeing in the new had been replaced by the ritual of a transfer of power.

In this, properly speaking, also lay the second, symbolic meaning of the combination. The New Year was not only the major holiday, but also the most ancient festival of the Russian calendar, dating back to pre-Christian times. The New Year was an agrarian celebration and until the seventeenth century was observed in September. It was Peter the Great, seeking to bring Russia into line with Europe, who ordered that the date when the New Year was celebrated be shifted to the end of December. The change of dates, however, did not alter the importance of the festival.

The sacramental significance of New Year's, or to put it another way, the subtext of the ritual, is death and revival. Nature dies, in order to be born anew. In primitive societies, the festival involves the ritual death of a god or a king, and a rebirth. Testifying to the power of this metaphor is the fact that the drama of Christ unfolds in a similar scenario.

Mircea Eliade views the closely related theme of the end/beginning of history through the prism of the relationship between the sacred-mythical time of the creation of the world and of great ancestors (*in illo tempore*) on the one hand, and profane time on the other. In his study *The Myth of the Eternal Return*, he describes the theme of a return to the beginning of creation, implicit in the rite of the celebration of the New Year, as central to mythological consciousness, basing his conclusion on numerous examples of such rituals, which he finds in one form or another in all mythological—that is, oral—cultures.

> Since the cosmos and humanity are renewed constantly and in all possible ways, the past is annihilated, sicknesses and misdeeds are expelled, and so forth. The formal side of the ritual varies, but the essence remains unchanged. Everything is directed toward a single goal: doing away with past time, banishing history, so as constantly, through the repetition of a cosmogonical act, to return *in illo tempore*.[18]

The theme of cleansing has a special significance for the New Year festival; with various tribes, this theme takes on different ritual forms ("Almost everywhere, the banishing of demons, illnesses, or sins coincides or coincided with a particular temporal boundary—the celebration of the New Year.")[19] On the other hand, in many cultures the New Year's rite also coincides with the rite of initiation and with the closely related ceremony of enthronement.

> For the aborigines of the island of Fiji, the creation occurs every time when a new leader comes to power; this concept, in more or less analogous formulations, has been preserved in other regions as well. Almost everywhere, the new rule is perceived as the rebirth of the history of the people, or even of history in general. With each ruler, however insignificant he might be, a new era begins.[20]

Putin's New Year speech as acting president was the culmination—premature, but nevertheless extremely dramatic—of the whole issue of the presidential election in Russia. On this occasion, the regime brought itself to speak of its own character and managed to recode the rite of the transformation of time into a rite of the transformation of power, at the same time demoralizing the opposition and working effectively on the deep strata of mass consciousness.

Compared with this profound legitimization of the regime, the election appeared as something predictable and insignificant. So indeed it became. As related by Lyudmila Resnyanskaya, the heads of public relations agencies admitted in private conversations that Putin's basic method was to "saw away" at the mass consciousness with paid mentions of his name in print publications in any context. It was enough for the regime to display its presence, and for Putin to figure constantly in news reports, in order to signify the inevitability, the predestination, of the outcome of the election campaign. The various steps by Acting President Putin (he rode the tractor and sailed the submarine) appeared one after another, and no commentators had time to react to changes on the information scene. Like the Western press during the wars in the Persian

Gulf and the Balkans, the Russian press passively followed the information lead provided by the government, not evaluating what was happening and placing it in a wider context and not taking any special pains to do so. Everything was perceived as simply standing to reason.

Responding to the hopes of a strong regime, the Kremlin group made a show of the most impressive capacities it had at its disposal. And indeed, what regime could be stronger than one resting on subconscious-historical strata of popular memory and rituals with profound roots in everyday life?

Standartenführer von Stirlitz and Peter the Great

In advancing a new politician to the center of the political stage, political forces always face a problem with "recognition" of the new image. During the first months of Putin's prime ministership, the theme of countless press articles in Russia and abroad was "Who are you, Mister Putin?" Writers played a game of trying to put together a consistent image based on the impression that the freshly minted prime minister created with his statements and actions. Seeking to position the heir in the political field, journalists plotted an image in relation to a fixed system of coordinates in which the central roles were played by the Chechen war, "economic reforms" (that is, attitude to business and businessmen), and the candidate's personal history. Putin had a taste for national-patriotic ideology, but his economic program, the preparation of which was one of the main media events staged during the nominating and campaigning, showed that in formulating his economic policies the prime minister was inclined to rest on the liberals.

On the level of mass consciousness, however, political discourse and the problematic constructed by the mass media do not mean a great deal. The recognition issue is best solved through a system of culture codes, which are at the disposal of the audience, and through comparison with the images of other public personas, both living and dead. A favorable political image is always a multilayered construct in which various "prompts" for mass consciousness are present on a symbolic level. Putin's history as a spy was doubly advantageous for him. This was first because Putin, who had in fact been a replacement for Primakov, was strangely enough perceived as his heir. Second, Putin embodied the image—very important for the Russian television audience—of Standartenführer von Stirlitz.

Table 4.3

Who Are You, Mister Putin?

Image	Standartenführer Stirlitz (Maxim Isayev)
Qualities	Love for the homeland, heroism, unflinching will.
Associations	Spy in Germany, age between 40 and 50.
Conclusion	A hero you can trust.

The latter is one of the central characters in Soviet grassroots mythology. Created by the writer Julian Semenov, this image was brought to life by one of the most popular actors of the Soviet epoch, Vyacheslav Tikhonov, in the television serial "Seventeen Moments in Spring." During the first showing of the series in the early 1970s, city streets would empty while it was being broadcast. It was a larger-than-life hit; "Seventeen Moments in Spring" attracted a greater audience than hockey matches.

The action of the series unfolds during the last year of the Second World War. Working in German counterintelligence, von Stirlitz (who is really the Soviet agent Colonel Maxim Isayev) drives the German nuclear program "Weapon of Vengeance" into a dead end using his sharp mind and unbending will. He forces a breakdown of peace talks between fascist Germany, Great Britain, and the United States; engages in intellectual games with the commanders of the SS and Martin Bormann himself, punishes traitors, and sacrifices his family happiness for the good of the homeland. Tortured by the desire to return home and be reunited with his wife, von Stirlitz subordinates his feelings to his duty, thus becoming a monument to late Soviet classicism.

It is not surprising that the German press was the most hostile in its reaction to Putin. On the front pages of newspapers and magazines, the photograph of Yeltsin's heir, together with the headlines, inevitably evoked associations with fascism. The headline of one of the articles asked: "Would you buy a used car from this man?" The image of the Soviet spy von Stirlitz, like that of Prime Minister Putin, was not made for the German audience.

The significance of von Stirlitz for the mass consciousness in Russia is comparable to the image of James Bond. The latter, as we know, embodies a successful businessman who is living a jet-set life and is not too concerned about the moral aspects of what he does—a sort of avenging angel in human form, and no stranger to human weakness. Both Bond and von Stirlitz often have to contend with alien-like forces and protect the world from destruction by diabolical powers. In this sense, Bond is a brother to Superman, Batman, and similar icons of twentieth-century mass culture. Their family is large, and its roots extend so deeply into history that it deserves to be the subject of separate genea-logical research that would trace the nuances in the transformation that such images undergo according to the context in which they ap-pear and the culture which has recorded them in its history. All that will be noted here is that such distant relatives of the superheroes as Achilles, Hercules, Kukhulin, and others appear in the most ancient of known literary sources.

Like Bond, von Stirlitz penetrated deep into the popular memory, but unlike Super-agent 007 he also became a character in the creative life of the population. Along with the heroes of other military and revolution-ary films, some TV series heroes (Sherlock Holmes was one of them), and Soviet leaders imbued with a powerful propagandist inspiration (Chapayev and Petka,[21] Lenin and Brezhnev), von Stirlitz became the hero of innumerable jokes and stories. Selections of the new adven-tures of von Stirlitz appeared in *samizdat* of the late 1980s. The spy hero was one of the most recognizable images of the Brezhnev era (it was Primakov's closeness to this era that the public found so impressive about him). If anyone missed the connection between Putin, who served in Germany, and von Stirlitz, articles in the press reminded them of the resemblance and helped create the association.[22]

In fact, the image of Putin had various connotations and parameters of "recognition"—among film heroes, military leaders, and political figures of the past. As a rule, the instilling of various images and fea-tures in political systems proceeds gradually. Sometimes the images are frozen in monuments that function as a sort of permanent propa-ganda (such as the huge memorial to Peter the Great erected by Yury Luzhkov on the banks of the Moscow River opposite the rebuilt Ca-thedral of Christ the Savior), while at other times the images, as suc-cessful devices, are borrowed from other political players. Politicians, as a rule, encourage some associations and try to expunge others. Peter the Great was one of the cruelest and most despotic emperors in Rus-sian history and yet one of the most enlightened. His image symbol-izes the power of the state (including the state as opposed to civil society), the greatness of Russia, the messianic ambitions of a politi-cal leader—and the enduring grandeur of his accomplishments, such as the city of St. Petersburg.

And what struck French analysts most about Vladimir Putin? Not the unexpected leap into the presidential armchair, not the black belt in judo, and not even the New Year's visit to the army in Chechnya. What really surprised them was the portrait hanging in Putin's office: a portrait of Peter the Great.

It may be that Putin's origins in St. Petersburg influenced this choice, or it may be that this portrait represents a certain hint, argues an observer for the Parisian newspaper *Le Monde*, reminding readers that Peter the Great defended his country from the Swedish threat and completely transformed its appearance, albeit paying for this with the lives of almost a third of Russia's inhabitants.[23]

The city of St. Petersburg, where Putin began his life's journey, is not simply an essential link between Peter the Great and the new president; the city is also a symbol in its own right. For everyone who has ever been in St. Petersburg, the city whose residents have always considered it to be Russia's cultural capital, there is no secret about the meaning of this symbol. St. Petersburg is an entirely planned city, constructed on a marsh at the command of young reformers headed by a young tsar. Its straight avenues intersect at geometrically precise angles. This is incontestably a city constructed in the grand style, mostly in the eighteenth and nineteenth centuries, the epoch of the rise of the Russian Empire. Moscow, decorated by Stalinist construction, embellished with the coronets of its hills and the necklace of its metro, has also taken on a style— at times just as magnificent and just as austere, but less insistent, losing itself in the winding, hilly streets, and little alleyways. Architecture expresses the relationships of power just like any other medium[24]—and in St. Petersburg it does so more graphically than anywhere else. In Moscow there is more chaos, more life. From the very beginning in St. Petersburg there has been more order, more authority—authority of a special kind, the despotic authority of an idea that Russia had to have a window to Europe: a capital on the Baltic Sea.

Founded on the basis of the tyranny of an idea, St. Petersburg from the start has been so uncomfortable that it would scarcely have survived had the emperor not transferred the capital from Moscow to the city he had created. In St. Petersburg one is stunned in the first instance by the fact that the city is alive at all, but second by the fact that by its very existence it expresses the triumph of will over nature, of action over inertia, possessing an enduring heroic charm.

Trying to establish parameters for the "recognition" of Vladimir Putin in the politician's beloved country not long before the elections, the journal *Vlast* compared the results of two surveys of public opinion:

> It must be said that the results of the surveys disheartened us a little. In the VCIOM survey, the prime positions were held by Peter the Great, Gleb Zheglov,[25] and Marshal Zhukov[26] (the fourth place went to von Stirlitz). In the ROMIR survey, the top positions went to Zhukov, von Stirlitz, and Zheglov (Peter the Great was not suggested as a candidate to respondents in this survey, and to judge from the figures, Peter's votes went to Zhukov). When we published the results of the surveys in May, we wrote that all the people who took the top positions combined the image of hero with that of conqueror: "Victory is the thing that consumed their whole lives and to which they sacrificed everything—including laws and the lives of human beings. The slogan of such a president might be 'victory at any price.' It appears that Russians have acknowledged through their preferences that they are ready to pay this price." The comments by the ROMIR analysts were similar: "A majority of Russians are thus ready to have an aggressive and uncaring leader. People are giving their preference to strength and severity, hoping that these will help bring order to Russia."[27]

The results of this study do not contradict in the least our hypothesis about the central place held by the image of von Stirlitz. The *Vlast* journalist stressed:

> First, the thing that puts any blood at all in the veins of the generally rather pallid image of Putin is his past as a spy. Work in Germany, devotion to the homeland, shedding a tear on Soviet holidays. Maksim Maksimovich Isayev, the very one.[28]

Out of all the above-mentioned associations, the one with von Stirlitz is the only one (with the exception of Zheglov) that falls outside the field of simple comparison, belonging instead to the province of shared experience, of empathy. Such a recognition already implies support. The first association was the most important. However strange it might seem, this "direct hit" on the image of a cult hero allowed Putin to acquire an identity.

On the whole, the image of Putin can be viewed as the result of a ten-year evolution of the Russian political system. Without laying claim to an exhaustive precision in these evaluations, we can trace the development of various qualities in a range of actors on the Russian political

scene and compare them with the qualities of the Putin image. Ultimately, it is no secret that the way Putin embodied in his image the most
successful strategies of political actors was an important criterion in his
selection as successor to Boris Yeltsin, and that enhancing this capacity
was a vital task for him both as prime minister and as acting president
during his election campaign. It is important to note that the contradictions between borrowed qualities that are obvious from Table 4.4 are not
a major hindrance in television politics. All the elements can be successfully acted out on the level of rhetoric and visual background, as
long as the audience lacks the possibility of relating words with deeds.
As a rule, the emphasis is not on achievements and decisions, since the
concrete always gives rise to contradictions.

In the 1996 presidential campaign, the principal motif underlying the
"virtual reality" of the elections was the solving of all problems. In the
2000 campaign, by contrast, the leitmotif was the forming of a consensus of the elites and the masses around the image of Great Russia with
all its component elements, including the creation of a front of military
actions (and also diplomatic conflicts), and of distinct images of "foreign" (ethnic) and domestic (political) enemies—the necessary compo-
nents for the nation-building effort. In constructing such enemies and
the narrative plots that define their place in history, people are mani-
festly defining themselves and their place in history as well; the self-
definition lends passion to the whole transaction.[29]

A New Type of Opposition

In the 1999 parliamentary election campaign, the main rivals—the warring parties of those in power—did not have particular differences on
the level of ideology, and it is possible to imagine that the achieving of
a consensus of elites took place quickly and painlessly. Alarmed by the
defeat of the Fatherland bloc, regional leaders made overtures to the
Kremlin as it celebrated its victory, and those who disagreed with what
was happening in the country were subjected to harsh media examina-
tion and criticism. The right-wingers were silent because they were counting on posts in the government (and not in vain—Sergey Kirienko became
the president's representative in one of the seven federal districts).
Yabloko held its peace because its leaders were afraid of ending up in
isolation. The Ministry of the Press intimidated the television industry
with warnings directed at ORT and TVC,[30] while the remainder were

Table 4.4

Innovations by Political Figures and Their Use by Vladimir Putin

Category	Political actors	Political message of actor	As acted upon by Vladimir Putin
"Old-Left" Patriots	Yury Luzhkov, Moscow mayor	Patriotism, expansionism, support of Orthodox church, chauvinism.	The Chechen war.
	Yevgeny Primakov, ex-premier	Great-power patriotism, links with intelligence, desire to build a personal power base.	Background in intelligence, Gusinsky arrest and administrative reform using military cadres.
	Gennady Zyuganov, KPRF	Raising the social prestige and salaries of scientists, doctors, and teachers. Expanding the role of the state in the economy and media.	Steps are taken to provide for a larger role of the state in media and economy. Salaries were raised a bit; more is promised.
Democrats	Anatoly Sobchak, St. Petersburg ex-mayor	For liberalism in the economy, democracy in politics.	Liberal advisers appointed. Putin attended the funeral of Sobchak, his former boss.
	Grigory Yavlinsky, Yabloko leader	Even-handed treatment for all economic players.	This slogan is used every time the newpower moves on one of the former "oligarchs'."
Populists	Vladimir Zhirinovsky, LDPR	Flamboyance, "street" language, dynamism, adventurism, gift for making enemies.	Dynamism, flamboyance bordering on the behavior of a poseur (visiting a submarine, driving a tractor, taking a flight on a jet aircraft in Chechnya.
	Aleksandr Lebed, governor of Krasnoyarsk Territory	Exaggerated toughness, macho language, harsh formulations.	"If we catch them taking a crap, we'll waste them right there in the shithouse"—this quotation is from Putin's press conference during the election campaign.

curbed by the "spiral of silence"[31] set in motion by the unending war in the Caucasus.

When Grigory Yavlinsky took the risk of calling for talks with the Chechens, he attracted a storm of accusations. Vitaly Tretyakov declared in *Nezavisimaya Gazeta* that Yabloko was an "anti-state" and "irresponsible" structure. Anatoly Chubais went still further. "The Russian army is being reborn in Chechnya," he declared. "Faith in the army is becoming firmly established, and a politician who fails to see this cannot be considered Russian. There is only one word for such a person—traitor. Whatever efforts Yavlinsky might make to justify himself will not change the essence of this."[32]

As a result, the only real opposition to the president's campaign came from two weeklies, *Obshchaya Gazeta* and *Novaya Gazeta*; from *Moskovsky Komsomolets*, which was maintaining an armed neutrality; and from a few journalists and political activists. Within an environment of the total subordination of the mainstream press to the regime's aggressive newsmaking, individuals emerged unexpectedly in the symbolic field and received opposition status. Surprisingly for many, the regime's main opponents during the election campaigning turned out not to be the official candidates, but journalists and private individuals. The most important role here fell to Andrey Babitsky, the correspondent in Chechnya for Radio Liberty. Babitsky became a prisoner in one of the infiltration camps run by the federal forces and, somewhat later, a hostage of pro-Moscow fighters.

The procedure through which Babitsky was exchanged for two Russian soldiers became a media sensation, because it had been a long time since Babitsky had contacted his colleagues or his wife in Moscow, and serious doubts were being voiced in the press about whether the exchange was taking place with his agreement. Babitsky unexpectedly provided a unifying symbol for journalists, who unleashed a campaign to protect their colleague. In its intensity, this campaign at times recalled the approach taken by the media in covering the Chechen war of 1994–96.

In a symbolic sense, the Radio Liberty correspondent was thus on an equal level with the president of Russia, providing an alternative pole of attraction and showing that real opposition extended beyond the bounds of the narrowly limited political field, where the regime could control the behavior of all the players. Central television channels portrayed Babitsky, along with Yavlinsky, almost as an enemy of the people. The fighters provided Babitsky with a false passport, and the correspondent was arrested while crossing the border, and he again spent time in a Russian prison. He was freed only after two weeks of scandals and a harsh wave of media criticism by Putin himself, who moved to correct the first one of those typical misjudgments of media events that was to mark his style during his first year in office. By the time he decided to intervene, the conflict between the authorities and the mass media had begun taking on threatening dimensions, especially considering the insistent demands for loyalty in time of war that the regime was placing on the press and public as a whole.

Aside from state television, where Putin dominated the news and the war dominated the agenda, the main events of the 2000 presidential campaign occurred on the Internet and at the city level. Scattered groups of private individuals spontaneously launched two campaigns—"against them all" (a.k.a., "against all parties") and "for a boycott of the elections." The campaign "against them all" was a continuation of the campaign "against all parties" started in 1997 by a number of political activists with artistic backgrounds, in particular, by the editors of *Radek* magazine, Anatoly Osmolovsky and Oleg Kireyev. During the 1999 parliamentary elections, this campaign resulted in several actions, including one in which a group of activists forced their way onto the base of the Lenin mausoleum (to this day, the mausoleum remains the principal attraction in Red Square). In Soviet times the country's top leaders assembled on this platform to watch long parades and demonstrations. Bursting onto the platform, the activists unfurled a banner with their slogan, "AGAINST THEM ALL!" and stayed long enough to create a media event. That evening, the event became a sensation on NTV news.

Another activity was led by the editor of the Web bulletin "Mailgetto," Oleg Kireev. In protest against the war in Chechnya, several activists threw bottles of red paint at the State Duma. This time, however, journalists stayed away, and the activists themselves did not get around to recording the event with a video camera, hence they received no TV coverage and no glory.

All those seeking the spotlight in both these actions came under the scrutiny of the Federal Security Service, the FSB, and were closely shadowed until the end of the presidential campaign. The theme of the persecution of human rights organizations and activists by the FSB that had become traditional during the second half of the 1990s, had an airing at an action held on March 8, 2000, by the Committee Against Political

Repression, headed by Larisa Shiptsova. This episode took place at the building housing the FSB's public reception room; hardly any journalists were present, and consequently, the event had no impact aside from everybody getting temporarily detained.

During the presidential election period, several groups of activists joined the campaign "against them all," with the result that several new political initiatives appeared on the Internet. These initiatives attracted extensive coverage in some Internet publications and also in *Novaya Gazeta*. The Mausoleum episode became a powerful media event—unlike significantly better-organized and better-attended antiwar meetings being held in the capital almost every week that received little or no coverage at all, marking clearly that "traditional" street politicking is unproductive in the media epoch. Of the campaigns conducted during the presidential election period, the most successful from the point of view of its use of media methods was the campaign for a boycott of the elections and of television conducted by the movement Union 2000 and the artists' group Osvod. While recognizing that to vote "against all" the candidates was a legitimate form of protest (this option is one of the most democratic features of Russian voting slips), the activists of Union 2000 and Osvod nonetheless did not consider such a strategy effective. In order for the elections to be ruled null and void, more people had to vote "against all" in the first round than voted for the leading candidate, and such an outcome did not seem likely. The main threat faced by the Putin campaign was that electors would not turn up to the polling stations; this was why the activists took up the call for a boycott of the presidential elections.

The participants in this campaign not only set up an Internet site but also held several smart media-events, including smashing television sets against the base of the monument to Karl Marx on Okhotny Ryad, opposite the Bolshoi Theater. This event was central to the opposition initiatives, since it provided an angle for coverage of the campaign for a boycott of the elections and state television as well as the campaign "against them all." Smashing television sets was a good image for TV, so all the major networks and local TV stations decided to cover the event. As a result, viewers of the state television channels were able to learn of the existence of the boycott initiative and the "Kremlin Wall" site operated by the "Net" movement, the main stronghold of the "against them all" campaign.

In their editing, television stations made no distinction between the campaign "against all," the campaign for a boycott of the elections and state television, and a march of prostitutes supporting former general prosecutor Yury Skuratov who was sacked because of a sex scandal; this latter demonstration attracted a horde of television journalists from state-controlled TV channels. The timing of this act coincided with a break between the end of the antiwar meeting and the beginning of the television-smashing act.

The route followed by the priestesses of love led from an antiwar meeting on Pushkin Square to the Bolshoi Theater across the street from where the television sets were being smashed. It is striking to note that before this march Moscow courtesans had never taken part in any form of political activity, nor have they since. The procession of women in dark glasses carrying placards was edited together with the other opposition events as a single topic, ensuring that all the actions would be viewed as absurd street stunts.

Superimposed on the shots of the street actions was the commentary of a news announcer who related the attitude of various political figures to what was happening. For their penetration of the political arena, the activists paid with a loss of control over the interpretation of their actions. In creating an image, they lost their voice.

The actions in support of a boycott of the elections and television drew abundant comment from political figures and even from the head of the Central Electoral Commission, Aleksandr Veshnyakov, who maintained that only registered candidates for president could actually campaign. Vladimir Zhirinovsky declared that the protesters had been bribed by self-interested oligarchs and by NTV, while the commentaries by leading television personalities were united in attributing the actions to forces who wanted to "destabilize the situation in Russia." Another television-smashing action opposite the building of the Moscow mayor's office next to the monument to Yury Dolgoruky (the former Freedom Square) turned out to be the end of the campaign. After receiving several offers to finance the boycott campaign from PR managers close to the Putin campaign, the organizers were forced to recognize that they had succeeded in making their mark on the political scenarios of the 2000 elections as a threatening image of the internal opposition, an image that could easily be converted to that of the "enemy within." The attempt to play the role of an independent party in the political spectacle, in circumstances where the central television channels had total control over information politics, was utopian. Their protest had easily been co-opted, and had become another signal drawing the attention of electors to the progress of a campaign that could have only one result.

Against this background, the minimalist project of Sergey Kuznetsov and Maksim Kononenko (at www.notmywar.ru) appeared quite successful. Without claiming to participate in the political spectacle, the authors of the project published an antiwar declaration, suggesting that anyone could put their signature beneath it:

> Whatever my political views might be; whatever my views on whether Chechnya should remain part of the Russian Federation; whoever I might consider guilty of the September terrorist acts in Moscow and Volgodonsk; whoever I might have voted for in the last elections and whatever their attitude to the war in Chechnya; and regardless of whether I hold a passport as a Russian citizen or am Russian in spirit, I do not want the things that are now happening in Chechnya to happen in my name. I cannot stop these actions, but I can say: THIS IS NOT MY WAR!

By the end of August 2000, 945 people had signed this public declaration, which may not seem like a lot, but the project was virtually unadvertised. For someone experiencing the relentless pressure of the militarist-patriotic propaganda on state television to see a long list of the nicknames and surnames of people sharing his or her views—a list so long that simply to scroll through it takes several minutes—means a great deal. This is enough for people to find support and reassurance, to overcome the "spiral of silence." Nevertheless, the main conclusion that can be drawn from the history of the antiwar and antielection actions is that during the 1990s an opposition of a new type appeared in politics, an opposition consisting of small organized groups of activists operating mainly outside the established political field, but at the same time capable of penetrating the symbolic space of the mass media. And media events that engage the attention of the audience cross the boundary into the field of politics. The combination of these factors is evidence of a new stage in the transforming of the political process into a media-political one.

Consequently, even the formal consolidation of the existing power relationships within the political system and the closing-off of this system, do not result in putting this area of social communication off limits. On the contrary, the rigidity of the new political configuration means that at times it is extremely vulnerable to unexpected changes in the symbolic field of the mass media, changes that may have an instant and devastating impact on the drama of the political spectacle.

After the Elections: Reconstructing the Media-Political System

The Kremlin group on the whole systematically managed to link the mass media to its agenda, and the owners of the mass media provided access to the channels of information. The owners of the media holding companies, however, proved to be unreliable partners; making any further use of their services would have meant letting a unique opportunity to strengthen the power of the state slip away. In terms of the election campaign, this could be summed up in the slogan "Law and Order." The image of "Great Russia," constructed around the figure of the president, had taken on its full shape. The task of the government was now to strengthen the new symbolic unity through reconstructing the media-political system.

One of the means of carrying out this task was to use the levers provided by the court system. Criminal proceedings were brought against Vladimir Gusinsky, who was charged with complicity in fraud committed during the privatization of the firm Russian Video.

According to an announcement by the public relations center of the General Prosecutor's Office, Vladimir Gusinsky was arrested "on suspicion of committing a crime covered by Article 159 of the Criminal Code of the Russian Federation" ("large-scale misappropriation of the property of another person by a group of individuals through deception or abuse of trust"). In the view of the investigators, Gusinsky, together with several leading figures from the federal state enterprise "Russian State Company Russian Video," had taken without compensation state property with a value of no less than US $10 million. When *Izvestia* went to press, however, the country's main law enforcement agency had not issued more persuasive explanations.[33]

Research by the mass media in the Russia of the 1990s was always somewhat restricted by a lack of information. An idea of the real state of affairs could be had only where there were obvious conflicts. The arrest of Gusinsky was one such case. This affair was seen as political not because everyone believed Gusinsky was innocent—anything and everything happened in the course of privatization—but because Gusinsky was incarcerated in Butyrskaya Prison, though the investigators might simply have extracted from him not to leave the country. The same issue of *Izvestia* where the previous quotation appeared also carried a declaration by eighteen of Russia's leading business figures making personal guarantees on behalf of Gusinsky. Uralmash owner Kakha Bendukidze; the heads of the Alfa group and Alfa-Bank Mikhail Fridman and Petr Aven; the president of the Interros group Vladimir Potanin; the general director of the company Vimpelkom (the cellular telephone service Bee-Line) Dmitry Zimin; Gazprom president Rem Vyakhirev, and other entrepreneurs vouched for "the appearance of Vladimir Aleksandrovich Gusinsky, suspected or accused, in answer to a summons from a person conducting an inquiry, an investigator, prosecutor, or judge."

Gusinsky remained in Butyrskaya Prison for several days, while Putin carried on with his tour of Spain. During this time various interpretations of events appeared, starting with "encroachment on the freedom of the press" and ending with the "dismantling of the old system," whose elements included the rival structures of the media-political system. When Gusinsky was at last released, the story circulated that the media magnate was prepared to sell Media-Most. As often happens, the rumors reflected the essence of the matter. Gusinsky had in fact signed a declaration to the effect that he intended to sell Media-Most in exchange for a guarantee that the criminal case would be dropped. The deal was certified by Minister of the Press, Television, and Mass Communications Media Mikhail Lesin and by the head of the firm Gazprom-Media, Albert Kokh. Of course, Gusinsky had earlier made a declaration in the presence of lawyers that the deal would be null and void, because it had been concluded "under the muzzle of a pistol," and once the deal was revealed hell broke loose, but we shall return to this marvelous story later, in chapter 6.

In parallel with this, Lesin's press ministry was taking action. The warnings delivered by the ministry to ORT and TVC during the election campaign served as a basis for refusing to automatically extend the channels' licenses. A contest was announced. No one doubted that ORT would win, but the press ministry was making claims against the Moscow television station over an insufficiency of local news. It took three meetings between Yury Luzhkov and Mikhail Lesin on neutral territory in the Pushkin restaurant, as well as separate talks with Vladimir Putin, before the conflict was resolved so that both ORT and TVC were able to win the contest.

The authorities had thus signaled a change in the rules of the political game. Henceforward, the owners of the mass media would have to realize that the authorities would no longer refrain from controlling the content of the mass media. Moreover, the regime would not be slow to resort to the methods of direct repression, and to the use of half-forgotten provisions of the Law on the Mass Information Media, to shut down any organization that did not accept the new rules.

Sociologists studying the mass media agree that television has a substantial influence on the political preferences of voters. According to a five-region study of the 2000 presidential elections by NISPI, television was the main source of information on the candidates. Meanwhile, other research into the influence of television on the political preferences of voters, cited in the same bulletin, indicates that television aids in the "recognition" of politicians, effectively lessening the distance between them and viewers. This has its most noticeable impact on such indexes as "familiarity with a politician" and "desire to vote"; in some cases it is important for "elements of electoral programs":

> Three weeks after the survey of the television programs began, regular viewers showed an increased recognition of local politicians who were mentioned frequently on the air. This result is not as trifling as it might seem at first glance. After the survey, regular viewers could not only recall more names of candidates and deputies, but also believed they knew these politicians better, even if there had been nothing in the broadcasts about the candidates' personalities, programs, views, and so forth.[34]

Meanwhile, the intensity of this influence is not the only significant index. For evaluating the role of the media in society (and also when a comparative analysis of the role of television, newspapers, and radio is made), it is also necessary to take into account the criterion of duration. Summarizing the results of research, Dmitry Konovalenko writes:

> One cannot help but recognize that in the modern world the mass media are among the most powerful instruments for the formation of the social space. The construction of reality becomes possible thanks to the use of a mechanism for nominating and operating systems of signs. To a large extent, the structure of everyday knowledge is set by the mass media, but the knowledge obtained with their help is as ephemeral as the fleeting images that flash across a screen. This is not even knowledge in the original, proper sense of the word, but the acquiring of particular information—short-lived, but perfectly functional in the course of a certain interval of time.[35]

Lyudmila Resnyanskaya and Irina Fomicheva, researchers on the journalism faculty at Moscow State University, agree with this conclusion. Comparing the impact of television and newspapers, they conclude that the effect of television is more powerful but less prolonged, while newspapers act more slowly but have a lasting influence. Television is able to impart sensation and arouse emotion, but this is something transient, since one television sensation is liable to be replaced by another. Putin's most important resource, the undeniable support he enjoyed from voters, was based on the television image of the leader (who posed in all kinds of places, e.g., on a battleship in naval uniform), and the parallel image of "Great Russia," which also was a TV-based construct. This resource was thus no more than a temporary advantage that had to be used to the fullest if the political system were to be reformed. The creation of seven administrative regions, together with the reform of the upper house of parliament so that places in the Council of the Federation would thereafter be held not by governors, but by their representatives, was one of the main thrusts of this reform. Something else also began gradually to be sketched in: the creation of a controlled party system. One of the country's best-informed political correspondents, Ivan Rodin, reported in *Nezavisimaya Gazeta* that the presidential administration was working at full speed to prepare a law on the financing of political associations at the same time as the Duma was preparing to reconsider the laws:

> "On Legal Guarantees for Opposition Activity in the Russian Federation" and "On Political Parties," which were approved by the lower house in 1995 and 1997, respectively, but which were vetoed by the Council of the Federation and President Boris Yeltsin. The latter was never in the habit of signing laws that played into the hands of the leftists who at that time controlled the State Duma, and who wished to consolidate their advantages in juridical terms.[36]

Thanks to the success of the Unity bloc and the Union of Right Forces in the elections, and also to the help provided by the State Duma when it adopted the laws—crucially important for Putin—on reform of the Council of the Federation and the tax system, the Kremlin was satisfied with the importance and usefulness of parties for strengthening the state system. At the same time, the necessary manageability of the party apparatuses could be ensured with the help of the above-mentioned laws and also through the traditional levers of lobbying that had been developed to perfection during the 1990s. Instead of the "media-political system," the new administration thus counted on getting a controlled media system and a clearly structured political system. This outcome would have made the political process more predictable.

A number of political figures turned immediately to the task of party building. First and foremost, these included the Kremlin administration and the Unity electoral bloc that had been established through its efforts. The Unity bloc was quickly converted into a party. Meanwhile Boris Nemtsov, who had become the new leader of the Union of Right Forces following the appointment of Sergey Kirienko to the post of presidential representative in one of the new federal regions, moved to establish an alliance with Yabloko. Here, however, things did not proceed without surprises, chief among them an announcement by Boris Berezovsky that he was establishing an opposition bloc which several other people had joined. Most observers considered that Berezovsky's new political initiative had a chance, taking into account his experience and his links with the Kremlin (some commentators thought he was acting on instructions coming precisely from this direction). Nevertheless, calm reigned in the political heavens—until, that is, the submarine *Kursk* sank.

The Kursk *Disaster*

The incident that resulted in the *Kursk* being at on the bottom of the Barents Sea occurred at 10:31 a.m. on Saturday, August 11. At that moment foreign seismic stations recorded a distant explosion. A second, powerful explosion followed two and a quarter minutes later. The Russian armed forces only started becoming anxious thirteen hours later, when the *Kursk* failed to make contact as scheduled. If this scenario is correct, it becomes understandable why Putin looked so calm at a meeting with Duma speaker Gennady Seleznev at 1:00 p.m. that Saturday, not long before setting off on holiday. At that time, no one yet knew of the catastrophe that had befallen the pride of the Northern Fleet.[37]

The *Kursk* situation hit the media only on August 14, when President Vladimir Putin was already on holiday in Sochi on the southern fringe of the Russian Federation. A submarine was on the bottom; how long would the oxygen in it last? The nature of the accident helped ensure that for several days the rescue operations would be turned into a television serial that the whole country watched with sinking hearts. The *Kursk* occupied the spotlight. In Sochi, Putin was isolated from the general tragedy, as he busied himself meeting with Russian scientific figures and preparing for a meeting of CIS heads of state. His decision not to go to the site of the tragedy was his greatest error since the beginning of the election campaign. It was difficult to imagine a worse contrast with the national catastrophe in the northern latitudes than the politician's white suit and the warm Black Sea. It is not surprising that Putin came under critical fire. The first to speak out was Boris Nemtsov, leader of the Union of Right Forces parliamentary faction, who described the president's behavior as "amoral." Ironically, two years earlier, Mentsov himself was criticized by the press for wearing white trousers while meeting Azeri president Geydar Aliev at the airport.

A "heroic" approach to the reporting of the tragedy continued for several days. Then the attention of the press shifted to the sparseness and inconsistency of the information coming from the armed forces. The rescue operations stalled. Meanwhile, offers of help were coming from abroad; these were first ignored by the armed forces, then accepted. Since the rescue apparatus was being brought by sea, however, it arrived only after a lengthy delay. Throughout all this time, different versions of what was happening were multiplying in the press, and passions were rising.

By the end of the first week after news of the sinking of the submarine first appeared in the press, indignation flared. Berezovsky's newspapers were especially prominent; the feeling emerged that the founder of the opposition coalition wanted to show everyone he was establishing not a mild opposition to the Kremlin, but a strong one. The newspaper *Kommersant* appeared with the front-page headline "Whose Honor Is Sinking in the Barents Sea?" and this was repeated by *Nezavisimaya Gazeta*. The reports on NTV became more and more critical. The feeling that Berezovsky and Gusinsky had again joined forces as former partners in the 1996 presidential campaign and in the fight for Svyazinvest was spoiled only by reports in *Kommersant* stating that Gazprom was about to take over NTV and Media-Most in reparation for debts.

Explaining his absence from the site of the catastrophe, Putin expressed confidence in the Russian experts and declared that the arrival of "high-ranking functionaries" would simply hinder the work of the rescue team. In an interview with an information agency the next day, a former submariner declared that he was disappointed in Putin: "It turns out that he's just a top-ranking bureaucrat, and I thought he was the supreme commander." Within a few hours this quotation had been beamed across the country, and the next day it was in all the newspapers. Television, whose main source of income and influence is its ability to hold the attention of its audience, was transformed into a single, giant apparatus for covering the rescue operations. The mass media gave detailed descriptions of what might be the experience of drowning in the cold waters of the Northern Sea. Under the regulations, submariners in case of a disaster are supposed to close the bulkheads and lie on the floor; unnecessary movements reduce the reserves of oxygen. Water may begin to gradually seep into the compartments. When one knows this, it is easy to understand why everything connected with the sinking of the submarine cast such a spell over the viewers. No one wants to die, and of all deaths imaginable, this one is the most horrible. People wept in front of their television sets.

No sooner had foreign divers gone down to the wreck, than the bad news became worse. That all the submariners had perished was immediately evident. Later, it emerged that the Norwegian divers could have entered the submarine earlier, if they had simply been allowed access to the site of the catastrophe.

Trying to bring the situation under control, Putin declared August 23 a day of mourning. But he had only to visit the settlement of Vidyaevo in Murmansk Province near the site of the disaster, for enraged relatives of the victims to insist that all the mourning arrangements be canceled; many of the relatives were certain that some of the submariners were still alive. The foreign rescuers poured oil on the fire by reacting indignantly to a declaration by the Russian armed forces that "everything possible" had been done to save the sailors. In a BBC interview, the senior pilot of British mini-submarine, Paddy Heron, stated: "We had the most modern equipment in Europe, specially designed to rescue the crew of a sunken submarine. And the Russians wouldn't let us use it." As Heron put it, "If a spark of life were still glimmering in any of the Russian submariners, they died only because we were sitting with our arms crossed."[38]

A statement by the head of the Norwegian rescue team, the commander of the country's armed forces Vice Admiral Einar Skorgen, was in similar spirits. Skorgen cast doubt on the most important excuses cited for the failure of the Russian rescuers. The escape hatch, he said, was not badly damaged, and neither was there any underwater current such as the Russian officers had referred to.

Journalists were moved by all this to declare that Putin had lost his Waterloo. Internet-based media were particularly tough on the new president:

> Over the past ten days, the best hopes of Russian society have been betrayed. The image of the gallant president, rushing tirelessly about the limitless expanses of the mighty state, examining all its burning questions and competent in everything from the mechanism of a rifle to the European security system, dimmed noticeably as soon as the president had to confront his first serious national problem.[39]

Along with the president's pre-election image, the image of "Great Russia" was also beginning to crack. The submarine *Kursk* had been making its way to the Mediterranean with the nuclear-powered cruiser *Peter the Great* and other vessels of the northern fleet. Instead, the cruiser became the headquarters of the failed rescue operation, at the same time as the very idea of moving the fleet without a reliable technical base and rescue service began to seem pointless and adventuristic. Perhaps, this simple conclusion and the impressive display of media power saved Putin from more embarrassment in the long run.

As had happened with the Radio Liberty correspondent Andrey Babitsky, who had vanished without a trace in Chechnya, the submarine *Kursk* grew into an independent media event that overshadowed the "star" Putin, pushing him to the sidelines of the unfolding drama as he hesitated and took his time to react. For a week, the new Russian president was fettered by a heavy sense of guilt, which was difficult for him to express. In an interview with the television channel RTR, Putin declared that he was "experiencing a feeling of guilt for the tragedy" of the *Kursk*. The president expressed his feelings: "No words suffice, it is hard to choose them, I feel as though I could howl."

Sharing this sense of guilt with the president were Defense Minister Igor Sergeyev, Commander-in-Chief of the Navy Vladimir Kuroyedov, and Commander of the Northern Fleet Vyacheslav Popov, who tendered their resignations (these were not accepted).

As in the case of Babitsky or even Gusinsky, the catastrophe that befell the *Kursk* was a media event from the very beginning—just like the crash of the Concorde a month earlier or any of the innumerable tragedies and catastrophes that the television industry loves so much. Falling under the influence of particular forces, however, this event took on a different resonance. Unhappiness and injustice resulted, but the president did nothing to remedy this.

The main complaint leveled against Putin and the navy chiefs ran: Why was foreign help not accepted immediately? One of the prominent on-line journalists Anton Nosik wrote eloquently about this at Postfactum.ru, setting forward the interpretation of the delay that was dominant in the press and that was no doubt correct.

> A delay which cost the lives, if not of the whole crew of the *Kursk* at least of those of its sailors who, after surviving the explosion and shutting themselves in the rear compartments of the submarine, were suffocating without light, food, or air in the icy arctic water. Or even of a single sailor who managed to reach the hatch. Even he alone might have been saved, if the services of the rescuers had not been refused. Someone must now accept responsibility for that refusal.[40]

There is a single refrain in this accusation: Putin should have known that the navy had no resources and that a rescue effort mounted on its own could not have been successful. If only he had been on the spot, not only where the rescue operations but also the most disturbing events of the media spectacle were taking place.

Everything Vladimir Putin did proved that he had no skills in public politics. As a novice to the political spectacle, however, he did not rush to learn how to play by the rules. He was in a position to change them. When Gusinsky was arrested, the Russian president was on a tour of Spain and Germany. When a terrorist act occurred in Pushkin Square, Putin did not visit the scene but merely came and laid flowers when everything had been cleaned up. Moscow Mayor Yury Luzhkov, it is said, "came running" (that pretty much sums up his charm). The mayor's office was close by: the Kremlin, however, was only a mile away.

In the cases of Babitsky, Gusinsky, and the terrorist act in Pushkin Square, as well as the submarine incident, the president should have known and understood things he clearly did not know or understand—the real facts concerning each matter and what it signified. The gap he was unable to bridge in this sense was not so much the difference between what was happening and what he did, but between the way he was expected to react and the way he did not.

Slowly but surely the task of media management was transformed into the control over the information system to be implemented during the guaranteed first presidency. Instead of using the logic of the media the way he did during the election campaign, when he was heavily tutored by Yeltsin's media-wise team of advisers, the president lost his grip and encountered an uncontrolled wave of public opinion, a wave that brought to the surface the smallest details of drama, conjectures, and commentaries. As the well-known scholar Aleksey Kara-Murza summed up:

> Vladimir Putin's rating was destined inevitably to fall, for one simple reason: the president did not conduct himself like a Supreme Commander-in-Chief. His conduct was beneath his status. Boris Yeltsin, who was not an artificially created leader, but one who had emerged spontaneously, would have acted quite differently. Putin did not have the flair for this. He was incapable of embodying the feelings of his people. He perhaps behaved this way out of inexperience, or because of his security service background. In any case, a failure to move in tune with popular sentiment is a very serious shortcoming for a politician of national standing.[41]

All that Putin need have done was to fly in for a few hours and say to people, "I feel your pain." The president shirked his role in the political spectacle. Instead of this, he occupied himself with other matters —ones he considered important but that involved neither the mass media nor the people who were following the daily drama. The president could not get his bearings in this conflict between the symbolic and the administrative. He was supposed to combine both elements, becoming the main hero in the serial. The court was supposed to be strung out behind him, in the spirit of Peter the Great. Then the topic of the Russian Navy would have become the president's trump card for the indefinite future.

While believing he was in control of the situation, the Russian president ending up in isolation. The honeymoon enjoyed by Putin and his regime almost appeared to come to an end. In a televised speech on August 24, 2000, the president blamed the mass media and the oligarchs "for everything"; particular suspicion was cast on Berezovsky, who had collected $1 million for the families of the submariners, and Gusinsky. In essence, only RTR, the second state television channel, remained totally on Putin's side during the crisis; RTR was even allowed to broadcast directly from on board the cruiser *Peter the Great*. In fact, former NTV channel news director Oleg Dobrodeyev, now in charge of the

VGTRK holding group, which included RTR, was personally editing Putin's footage in a TV van when the president met with the submariners' relatives.

The drama, which was not expressed in the form of a struggle between players on the political field, was transferred by the mass media onto a different territory. The relatives of the submariners in the settlement of Vidyaevo, on the shores of the Arctic Ocean, became the most important people in Russian politics. Coping with them was difficult even for the military. A speech by Commander in Chief Kuroyedov to people gathered in the House of Officers aroused a sense of the absurd in journalist Andrey Kolesnikov:

> "Do you think the lads are alive?" he was asked.
> And do you know what he replied?
> "A good question! I'll answer it as plainly as you've asked it. I believe to this day that my dad, who died in 1991, is alive."
> Then another question was put to him. Also, no doubt, a good one.
> "Why didn't you ask immediately for foreign help?"
> "I can see," he replied, "that you watch Channel 4 more than Channel 2."[42]

Putin met with just as charged a reception. Kolesnikov described how long it took the president to answer questions from the audience on the progress of the rescue operations during a lengthy dialogue, which all the television channels, including the state one, were banned from filming. At the meeting, the president announced that the relatives of the victims would be paid compensation equal to ten years of an officer's average salary and promised apartments in central Russia to all who wanted them.

People began waiting for the president at five o'clock in the afternoon. He arrived at almost nine, but no one even thought to complain, because none of this was the main thing, and after all, he had come. Now they were preparing to tell him everything.

"He's suicidal!" exclaimed an astonished old woman at the entrance to the House of Officers. "Anyway, he's come, and now we're going to tear him to pieces!"

The meeting continued for two hours and forty minutes. Putin left it as president of the people who moments before had been ready to rip him apart. The next day all the relatives filled out declarations requesting a monetary advance amounting to ten years' average pay for an officer. At the request of the relatives, Putin canceled the memorial meeting had aroused such anger when Kuroyedov spoke of it.[43]

Efforts to control the flow of information, just like attempts to create a controlled political system, are dangerous for the very reason that a new threat can arise out of nowhere, just when no one is predicting trouble. It is no surprise that Gleb Pavlovsky, in an interview with a political observer for *Russky Zhurnal*, expressed wonderment at the senselessness of the "information war" linked to the events surrounding the *Kursk*. There was, of course, no information war; all that happened was that the mass media did their job well and the president did his poorly. And, however great the *Kursk* catastrophy appeared to be, it actually did not hurt Putin politically because by that time his control over the political system was already complete. Media can make a lot of noise, but little change if there is no vibrant democracy. The situation can be viewed not just through a prism made up of the positions taken by the actors in the political spectacle, as was done by the professional critic and scriptwriter of the Russian electoral serial Gleb Pavlovsky, but also in a thoroughly functional manner. In this case, according to the film critic Sergey Kuznetsov, the function of the mass media was to lay bare the theme of death, encouraging the viewer as strongly as possible to sympathize, but at the same time performing a ritual exorcism of death. The submariners remained a focus of the viewers' attention just like Princess Diana and the Chinese student on Tiananmen Square.

The energy generated by the fear of death is redirected into a psychologically harmless and socially acceptable channel, being transformed, for example, into indignation (at poverty, at the leadership, at foreigners, and so forth), or into tender emotion (Berezovsky collected a million, Nemtsov condemned Putin, Luzhkov pledged money to the families). This is what people usually have in mind when they talk about political dividends. As we can see, however, the mechanisms are somewhat more complex in this case as well; it is simply that journalists, like ordinary people, have psychological defense mechanisms that prevent them from directly empathizing with the death of someone they do not know personally. By redirecting the energy of horror in one direction or another, the mass media themselves act as a powerful mechanism for the psychological defense of society.

It should be noted that in a secular society, the mass media play the role of the church; reporting death and showing it, they simultaneously switch the energy of the viewer into another channel. Nevertheless, there is a difference; the energy of the religious person is redirected into the area of God and eternity, and that of the television viewer into the area of politics and the immediate. The latter, of course, is much more akin to jeering at the memory of the victims, but I repeat, the secular mass media simply have no other option.[44]

The way the mass media "obsess about" any tragedy at great length means that the tragedy becomes overgrown with masses of detail and therefore, with the help of the political spectacle, becomes transformed in many ways from an irreversible event into a series of understandable situations and soluble problems.

It is not only that the mass media work with the theme of death; what they do is block the unknown and unspeakable, wherever that is, helping their audience to avoid it, distracting people in the most diverse ways. Yet before they start doing that they must get the audience hooked.

Once we acknowledge this motive, we come to understand that the only way the media can stay effective is by becoming unpredictable. Yet it is quite the opposite of what the new administration seems to demand from them, at least in the political field. Incapable of changing the tactics that distance the president from the media agenda, inflexible and intolerant, the executive power has alienated the sophisticated urban milieu (that used to be called *intelligentsia*) but still retains high popularity in the provinces. The existence of an inert audience with post-imperial values lets the new president rest in the position of power, insisting on changes in the media system without learning the lessons well.

The Focal Point—Great Russia

Where the real influence of viewers on the life of society is concerned, the political spectacle has the function above all of substitution. According to democratic ideology, elections, which in many ways justify the attention paid to politics, give voters a chance to influence the policies of the government. But instead of being a weapon of influence in the hands of voters, the elections on many levels can be regarded as a ritual of legitimization.

Elections are powerful symbols, myths, and rituals in several important respects. Chiefly, they symbolize the will of the people and therefore sanctify the entire governmental process as democratic because they can be cited as the basic influence upon all of it, directly or indirectly. The officials who act and prescribe policy are either elected themselves or appointed by those who are, and in principle the electorate can change politics by removing from office those officials who have pursued policies the public does not like.

This reassuring account only rarely has much bearing on actual governmental operations. Harmful or disastrous conditions can only occasionally be traced to the actions that generated them, and it is easy to create misleading impressions about causes and effects in this regard. Policies that have only a trivial effect on the well-being of the population, or none at all, often become crucial in election decisions because they evoke strong emotions. Voters invariably confront a record that includes some actions they like and some they dislike, and only the rare voter knows the record in any case. It is apparent that elections legitimize governmental actions much more effectively than they influence them.[45]

Nevertheless, elections, like any social institution or ritual, represent a channel of communication. From this point of view, the symbolic meaning of elections can be regarded as real. Elections serve as a catalyst for the crystallizing of social expectations and a sense of national identity. This chapter argues that the electorate campaigns of 1999–2000 became a focal point for a new Russian national identity, which can be described as "Great Russia." The language of images and spectacles that marked the election campaigns meant far more for the new "Russian idea" than a decade of discussions on this theme, or the work of a special commission of court intellectuals set up by Boris Yeltsin in the middle of the nineties.

This chapter has traced the contribution made by several politicians and events to the forming of this image. In order to put some final touches on this picture, a few details must be added here. The national symbols of Russia are the two-headed eagle and the flag of the Russian Empire, together with the rewritten Soviet national anthem. Their symbolism rests on the idealized image of prerevolutionary Russia and the imperial period of the Soviet epoch, which is entrenched in history courses at schools and institutions of higher learning responsible for reproducing the social structure, as well as in the language, the monumental propaganda that helps to visualize this construct: the Kremlin (although designed by Italians, it definitively has some "Russian" feel to it), the Moscow Metro, the palaces and gardens of St. Petersburg, and so on.

The logic of legitimization of the social institutions of the Russian Empire also made it necessary to rehabilitate the Empire itself. On August 20, 2000, the last Russian Emperor, Nicholas II, comprehensively demonized in Soviet history, was canonized by the Orthodox Church as a martyr, a degree of holiness approaching sainthood. This postmortem rehabilitation was needed to allow a stronger reliance on symbols as evidence of a continuation of traditions: on August 25, 2000, the George Cross, the military order of the Russian Empire, was reintroduced to the army as a decoration.

The other elements making up this image are the cultural codes and events that figure in a common cultural memory: the "great Russian literature," which is still taught intensively in schools; the best Soviet films and serials, repeats of which are still shown on television; and finally, shared holidays, the most important of which inevitably remains New Year. The political spectacle, disasters, wars, and enemies all lend dramatic tension to this image of the new Russia. The enemies, as usual, are chosen on the basis of their nationality and external characteristics; they are natives of the Caucasus Mountains, victims of the turmoil in that region, who in line with the rule "blame the victim" are accused of creating the problems there. Enemies, as we know, are everywhere; this is something that anti-Semitic newspapers will always tell us, as will Russian generals who explain the tragedy of the *Kursk* as the result of a collision with a foreign submarine.

Naturally, such a construct-image evokes extremely contradictory feelings in citizens. The creation of a new Russian style has aroused comment, criticism, and debate at each stage, starting with the erection of a huge monument to Peter the Great on an embankment in central Moscow, and ending with the war in Chechnya. However, the logic of those who debate and comment upon this image differs from the logic of those whose attention the authors of the new style are trying to attract. What we can see here is perhaps the traditionally strained relations between the urban intelligentsia and the mass of people who more often than not take the side of the government.

For the masses, the political spectacle is always a show whose purpose is to impart meaning to such concepts as "Russia," "the state," and "authority"—in other words, the creation of a definite image of social reality, an image that has a social-therapeutic significance. For the mass of viewers, the media and public politics are a mechanism for bringing order to social life, a means of utilizing negative emotions, and simply a way of filling up an excess of spare time. They are the consumers of meaning, while the urban intelligentsia, as producers of meaning, tends to reflect more seriously on what is happening.

Journalists and intellectuals try to make sense of the political spectacle, and on a global level, of everything that is going on; by virtue of this, they devise a construct. Just as a critic constructs the content of a work of art, commentators on the political spectacle use the material of this tragedy-comedy-drama in order to produce one or another "meme," to publish the results of social analysis, and to propagate their view of social good (or to borrow some irony from psychoanalysis, their "trauma").[46] The conflict between the intelligentsia and the government raises the temperature of the political drama, and accordingly, helps draw additional attention to the political spectacle.

On the one hand, convictions divide people, but on the other, conflict itself allows people to come in contact with each other. This struggle draws people together, because it provides common themes for discussion; each group and each person has the chance to use these symbols for self-identification. And so it goes.

The image of "Great Russia" is important not just for its content, but also for the sense of order it brings to the symbolic field. This feeling of "certainty" that has been restored after ten years of "chaos" not only reduces social stress and simplifies conformism, but also provokes criticism, which impels long-term change. As the political system acquires firm shape, the economy and cultural life attract more and more attention. The latter is reviving right before our eyes, under the influence of powerful politicized investments in culture by the state, political parties, the entertainment industry, and millions of people whom boredom and loneliness drive into the cinemas and bookshops, stadiums and concert halls, or . . . onto the Internet.

As government reasserts its traditional dominance of the social field, the traditional opposition stance of the intelligentsia and of the cultural elites is reemerging as well. Cultural life is thus becoming a site for the development of alternative identities, and potentially, of a new concept of Russia, on the personal level. It is a slower process that may appear harder to monitor, yet the only one that can possibly make a difference . . . that is, until the contradictions mount and come to the surface to bring some tensions into the social order and produce change.

5

The Internet in Russia

The first time electronic mail became widely known was in August 1991. According to the study "The Internet for Journalists":

> [D]uring the August 1991 putsch in Moscow, when reactionary political and military figures were trying to restore the old system of Soviet rule, all the traditional means of communication—telephones, television, radio, and the press—were cut off. However, the computer networks that had by that time appeared in the Soviet Union had not been affected by the censorship and managed to issue a sea of information about the events in Moscow. According to Aleksey Soldatov, the president of Relkom (now the largest computer network in Russia), during those tension-filled August days Relkom dispatched 46,000 items of information all over Russia and abroad, when all other media channels were closed.[1]

The development of the Russian Internet began in the mid-1990s. It would perhaps be more correct to say the Russian-*language* Internet since, particularly in the early stages, the well-known figures on the Net (the "Net authorities") included large numbers of emigrants living in Israel, the United States, and Canada.

Among the early sites, two main types stand out: specialized amateur or personal sites, and pages devoted to Net reviews compiled by various authors who were engaged in studying the Net and in publishing regular surveys of it. Here is how Anton Nosik—later a leading Internet publisher and head of *Vecherny Internet*, one of the most popular daily Web reviews—described the birth of the new genre:

> Since the day last autumn when Ivan Paravozov posted his first notes on the server *www.ok.ru*, the appearance of new surveys and observers throughout Russia has taken on the character of an epidemic. The first

initiatives came from the publishers and observers themselves, but readers soon began demanding literature of this type, and many Internet groups began to create the Web reviews on their servers simply because they saw this as a way of getting their names known and expanding their existing resources. For Web observers, the "head-hunting" season has probably not ended to this day; every week new headings of this sort, resulting from both individual and corporate initiatives, appear on the Russian net.[2]

In parallel with this, the most regular and popular Russian Net publications, including surveys of the Net, were uniting in common blocs of "dailies" and "weeklies." On March 19, 1997, a manifesto of the first such union, by the most popular daily sites, appeared in *zhurnal.ru*, the main mouthpiece of the Russian Internet community at that time. The aim of this move was to put the logotypes and hyper-references of all the sites in a single "line-up" that would be present on the sites of participants in the program and available to all who wanted it. The initiators of the union were Aleksandr Malyukov and Leonid Delitsyn (soon to become the head of the Internet advertising agency Sputnik). The idea arose during a discussion on the IRC-Channel, since Malyukov at that time was in Finland and Delitsyn in the United States.[3] As the number of projects in the "dailies" and "weeklies" increased, the single line-up was replaced by an overall navigation system with a "rotator."

The Russian Internet in its "amateur" phase continued a whole series of popular and "underground" traditions, beginning with jokes and ending with *samizdat*. During the first years of the Net, up until 1997–98, only Internet providers could count on making money from the appearance of the new communications medium. People were drawn to the Internet by other interests and strategies as well. The most important attraction was e-mail, which spread rapidly following the appearance of convenient graphic interfaces such as Eudora, Outlook Express, and Netscape.

One of the causes of the rapid spread of the Internet and computer technologies in Russia was the crude state of legislation on intellectual property and the lack of precedents for prosecution of people who breached these laws. The government pretended to ignore the spread of unlicensed audio and video recordings, as well as computer programs. At the "Gorbushka," the huge music and computer market next to the Gorbunov House of Culture, anyone who wanted could (and can to this day) acquire any programs along with the operating codes. The result was that graphic and HTML editors became available to anyone at a price of US $1–2 a dozen.

Amateur designers created Internet pages for their friends and anyone else who wanted them, either free of charge or for petty sums. The first Net games and poetic servers appeared. One of the first serious-content projects was *zhurnal.ru*, published by a collective of writers headed by Dmitry Itskovich, Yevgeny Gorny, and Mikhail Yakubov. The first issue of *zhurnal.ru*, in 1996, carried a document typical of the first years of development of the Net—a "Declaration of the Independence of Cyberspace," written by John Perry Barlow, proclaiming that the construction of a new "civilization of consciousness" had begun:[4]

> Governments of the industrial world, you are weary giants of flesh and steel; my homeland is Cyberspace, the new home of consciousness. In the name of the future I ask you, whose whole being is in the past: leave us in peace. You are not wanted among us. You do not possess supreme power where we are gathered. We have not elected a government, and it is scarcely likely that we will ever have one; therefore, having authority no greater than that with which liberty itself speaks, I make my appeal to you. I declare that the global social space we are constructing is in its nature independent of the tyrannies to which you seek to bind us. You have neither the moral right to wield power over us, nor methods of compulsion that could really frighten us.[5]

The declaration testified to the appearance of a new utopia. In the Russian Internet community, there were no doubt many people who took a skeptical attitude to such enthusiasm. But it would have been hard to find anyone who had not read the declaration or who did not at least know of its existence.

Among other large-scale projects, the site of the Internet provider Cityline deserves to be mentioned; it was on Cityline that the earlier-mentioned *Vecherny Internet* appeared, as well as *Paravozov-News* and Sergey Kuznetsov's "Senoval." Just as newspapers in the sixteenth century were issued by post offices, Internet providers became an important source of investment for Net content projects.

Pioneers

The first wave of "amateur" Internet projects was quite high-powered and productive, and the impulse of development that went into these projects largely determined the nature of the Russian Internet enclave. In 1994, for example, Maksim Moshkov's electronic library appeared;[6] this was the most complete collection of digitalized texts in the Russian language. Moshkov worked out a simple and flexible approach to the question of copyright; he announced that he would remove from the library any materials to which an author or a publisher made claims. As contacts were established between the library and authors, more than thirty authors agreed to have their texts available on line, and only two asked that they be removed. This was evidently aided by the fact that the electronic library recognized the right of authors to have their names on the works, and published the works without any editing.

The library now contains around four hundred megabytes of text (in the ultra-simple txt format), of which some three hundred megabytes consist of literary texts in the proper sense, while the remainder represent the content of several additional headings (a UNIX library, plus sections on waterborne tourism, and the works of songwriters). The library is brought up to date once or twice a week with the help of users, who post not only ideas ("what should be listed") but also texts (Moshkov has long since ceased scanning materials). Lists of new acquisitions by Moshkov's library regularly appear in the electronic *Russky Zhurnal* and other Net publications.[7]

The initial selection of texts in this and other libraries reflected the tastes of their compilers, initially the technical intelligentsia. Science fiction (Arkady and Boris Strugatsky, Isaac Asimov, Roger Zhelyazny, Ursula Le Guin, Tolkien, Philip Dick, and others; later, William Gibson), Russian and foreign classics (Fedor Dostoevsky, Mikhail Bulgakov), esoteric texts (self-instruction books on yoga, the works of Carlos Castaneda, and so on), and applied psychology (neurolinguistic programming, and so forth) were all mixed into a single selection and even published in large editions as collections of texts on CD-ROMs, which could also be bought at the Gorbushka. Here is what Moshkov himself writes about the process through which the library came to be established:

> This library was not selected by a publisher prepared to publish anything as long as people bought it, and not by writers to whom it meant nothing who used the library so long as their words were given to all the subscribers. This is a library for readers, compiled by readers with the help of readers. This is the source of its strengths and shortcomings. What the library contains is not classics and not run-of-the-mill writers. Here there

is a great deal of science fiction and esoteric writing of all types. Here you'll find bestsellers, but not all of them, only those of high artistic quality. Here there are many books that have become widely known, celebrated, and remembered.[8]

Later on, scholars started to get interested in the Internet, and the range of works expanded to include texts of interest only to specialists or connoisseurs. Moshkov's library and others (for example, the library of Russian science fiction) have numerous mirror sites on the Internet and are quite popular. It is hard to determine the overall number of libraries, but on the "Literatura" site alone,[9] references can be found to a hundred electronic collections, including many specialized ones, from historical and philological libraries to collections on marginal culture.[10]

The Russian library projects resemble the well-known English-language "Project Gutenberg," mainly because the texts are stored in simple text-file format. The main differences are in the area of content. Because of their flexible approach to the question of copyright, Russian libraries are not limited to classic works, and their significance is therefore much larger. They represent a priceless contribution to the viability of Russian culture abroad, where paper copies of most books are not available and also a mass of reference information that can be searched by keywords. Meanwhile, as can be seen from Moshkov's statements, decisions on the publication of texts are made in decentralized fashion, and this ensures a high rate of renewal. The library receives about a hundred messages per day, and of these, somewhere between ten and thirty are accompanied by books. "If things continue like this," Moshkov says ironically, "they'll start sending me copies automatically, as if I were a real librarian."

The high rate of usage that Moshkov's library attracts is explained by the close match between the collection of texts and the preferences of the readers. The library is number one among all sites that deal with literature, according to Rambler's Top 100 rating system. It is visited by half a million Internet users per month. Since its conception it has managed to attract almost eight million visitors. To this must be added visits to the remaining twenty-six small mirrors; statistics for these are not available, but they can be estimated at a further 10 to 20 percent on top of the base number.[11]

Moshkov's library has thus become one of the most important infrastructure projects of the Russian Internet. This popularity might appear to pose an obvious threat to the interests of publishers. In principle, it is possible to read the whole text of a novel from a computer screen or from the handheld organizer, according to the latest fashion, but more often people simply buy the books they like in bookstores. It is not surprising that Moshkov sees among the future sources of financing for electronic libraries not just grants and the "personal funds of the librarians," but also the advertising and sale of books in print format.

In Russia, the Internet has become one of the channels through which the globalizing of the information space is proceeding. With access free for the major foreign commercial media, including such high-quality publications as the BBC, the *New York Times*, and the British *Guardian*, any Russian user of the Internet can check the information appearing in the national media and weigh the situation from a different point of view. It is no longer necessary to speak a foreign language in order to do this, since many foreign press publications are available in translated form on the site *inopressa.ru.*

Of course, only users of the Net now have this possibility, and they number no more than three million at most. We can, however, assert that cyberspace has the potential to radically strengthen the positions of the individual and of small social groups within the information system. On the Internet, users have received access to independent sources of information, and the chance to establish communities and communicate directly. This opportunity has been taken up enthusiastically. On the basis of various private initiatives, a parallel information system has begun taking shape on the Net; some scholars in the West compare its impact to that of the youth counterculture of the 1960s. Despite arguments over "virtuality," the Internet in fact has helped give material form to the sort of communicative practices that earlier were elusive elements of speech and of horizontal communication.

Tools such as ICQ and IRC channels, guest books on authors' sites, forums of all imaginable kinds, e-mail lists, chats, and personal Web page builder kits have been taken up and used on a massive scale, and the Internet has become a lively interactive medium. The circle of users of the Internet was narrow at first, and the various Net personalities quickly got to know one another, "virtually" at first and then "in [live] 3–D format." This led to the formation of a small group of "pioneers." Some of the "pioneers" were luckier than others, but still at least some of them rose to the status of Internet celebrities. As more people join in using the Russian-language Internet, the status of pioneer has become less significant. Nevertheless it remains, though resting now on the statements and articles of the pioneers who have achieved success, above all commercial success.

A typical success story is that of Anton Nosik, a former Web observer who later became editor in chief of such large information projects as *gazeta.ru*, *vesti.ru*, and *lenta.ru*. Nosik also participated as a consultant in the launch of the project *memonet.ru*, belonging to the Media-Most holding company. He currently holds the top position at Rambler Internet holding—the largest Russian-language Internet portal. Artemy Lebedev, considered Russia's best-known Web designer, is a college dropout in a bandana who began on his own. After several years of determined work, he was able to turn his name into a trademark that customers take pride in as a sign of quality. Lebedev set up his own studio and two Internet advertising agencies, as well as undertook a multitude of noncommercial projects, which have included, for example, a site devoted to the Moscow Metro.[12]

Other pioneers who deserve mention include Roman Leybov and Sergey Kuznetsov. Both work as journalists, though this is really too narrow a way of describing their activity on the Internet. Leybov was the first person in Russia to establish a totally interactive project, which he called "Roman."[13] Anyone who wanted was invited to take part in creating a hypertext; participants were to provide a reference to the first paragraph, written by Roman himself, and then to write what they liked, starting from any word in the first sentence or in the numerous continuations. About twenty people took part in creating a hypertext novel. Reading the resulting novel was almost impossible; in their search for an individual style, the participants copied the language of their favorite writers. The appearance of a new technical tool did not change the relationship between talent for prose writing and graphomania. The result of the penetration of literature onto the Internet was rather to encourage the appearance of a whole industry of Internet literary criticism (featuring Vyacheslav Kuritsyn,[14] Max Frei,[15] Ivan Davydov,[16] and others, not to mention the numerous authors who took part under the corresponding heading of Internet publishing).

As well as being responsible for "Roman," Leybov was also the author of the project "The Garden of the Diverging Hokkus"; here, anyone who wished could compose a hokku verse on the basis of a given first or last line. By August 2000 the number of such works was around 20,000. For the past few years Leybov has been writing the column "Exile for

Life,"[17] later to become a weblog of *lifejournal.com*. His main peculiarity is his wonderful use of the Russian language and exquisitely restrained ironic intonation. Leybov's expertise in literature and his interest in language leads him at times to apt and unexpected observations. In each column, readers are urged to try to guess the author of particular verses, and so forth. Since 2000, Leybov has been in charge of the "Net-Culture"[18] section in *Russky Zhurnal.*[19]

Sergey Kuznetsov, who made his debut as "Senoval" on the server Cityline, has become one of the most popular journalists on the Net. Indeed, Kuznetsov has become a sort of barometer of the Internet; the very brightest content projects are determined on the basis of where his work appears. After spending several years editing the section on cultural life in Moscow in *Russky Zhurnal* and the culture sections of *gazeta.ru* and *vesti.ru*, Kuznetsov, who is well known outside the bounds of the Internet for his work as a film critic, went off to write reviews for the new information and entertainment site *pole.ru*. Besides the project *notmywar.ru* that was mentioned in the previous chapter, it is worth mentioning Kuznetsov's efforts to use interaction in the project NasNet.[20] For example, the heading "Project Nineties," on the history of the 1990s, was constructed almost completely on the basis of material sent to him by readers.

Another of the pioneers of the Russian Internet was Olga Lyalina, who became well known for her art project "My Boyfriend Came Back from the War."[21] This project remains one of the best attempts yet at exploiting the peculiarities of the Internet in order to create works of art. Curiously, the project was initially conducted in English, which was also the language in which Lyalina's whole server *teleportacia.org* operated; this suggests the degree to which artists are becoming integrated into international artistic discussions. A museum of Internet art is to be found on the same site.

Of the other art projects on the Russian Internet, it is worth mentioning the work of Aleksey Shulgin and Andrey Velikanov. Velikanov's project "Choose Yourself an Enemy"[22] is a timely and accurate statement that exploits both the interactive potential of the Net, and the topical theme of the construction of a national and personal identity. This list would have been incomplete without *Mult.ru*—a series of flash-animated cartoons that won five prizes at the National Internet Academy Award in 2002. Oleg Kuvaev, an artist from St. Petersburg, did it alone and needed no advertising or marketing campaign to succeed. When *Mult.ru* received its first prize from Rambler as the "Debut of 2001," it had already grown into a giant, visited by more than half a million people per month.

Politics and the Internet

Considering the intensity of political intrigue in Russia during the 1990s, it is not surprising that political experts were among the first to discover the new possibilities opened up by the Internet. The Net proved to be a useful weapon for political consultants waging their information wars; information could be published on it anonymously and then cited as a source. Large quantities of contentious and unreliable data obtained through illegal methods began appearing and became widely known due to publication in the press. At first, one or two paid publications in Moscow newspapers were enough to set journalists themselves delving into the "source," and extracting new discoveries from it. Two examples will illustrate how this scheme worked.

The first is the site Kogot (meaning "claw")-1, and the second, Kogot-2. Both are widely known not just among users of the Net, but also among readers of the print media, and they are therefore worthy of attention. The Kogot site existed for only one day, November 28, 1998 (a permanent, though edited, mirror of Kogot can be found on Anton Nosik's *Vecherny Internet* site).[23] Published on Kogot was a list of the "Russian elite," with their home addresses and telephone numbers. Also published were transcripts of the pager communications and telephone answering machine tapes of prominent figures ranging from *Moskovsky Komsomolets* journalist Aleksandr Khinshteyn to former head of the State Property Committee Alfred Kokh, and also secret information about former Chief Prosecutor Yury Skuratov, Interior Minister Sergey Stepashin, and more.[24] Apart from everything else, the site carried a transcript of a telephone conversation between Boris Berezovsky and Tatyana Dyachenko, the daughter of President Yeltsin.

The site became famous when *Moskovsky Komsomolets* and other publications carried references to it in one context or another. Strictly speaking, the context was unimportant; one way or another, the site instantly became one of the most popular on the Russian Internet, and only the lack of foresight of the organizers in locating Kogot on Russian territory prevented the information it contained from being universally available. In any case, the most interesting item on the site, Berezovsky's conversation with Dyachenko, was published in *Moskovsky Komsomolets*. The people who created the site Kogot-2 included various errors in it (whether their own or those of predecessors is hard to say). The site *www.krasnobykow.com* was located outside Russia and had its own domain. This site published analytical and practical material about the Krasnoyarsk entrepreneur Anatoly Bykov, who was openly opposing Krasnoyarsk governor Aleksandr Lebed. The conflict between these two was based on the economic interests of the businessman and the region, but the site was given over completely to the topics of crime and politics. Especially for the convenience of users, all the documents were grouped into two archives for anyone to download.

Who made use of these materials? Most of all, the media belonging to parties with an interest in the conflict. The compromising materials, however, were also interesting for the commercial mass media either on the all-Russian or the regional level. For those players in the media-political system who could not boast of a serious presence there, it was no doubt the ability of the Internet to serve as a communications channel for putting information onto the sounding-board of the commercial media that represented the main attraction of Internet *kompromat*.

Cases in which compromising materials have been "thrown" onto the Internet are too numerous to be listed in any detail. All that can be done is to note a few cases in which the Net was used during elections as a powerful propaganda weapon. To show the seriousness of their accusations, the authors were forced to renounce their anonymity. Gleb Pavlovsky thus created the site "United Criminal Group," about the leaders of the Fatherland-All Russia movement.[25] The site provided summaries of all the accusations leveled against the movement's leaders Yury Luzhkov and Vladimir Yakovlev, the mayors of Moscow and St. Petersburg, respectively. Demonizing these two helped create the image of corrupt regional bosses for whom, it could be said, Yevgeny Primakov had agreed to act as the political "roof."

Accusations of vote-rigging (which were just as soundly based in the case of the regional leaders as in that of the government) allowed Pavlovsky to justify the need to "monitor the figures" through exit polls— that is, through surveys of people who had already voted. Conducted and published on a "real time" basis on the day of the elections,[26] exit polls could in the view of Andrey Raskin affect the results of the voting.[27] Although the numbers of users of the Russian Internet is not great, the appearance of survey results on the day of the elections created a sensation, enhanced to a considerable degree by the instant reaction of representatives of the Central Electoral Commission, which demanded that the site be closed forthwith. There could be no better way of drawing attention to the site than to have its contents quoted in scandalized tones on television, and Pavlovsky was assured of this.

It would, however, be hard to find anyone in Russia convinced that the effect of a survey of voters exiting the polling stations could be serious or decisive. If we are to take Pavlovsky's action in the context of another history, that of Internet journalism, the political consultant Modest Kolerov is inclined to welcome what his colleague did. As Kolerov puts it, the openness of any and all information and the fact of operating in real time are inherent, crucially important virtues of Internet publishing, and the issuing of the survey results simply reinforced this point. By contrast, Mikhail Yakubov, the programmer for the Internet company Agava who is known to some "pioneers" as "Qub" and to others as the "manager of the Internet," thought Pavlovsky's action had more significance as a provocation. Indeed, to a wave of public indignation, the Press Ministry came out with a proposal to introduce compulsory licensing for Net information organs—that is, regulation of the Internet. Discussion of several variants of a law on the regulating of the Internet became the "hot topic" of 2000.

Several sites devoted specifically to *kompromat* have now opened. One of them, the "Home Library of Kompromat,"[28] was founded by Sergey Gorshkov, while the other, named the "Bureau of Federal Investigations" was set up by "Free-Lance Bureau"[29] journalists who had earlier conducted investigations for publications of Artem Borovik's Top Secret group. For Gorshkov, assembling a library of published compromising materials has become something of a hobby, but the journalists of the Free-Lance Bureau are trying to establish something like a specialized "yellow press" publication on the basis of a library of *kompromat*. They claim to have managed to outbid others for "the database of the Most group" (this must be regarded skeptically; the real collectors of the material are unknown), and part of this database has been published on the site together with a full list of information said to be in the possession of the journalists but that has not been made available to Internet users. The market for *flb.ru* is made up of enthusiasts for conspiracy theories and of people with an interest in rummaging in the history of the 1990s (the "Most database" ends with 1998). It is possible that the creators of the site count on making money through selling information to interested people.

Kompromat, of course, is the crudest of all possible instruments for working on public opinion. In the long term, a far more precise and effective means of influencing the views of the public is to set up information organs. The Internet has made this simpler. The net has allowed Gleb Pavlovsky, one of the leading political specialists of the 1990s, to construct a "virtual holding company" independent of the media empires; this has already taken on a good deal of significance, and its importance can only grow.

Pavlovsky's first enterprise was *Russky Zhurnal*,[30] founded in 1997. Free from the limitations of paper periodicals, which require a mass readership to cover printing costs, *Russky Zhurnal* was aimed from the very first at a more demanding audience. Many of the "pioneers" of the Internet helped edit the publication, each day replacing the book reviews and once a week renewing the analytical and cultural sections. Thanks to its popularity among the intellectual elite, *Russky Zhurnal* by the end of the 1990s had become a leading intellectual review—the bright façade of Pavlovsky's PR group—independent, but with limited readership. For Pavlovsky's "virtual media holding," *Russky Zhurnal* is of importance rather as a sort of intellectual portal that makes it easier to launch additional projects, including paper publications such as *Intellektualny Forum*.

Among Pavlovsky's other projects, it is worth noting the servers *smi.ru*, which is devoted to the media news, and *vvp.ru* (from Vladimir Vladimirovich Putin), set up especially for the presidential elections. The latest of the political specialist's projects, and probably the most ambitious, has been the site *strana.ru*, dedicated to Russian news. A distinguishing feature of the site is its thoroughly official treatment of events; in this sense the "strana" journalists have shown themselves to be more royalist than the king.

Pavlovsky's Foundation for Effective Politics is one of the first consulting firms to provide its clients among the first ranks of political elites, with the opportunity to set up Internet pages.[31] The foundation has been the joint initiator of, and an investor in, many projects of Anton Nosik, including for example *gazeta.ru* and *vesti.ru*. The alliance with Nosik has allowed the Foundation for Effective Politics to count on the collaboration of the Internet media when this has been necessary. Here, however, before passing on to the next topic, we need to say at least a few words about the techniques used on the Internet for the purpose of manipulating public opinion.

Faced with the need to analyze vast quantities of media content, political experts have worked out techniques for identifying key emerging opinions. Through their practical work, analysts have come to isolate and analyze opinion blocs, defining the essence of the articles and televised statements. In their form, these opinion blocs are reminiscent of "memes"—a concept created by analogy with the "genome" of Richard Dawkins. A "meme" contains a particular assertion that makes it possible to order a certain set of facts in one fashion or another.

> A meme, as a rule, provides a sense of the authenticity of knowledge, since it rests on information that is difficult or impossible to verify. Under the conditions of a specialized society, which typically combines an excess of information with demands for expertise on every question, memes spread like viruses. For many years now, political consultants have viewed the "battle of ideas" from this angle. Work in the field of ideas of the mass media can thus be understood as a complex of measures intended to neutralize, replace, and disseminate "memes."

Everyone who reads newspapers regularly has had occasion to note a certain difference between the headline of an article and the content. Headlines, like billboards, are often used to express in compressed form the kind of symbolic formulas that in principle might not be corroborated in the article. It is enough that such a text should capture the attention and remain in the memory; then it will be recalled in conversation with friends or relatives, and so forth. How are such techniques employed on the Internet? They are in fact used extremely widely, since thanks to memes it is not only various electronic publications that exert influence within the setting of the Net, but also the whole mechanism of the banner advertisement, which makes it possible (often free of charge or for insignificant sums) to achieve extremely wide distribution for one opinion or another. One public relations consultant acknowledged in a private conversation that he once fulfilled an order from a client in precisely this fashion. Using the system of banner exchange, the agent draped right across the Internet a colorful banner advertisement bearing the words "the latest scandal in (name of a company)." In fact, banner advertisements can readily be used to discredit particular targets or to draw attention to one or another problem. During the campaign against Vladimir Gusinsky, for example, Gleb Pavlovsky's site *smi.ru* constantly used banner headlines, such as "NTV Sold," that led to surveys of articles in the newspaper *Kommersant* that were far more restrained in tone and content.

Another method for implanting a meme is to insert it as a headline on one of the leading pieces in any of the first five (by readership) net publications (*gazeta.ru*, *vesti.ru*, *lenta.ru*, *polit.ru,* and *rbc.ru*). Making its way onto the *Rambler's Top 100* ratings list, the article will be featured as one of the top ten, and in the course of a day the headline will be read by tens of thousands of people—absolutely free of charge. Few will want to check out the correctness of the assertions contained in the headlines, but everyone will read the headlines.

This does not mean that the *Rambler's Top 100* is used exclusively or even mainly for the purposes of exerting influence. In fact, this ratings list plays the special role of an open space where one can easily identify the way particular publications of various Net information organs compete for readers' sympathy. The question of where an article or item of information was published, in which of several leading Net outlets, is not important. If the item arouses the interest of readers, it has a chance of rating among the first twenty of the day, and will thus help provide an idea of what the readership is interested in—and hence, of what makes up the agenda. Here, too, there are particular tricks being applied. Fierce competition leads to faster rotation of headlines in the popular rating systems such as *Rambler's Top 100*, where they can change every half an hour.

For an item to be noticed, it generally needs a "booster," ideally in several Net newspapers and journals at once. In the words of Modest Kolerov, the information techniques on the Net are like a soccer match in which the players kick the viewer back and forth like a ball. The more players there are, the more balls find their way into the goal.

Gold Fever: Commerce on the Internet

In the forming of the Russian mass media system, the political process had a definite significance, but in the case of the Internet the economy was more important than politics. This does not mean that politics had no impact on the Internet; there has been, is, and will be political money on the Net, just as there will be attempts to influence public opinion in one way or another. The political context, however, was never definitive for shaping the infrastructure of the Net in Russia, and herein lies the basis for the unquestioned advantage the Net enjoys over the mass information system.

Internet fever came relatively late to Russia, only in 1999 and, as the later development proved, even that was too early. Prior to this, the Net lived in people's expectations. In late 1997 and early 1998, it seemed that investments were just around the corner, but the 1998 crisis had a serious effect on the advertising market, and by undermining the banking system, made investors pessimistic about the development of Internet commerce. In fact, the problems with the banks spurred the development of electronic payment systems. Russians in general barely use credit cards. E-shops offer many different options of payment, but so far most of them still have to deal with cash that couriers bring from clients after the goods are delivered. Needless to say, this is the biggest barrier to the development of the Internet sales market in Russia.

As a result, the commercial exploitation of the Net was delayed for several more years. By the time the first venture investors appeared in the marketplace, "favorites" had already emerged on the Web sites that were the leaders in their categories. It was on the buying-up of leaders that investors based their market strategies, which were oriented toward the so-called American model of Internet business, constructed around powerful portals whose popularity is ensured by the presence of a search engine, electronic mail, and other services available free of charge.

By the late summer of 2000, the main "leaders" had already been bought up, both among the search engines and the most popular entertainment projects. Drawing up a balance sheet of a turbulent year of Internet development, observers for the newspaper *Vedomosti* stated:

> The mass hysteria around the Russian Internet projects is gradually declining. Not in the sense that money has ceased to be invested in projects with the ending ".ru." To the contrary, analysts expect that next year far more money will be invested in the Russian Internet than this year. Evidence for this is provided in an analysis that appeared in Troyka-Dialog on July 12. Each day, however, this process is becoming more and more manageable and predictable. The Russian Internet has clearly outgrown its childhood illness, that is, the fever.[32]

Another feature that distinguishes the Internet from the mass media is the enormous importance of foreign investors. Even the Russian investors, who have invested money in high-tech projects, starting with mobile telephone operators and ending with net portals, counted first and foremost on a high market capitalization, something that is possible only if shares are sold on foreign markets, above all in the United States. It was precisely for this reason that the 1998 crisis had such an impact on the development of the Internet; investments in the Net involve staking large sums on future profits, and the money for such projects did not exist in Russia. When a few Russian companies were able to sell shares abroad, the rules of the game changed for them. For example, after two Moscow mobile telephone operators managed to sell shares on the New York Stock Exchange, their market capitalization totaled on the order of five billion dollars. After a few such deals, "hot money" began appearing on the Russian Internet as well. Aggressive investors appeared on the market in the mid-1990s and immediately set about buying up all the projects that held the top five positions on the popularity lists. As a result, several large Internet holding companies had taken shape by mid-2000.

One of the leading players on the Russian-language Internet is the firm *port.ru*, with its portal of the same name. The company's most successful early project was *mail.ru*, the Internet server of the postal service. This server rapidly grew to more than 4 million users. In 2001 all the Internet projects of *port.ru* were consolidated under the *mail.ru* brand except for *molotok.ru*—an Internet auction site.

The strength of such *mail.ru* projects as *talk.ru* and *ruki.ru* lies in the way they are oriented toward "horizontal" communication, among users of the Internet. In essence, both projects represent programmatic envelopes whose content the clients bring with them. As a result, some private initiatives are receiving support and popularity, and the server is providing real help to its users. According to the 2000 results, for example, the best forum on *talk.ru* was Sergey Shayakhmetov's project "Poputka."[33] The purpose of this free service was to unite commuters making daily trips on their own with people who needed to go somewhere, if possible by means other than public transport.[34]

"Russian funds" acquired Rambler,[35] one of the first and best-known Internet search engines. Rambler is also the home of one of the most popular Internet rating systems, the *Rambler's Top 100*,[36] not to speak of the English-Russian and Russian-German dictionaries that have appeared relatively recently. Hosting a number of strong services, Rambler Internet Holding also owns 70 percent of *lenta.ru*, the leading Web-based news service. In 2001, 43 percent of the holding company was bought out by First Mercantile Capital Group, whose representative, Yury Lopetinsky, wants to become the general director of Rambler.

Ru-Net Holdings owns the Net bookshop Ozon,[37] as well as a part of Yandex,[38] one of the leading search systems on the Russian Internet. Other assets of Yandex company include the projects of the free host *narod.ru*, and the Internet bookmark storing site *zakladki.ru* with its complete set of allied projects (postcards, free electronic mail, and so forth).

Of all the large Internet investors, only Golden Telecom combines big stakes in Internet providing with investments in net projects properly considered. Golden Telecom is clearly using the strategy of the company America On Line, which recently merged with Time Warner. Golden Telecom first began to be talked about when it acquired one of the oldest and largest Russian Internet providers, Glasnet, whose history dates back to the very beginning of the Russian Internet. The next step by Golden Telecom was a powerful advertising campaign aimed at bringing the Internet to the masses under the brand name Russia On Line. Offering the lowest charges for Internet service, from 40 cents per hour, the company touched off a price war.

When Golden Telecom purchased the portal *infoart.ru*, the search engine and catalog of the company Agama (*aport.ru* and *@rus*), the newspaper *Vedomosti* argued that the period of "gold fever" on the Russian Internet was over. In the view of journalists for this business publication, no other large Net projects remained to be bought up. This was of course an exaggeration, since outside the bounds of this survey there remained such resources as "Cyril and Methodius,"[39] a company that had established a portal with all the additional options on the basis of an electronic version of the encyclopedia of the same name.

The *Vedomosti* review mentioned two more large players. These were the portal *memonet.ru*, owned by the Media-Most group and including the first jokes site[40] (which differed little from dozens of others, except for its legendary but clumsy interface); and the project *eStart.ru*, owned by the group Independent Media, of which *Vedomosti* was itself part. To judge from the first assessments of Independent Media's debut on the Internet, the company, which was trying to use Net versions of its press publications as bait, was headed for a fall in this area:

> The heads of the eight companies, of course, expect new faces to appear in the market. Most of all they are awaiting the arrival of large American companies such as Yahoo! or Lycos. Both have long been present in Latin America and Western Europe. Lycos recently extended its reach as far as Southeast Asia and India, opening its department Lycos Asia in Delhi. No one believes, however, that the American giants will come on their own and start building companies from scratch, and each of the eight is sure that theirs is the company with which the giants will collaborate.[41]

One way or another, the commercialization of the Internet in Russia has picked up speed, and this has been reflected in the size of the transactions. For example, the purchase of two portals of the company Agama cost Golden Telecom $25 million to be written off as losses in 2002, according to the rumors circulating on the market. Looking back on Russian Internet development from 2002 one can see that the "gold rush" has been misguided simply because it was based on attitudes in the West, where Internet penetration has been climbing from a quarter to a half of the population, while in Russia it has barely reached 5 percent in 1999. If the Russian Internet was to see a legitimate and not imported Internet fever, it would have to start right away. How the commercial appropriation of the Internet will proceed in the future is still difficult to say. Many observers agree that the "American" model of Internet business (portal plus electronic commerce) is not suited to Russia, since there is not enough Net advertising to cover the costs of maintaining large companies, while the necessary preconditions for the development of online trade on a serious scale (the habit of purchasing goods from catalogs, and a broad distribution of credit cards) are simply absent. Nevertheless, the very existence of large players, and their need to develop projects—whatever the ultimate result of their efforts might be—is creating the conditions for an increase in the advertising revenues that can be used for content resources. And within the framework of this study, it is these content resources that are mainly of interest to us.

Before moving on to the topic of Internet journalism, it is worth mentioning the information agency Rosbizneskonsalting (*rbc.ru*). This firm is at the same time a powerful player in the market for commercial information and a sort of information portal, having a limited but rather affluent readership among people with an interest in economic news. An effort to broaden this audience through issuing the electronic newspaper *Utro Rossiy*[42] had mixed success; although materials from *Utro Rossiy* make it into the top ten on the Rambler list, but less often than articles of competitors.

Curiously, it was fierce competition and a reputation as a second-ranking player on the information market that drove Rosbizneskonsalting onto the Net. Everything changed during the crisis of August 1998, when the agency became the main source of information for people searching the Internet for news about the state of the stock market and for news of the reaction to the crisis in Russia and abroad. Rosbizneskonsalting jumped at the opportunity to convert itself from the news agency into the free Web-based news service and immediately became the most popular information source on the Internet in the area of the economy. Meanwhile, the agency remains independent, and according to the company's official information releases (with which many would take issue) even makes a profit.

Here it would also seem appropriate to mention "b2b" (business to business) and infrastructure projects, which represent very important trends in the commercial development and use of the Internet. This topic, however, is excessively broad, and in part lies outside the bounds of this study; it will therefore simply be noted that with the help of the Internet, the management and communication techniques of all participants in business—whether stock exchanges, banks, suppliers, or real estate agents—are being optimized.

Everything that has been said above also applies to "b2c" (business to consumer) projects. Here the success of the insurance company Renessans deserves mention. As acknowledged by the company's managers, with the help of the site *renins.com* Renessans managed to earn half a million dollars from automobile insurance in 2000 alone. This and similar success stories have created increased interest in the Internet, and the commercialization of the Net, once consisting of isolated initiatives, is turning into an avalanche.

Naturally, the importance of infrastructure projects should be evaluated not only from the positions of those involved, but also from the point of view of their influence on changes to the socioeconomic relations of society. The founder of the project Libertarium, Anatoly Levenchuk, considers that all Internet sites are infrastructural in character, since they are accessible on any terminal, twenty-four hours a day, seven days a week. The net is laying the foundations for new economic and social relations, for a new information architecture, and a new economy.

While overall Internet usage appeared insubstantial, the fact that there was very little (if any) money to be made on the Internet discouraged major traditional media in Russia from launching ambitious web-based operations. Acting prudently, however, the traditional media left a window of opportunity open and just waited long enough for the Web-based media in Russia to develop and secure leading positions.

Although traditional media companies tried to establish their Internet operations, they lacked the expertise needed to truly adapt the content of the parent companies to the Internet. Simply putting the contents of

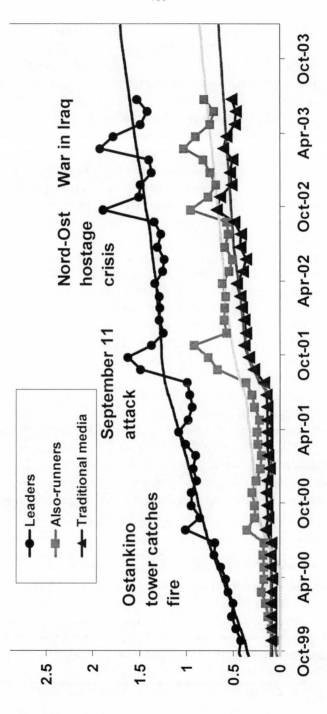

Figure 5.1 On-line Media Audience in Millions

Source: Rambler's Top 100.

the newspaper up on the Web site did not work. Thus, traditional media initiatives became hostage to the genres and styles of the parent companies, primarily newspapers. Featuring long articles and clumsy interfaces, the newspaper sites proved to be weak competition for the leaders of the emerging on-line news media industry.

The gap that appeared between the Internet-based news media—such as *gazeta.ru*, *lenta.ru*, and *rbc.ru*—and the Internet projects of traditional media companies looked almost impossible to bridge. Yet the latest research, conducted in 2002 by Rambler analyst Leonid Delitsin, shows that the traditional media companies' Web sites are rapidly catching up.

The reasons for this are clear—the older media learned that a Web site demands special treatment and they hired professionals who knew how to compete with Internet heavyweights. In fact, to do that they merely copied the newer methods and applied them to their products. While sitting on mountains of content that is paid for by the paper-based operations, newspaper Web site operators were quick to join banner-exchange networks.

According to Rambler's Top100 rating system, after September 11, 2001, the news traffic on the Internet, doubled to reach 30 percent of all Internet usage, and these newspaper sites were discovered by the information-hungry surfers. Unlike most other Internet news sites, they featured original content. They were not updated as quickly as those on *lenta.ru*, but they were more thoroughly prepared and rich with analysis.

Currently three newspaper sites have been able to climb up into the top twenty of the news and media category in Rambler's Top100 rating system—those of *Komsomolskaya Pravda*, *Izvestia*, and *Nezavisimaya Gazeta* (positions 7, 9, and 13, respectively). Yet, unlike the Internet news projects that still remain more popular than newspaper sites, they have an enormous potential for growth. This potential resides not only in their loyal audience, which is getting wired fast, but also in their ability to use advertising space in parent newspapers in exchange for promotion on the Internet by the leading portals interested in off-line promotion.

The State and the Internet

The problem with SORM-2 would not have existed, or more exactly, we would have learned of it considerably later, if it had not been for Anatoly Levenchuk, the founder of the project Moskovsky Libertarium. Learning that the necessary government decrees were being prepared,

Levenchuk in the summer of 1998 planned a campaign against the system of investigative measures and mounted so effective a struggle that the topic of bugging devices became as firmly implanted on the Internet as those of *kompromat*, pornography, and hackers.

SORM is a surveillance system. Telephone lines and paging services have long been monitored, but in the case of the Internet the introduction of surveillance was a much more painful process, for several reasons.

First, relatively expensive equipment (costing from ten to twenty thousand dollars) had to be installed and paid for by the provider of Internet services on the basis of laws enacted by the government. The cost was insignificant for large companies, but for small providers it amounted to a direct road to bankruptcy. No one was prepared to listen to their complaints, though in fact the only argument that law enforcement had was the threat to cancel licenses; formally speaking, the FSB had no right to the providers' money.

The second reason was that the technical requirements, which included a direct connection to the server of the FSB administration, provided no guarantee that the confidentiality of messages would be observed. In other words, if someone in law enforcement wanted, he or she could gain access to personal communications without even having to establish a need.[43]

Third, the ideology of the Internet has traditionally been built around the counterpoint of "civilized consciousness" to national governments with their harsh surveillance strategies and interests. The possibility that law enforcement would interfere in private life was widely perceived as a real danger to the atmosphere of total freedom that had reigned on the Net.

The Volgograd Internet provider Bayard-Slaviya Communications poured oil on the fire by refusing to cooperate with the FSB, leading to the cancelation of its license and a lengthy court battle. While this court case was under way, the license was restored, but for the introduction of SORM-2 the Volgograd case was more of an exception than the rule.

An attempt by activists to bring a case to the Supreme Court ended in failure when the court refused to admit it for trial, arguing that the decree relating to SORM-2 did not constitute a normative act. The story of SORM-2 is thus simultaneously the story of a successful Internet campaign by Anatoly Levenchuk and other Net activists, as well as a case of successful state penetration of the Net. At first glance it might seem that the government had scored the ultimate victory, since the system was, after all, set in place. The fact that the topic was actively discussed by

Internet users meant that questions of encryption technology were placed on the agenda, that information on encryption programs appeared along with calls for installing them, and that demand emerged for "protected" Internet postal services.[44] The public was thus warned about the introduction of SORM-2, though surveys have showed that only a few people have used encryption programs or other means for defending private information.

The scandal with SORM coincided with the appearance of Echelon, a system of global surveillance supported by the governments of the United States and Great Britain, and about which a great deal has been published in the press. Internet users in Russia, however, have not come to grips totally with the fact that it is not only the government that can spy on Internet users. Moreover, marketing companies and other suppliers of information are threatening users with spam and special-purpose advertising, at the same time as law enforcement agencies are threatening direct interference in users' private affairs.

It seems unlikely, however, that the situation in Russia has differed radically from that which has arisen in other countries. Everywhere, openly or not, the Internet is being regulated and equipment installed to allow the guardians of law and order to intercept messages.

In Russia, unfortunately, the state is not yet making use of the other possibilities of the Internet, in particular the potential that new electronic technologies offer for reforming the system of power. In fact, the logic of the Internet is simply incompatible with the way the Russian state machine is organized; it is largely oriented toward its own reproduction and has a solid reserve of inertia. Despite the appearance from time to time of government proposals for regulating the Internet, for introducing the compulsory registration of Internet media with the Press Ministry and so forth, the worst expectations of Internet users have not yet been confirmed. In a meeting with Vladimir Putin on December 28, 1999, and also at the roundtable discussion "The State, Information, and the Internet" with the Russian government on May 12, 2000,[45] representatives of the Internet community received assurances that freedom of information on the Net would not be infringed.

It may be that there is simply no need for such restrictions. The Internet cannot have a serious impact on the political process without the aid of the mass media, and the development of events since the elections shows that the state has the ability to control the most important channels of information, such as state television. If this were not done, regulating the Internet would not help in any case. According to research data from *monitoring.ru* for the year 2000, 9.2 million people in Russia accessed the Internet at least once, and this represented the maximum audience. Some 2.5 million Russians visit the Net on a weekly basis, and only 1.8 million log on for at least an hour per week. The most active users, those who surf the Russian Internet for no less than three hours per week, numbered only about 900,000 throughout the country.[46]

Of course, the number of Internet users is continuing to increase rapidly; between February and May 2000 alone, their number increased by 2.6 million, and preliminary forecasts suggest that by the end of the year the maximum audience will stand at 11 million people. In March 2002 the monthly Russian audience stood at 5 million people according to Rambler. However, the true audience of the Russian Internet includes everyone who uses Russian-language sources on the Net, since national boundaries apply to cables and domain names, but not to the communications.

The spread of the Internet is like water wearing away a stone. Although this is happening quite slowly, the Internet is now playing the primary role of permitting the survival of diversity in the information system and of expediting communication for the people who find this really necessary. Against the backdrop of the reconstruction of the image of Great Russia, an image that dominates the symbolic field, it is also sufficient that the Net allows communities and reference groups to exist outside the boundaries of political discourse and to work out their own cultural codes. Combining the role of *samizdat* with a social communications industry, the Net is perhaps required more by a vocal minority than by a silent majority. But in some cases (for example the war in Chechnya), this is already very important, since it leaves a window of freedom in the communications system, and does not allow the majority to drive dissidents into a "spiral of silence."

At the same time as the media-political system is being consolidated in Russia, the Russian-language Internet is showing more and more life, and developing increasingly complex forms about which it is difficult to say anything specific. Although this "virtual Russia" has very diverse forms, on the whole it is quite different from what the word "Russia" is normally understood to mean. As of mid-2000, the Net was inhabited by the most active, modern, and educated of the younger citizens of Russia and other countries. The Net is still only beginning to develop, but it has already become an important new factor in society's information system. The views of the people who now inhabit the Net are different in many ways from those that the media-political system perceives and reproduces as the social norm. This is not to mention the fact that with the appearance of the Internet, the idea of the social norm as a standard system of views characteristic of a particular national state has lost its essential force. There are too many cultures and points of view existing simultaneously in cyberspace. In speaking of the Net, it is hard to speak of anything common or general except for the technical parameters of the messages transmitted, and the basic system of signals, which in a computer consists of the numbers one and zero.

The rise of the Internet has had an impact on many aspects of social life, above all on the economic infrastructure and the technologies of administration and entertainment, as well as other areas. If there are important changes implicit in the Net, however, they need to be posed in a long-term sense and in the context of other social processes. At present the new medium is just at the beginning of its development. It may be that the Net, like television, will act as a catalyst for particular changes, and that these will be substantial. If such changes occur, however, they are more likely to be in the area of private life than of people's social existence. Their character may also be extremely diverse, but like the actual content of our personal lives, this depends to a large extent on each of us as individuals. It is in this that the charm of the process lies.

Cosmopolis

Marshall McLuhan was the author of a particularly apt metaphor for the television media-sphere, which he described as a global village. This definition was coined in the mid-1960s, when television was only beginning to occupy the dominant place in society that we now think of as its due. The events of distant lands were lighting up the small screen, while the Beatles were appearing on the Ed Sullivan Show and acquiring instant popularity. Wars, coups d'état and disasters, the Cuban missile crisis, and the Kennedy assassination were all played out in televised images that invaded people's private worlds and aroused a multitude of emotions. One could endorse McLuhan's observation that the media had become the nerve system of modern society.

Which peculiarities of television were instrumental in shaping the concepts of the "global village" and the "nerve system?" Above all, the ability of television to evoke an emotional response in the viewer.

McLuhan himself suggested several esoteric explanations for this characteristic of the medium. In his opinion, the viewer's powerful emotional response to television was aroused by the very technology used to broadcast images. The picture consists of dots that are renewed twenty-five or thirty times per second, depending on the broadcasting system. The subconscious attention of the viewer is concentrated on solving the problem of forming a complete image from these flickering dots; this also explains the complete involvement of the viewer, and the powerful, almost hypnotic effect of television. Once the Internet appeared, however, it became clear that television did not offer the viewer the chance to participate in what was happening. All that was possible was to find out what was occurring somewhere, to experience certain emotions as a result, and to discuss everything with the neighbors; to actually *do* anything was fundamentally impossible. On the contrary, it could be said that television effectively filtered out any "grassroots activism," along with all the peculiarities, inconveniences, and obscurities inherent in that phenomenon. Meanwhile, television did not allow grassroots activism to penetrate the world of hyper-real political personalities and corporate leaders.

The isolation of viewers from one another differed to a degree from the isolation of the viewer from TV-reality and was quite comparable with the distance that dwellers in a village maintain from one another. Ultimately, everyone was alone with his or her emotions in front of the screen.

The Internet, by contrast, offers transparency and the opportunity for participation; at least technically, and in theory, it also offers the overcoming of distance, even if not always or for everyone. As before, of course, everyone sits on his or her own before a screen, but now there is also a keyboard. As a result, there is the possibility of establishing contacts and of entering into relationships that often cross over into the sphere of the real.

This is where the real transformation that the Net has brought to the media system can be seen most clearly. In cyberspace, society appears as a complex, self-developing, interactive system that has fundamentally different, urban characteristics. In place of the imaginary unity of tele-reality, which is formed out of the mutual influences of television styles and genres, of broadcasting networks, of the power centers of society, and of the interests of the owners of television channels, the Internet represents an endless variety of cultures and styles. The Net resists all generalizations. It does not belong to anyone. Like life, it belongs individually to everyone. Any attempt to generalize about it is doomed to be imprecise or incomplete, since the only common elements in the Net are the lines along which signals are transmitted, the programs, and the basic system of signals consisting of ones and zeros. Everything else is individual and particular.

In most cases, when the subject matter is neither masterpieces of media art or flirtations, the Net does not have the depth of emotional involvement that characterizes television. The reasons for this are obvious; they are implicit in the current carrying capacity of the telephone lines (which in Russia remain the major route to the information-highways) and in the possibilities available to the producers of content, who have given a second life to printed text as a means of exchanging ideas.

The "virtual reality" of the Net is, of course, far more real than the social conventions that we accept as proper and project onto the surrounding world. The content of the Net is at least visible. Moreover, this content is often far more intelligible and accessible to us than other parts of our environment. An endless multitude of facts exist around us in any case, without in any way attracting our attention; meanwhile, the events, products, and phenomena in cyberspace are at least provided with commentary in the form of text, that is, interpretation.

The urban space is discrete and segmented. Instead of a narrow circle of acquaintanceships arising out of territorial limitations, a city offers an intricate network of horizontal and vertical links, a whole spider's web of unseen connections. Orienting themselves within this, urban dwellers gain access to an endless variety of cultures, types of activity, and forms of leisure, communication, and entertainment. The Internet has become something like a graphic envelope for urban civilization, allowing us to visualize this diversity, to expedite and accelerate the process of communication. The Net wipes out the distances between cities, while air travel connects this global urban space through the channels of physical teleportation (even if this is neither instantaneous nor cheap), transforming distinct settlements, nestled as before in the age-old curves of rivers and gulfs, into a single cosmopolis.

As Manuel Castells notes, the main distinction of the period around the beginning of the third millennium is between the people who are included in this expanse of information currents and those who remain on its periphery. For the latter, the fragments of traditional national models such as "great Indonesia," India, or Russia may come to serve as a consolation. The conflict between these cultural realities is still only beginning to take on its outlines. In time, we will discover how it culminates. For the present, only one thing can be said: the cosmopolis is in a period of rapid construction, and at this stage, the new architecture of the social system is crystalizing. The key positions in the new reality will be taken by the people who can adapt themselves best to meeting the demands of the system's users. The Internet is now in the first place a new industry of social connections, an infrastructure of knowledge and technology that can act as the basis for an information society, or as people still describe it, a knowledge society.

6

The Media System

This final chapter will review the Russian information system as it evolved during the 1990s. We shall concentrate on the strategies employed by various actors in the media system during the 1990s. This will make it possible to present various points of recent history that were not discussed in the earlier chapters.

As in the previous chapter, we shall extend our investigations beyond the bounds of the media-political system. As well as the state media and the largest politicized media holding companies, we shall touch on the commercial and alternative mass media, as well as on a number of successful and unsuccessful attempts to intervene in the Russian media system on the part of foreign entrepreneurs and investors.

The Role of the State in the Media System

During the 1990s, the state on the whole remained the decisive factor shaping the new system of mass information media. The logic of resistance to the all-union officials, along with the personal conflict between Boris Yeltsin and Mikhail Gorbachev, meant that the new Russian government from the very first supported the independence of the press. The formation of the first Russian Ministry of Information, headed by former *Moskovskaya Pravda* editor Mikhail Poltoranin, laid the basis for the first privatization of the mass media and for the final collapse of the Soviet propaganda machine.

The new Russian state began by providing itself with its own television channel, initiating the setting up of VGTRK. Later, it received the "Ostankino" first channel and the educational fourth channel as part of its inheritance from the USSR. In the area of print publications, however, the position of the state media was far weaker. For several years

Rossiyskaya Gazeta, founded in 1990, and *Rossiyskie Vedomosti*, established a couple of years later, remained the only state information organs in the new Russia. In addition, *Rossiyskaya Gazeta* was controlled by the Supreme Soviet, which was hostile to the executive branch. On the whole, however, partnership with the freed-up community of "democratic" journalists ensured the new Russian authorities the support necessary for recreating the state media system. The first Russian president's mission of liberating the press, and the disdain he developed for the content of television news programs and newspaper commentaries, meant that his attitude to the press was lenient, and that freedom of expression remained intact. For a long time to come, journalists in Russia would remember Boris Yeltsin kindly.

State Print Publications

Prophecies that the conservative publications in Russia would be unable to withstand the competition on the information market and would go bankrupt and be shut down were borne out in the case of only one state newspaper, and then only in part. Aside from the government's *Rossiyskaya Gazeta*, the presidential administration owned *Rossiyskie Vesti*, which had been founded by the executive branch in 1993. In an environment of falling circulations, both publications continued to appear in print runs of several hundred thousand copies, with financing from the budget. Early in 1998, however, the editors of *Rossiyskie Vesti (RV)* changed the newspaper's official sponsor and switched to a weekly publishing schedule. Late that year, the newspaper again appeared, this time as a publication of Nikita Mikhalkov of the Union of Cinematographers and of Pavel Borodin of the presidential administration. Unconfirmed reports held that Mikhalkov had been financed in this purchase by Boris Berezovsky. However, nothing has come of it and little has been heard of this paper ever since.

Few people can have learned of the divorce between the presidential administration and *RV* with sadness or foreboding. The justification for putting out two loss-making government newspapers at the same time was doubtful. Advisers agreed that the function of the newspapers was to defend the interests of various government bodies. The way in which the two state publications fought for their survival, however, is interesting in itself, since market methods did not figure among the weapons employed in this struggle. In stylistic terms, moreover, both newspapers were bastions of conservative journalism, stubbornly persisting (though to varying degrees) with Soviet concepts of publishing for the masses.

During the conflict between the Supreme Soviet and President Yeltsin that emerged as early as March 1993, *Rossiyskaya Gazeta (RG)* was the mouthpiece of the parliament. After the events of October 1993 and the subsequent parliamentary elections, *RG* was handed over as a trophy to the control of the Russian government. The newspaper distinguished itself in this capacity as well. On November 19, 1993, the celebrated article "Snow Is Falling" appeared. In this article, Mayor Luzhkov and organizations friendly to him (in the first instance the Most financial group) were accused of making preparations to remove President Yeltsin during the forthcoming elections. The publishing of this article was interpreted as a maneuver by Presidential Security Service chief Aleksandr Korzhakov. This was confirmed following the sensational operation mounted by the Presidential Security Service against the security guards of the Most group. During this operation, the Presidential Security Service clashed with agents of the Moscow administration of the Federal Security Service. Following the replacement of *Rossiyskaya Gazeta* chief editor Natalya Polezhayeva by Sergey Yurkov, a former editor of *Rabochaya Tribuna*, *RG* ceased taking part in such excesses.

Valery Kucher, the chief editor of the newspaper *Rossiyskie Vesti*, had awards bestowed on him for establishing a "democratic official newspaper." *RV* was not, in fact, at the center of scandals such as those that shook *Rossiyskaya Gazeta*, but consistently assumed an official-democratic position. During the 1996 presidential elections, the newspaper naturally supported the party of the government and its candidate Boris Yeltsin. In April 1996 Kucher was appointed head of the press service of the presidential administration, while retaining his post of chief editor of *Rossiyskie Vesti*. This showed that the newspaper was being used in practice as an official election campaign organ—that is, as a propagandist, agitator, and organizer, in full accord with Lenin's vision of the role of the party press.

The rivalry between *Rossiyskaya Gazeta* and *Rossiyskie Vesti* was incessant, at times growing more intense as discussion took place on whether the federal budget needed to maintain two newspapers. This struggle unfolded not only in the area of circulation, but also in that of efforts to find patrons in the structures of power. It may have been the precarious position of *Rossiyskaya Gazeta* that at a certain point induced it to take part in "palace" intrigues. Ultimately, however, it was *RG* that remained as the sole newspaper of the Russian executive branch, winning out in competition with a fellow publication that put greater efforts into saving its face. The reasons why the executive powers preferred this publication to its rival were, nevertheless, different. The established legal practice was that decrees and laws entered into force once they had been published in *RG*; *Rossiyskie Vesti* lacked this competitive advantage. Meanwhile, the propaganda impact of both newspapers was equally low compared with the broad spectrum of information services that the large media holding companies offered the authorities.

As well as its newspapers, the state has published two journals, *Rodina* and *Rossiyskaya Federatsiya*, which do not play a significant role in the media-political system. The journal *Rodina* is notable for its good quality and fills the niche of a historical publication. It often publishes the results of historical research, archival materials, and other documents of interest to students of the Russian state.

State Television

For a considerable time, Boris Yeltsin's prime concern was to fight to obtain his own television channel. In May 1992, as a result of tough negotiations with Gorbachev, the new born Russian state received the second channel and six hours of broadcasting per day. The conflict between the two state channels "Ostankino" and RTR (the flagship of VGTRK, the All-Russian State Television and Radio Company) defending the interests of Gorbachev and Yeltsin, respectively, did not continue for long. In the same year Boris Yeltsin won control of the all-union channel, entrusting its management to Yegor Yakovlev. The power accumulated in this way proved sufficient to ensure the new government a dominant position in the information field.

The first "television bosses" had their own ideas on this score. The concept of the "fourth estate" remained extremely popular, if only because the chief editors of the main media organs were political allies of the president, who was heavily in their debt. If the government in the first half of the 1990s showed any desire to gnaw away at journalists' creative freedom, it was enough for the journalists to kick up a row about attempts to bring back Soviet censorship for this desire to be suppressed. For years the government avoided touching the founder and long-time director of VGTRK Oleg Poptsov, that is, until Poptsov was finally replaced during the first war in Chechnya. It will be recalled that

Eduard Sagalaev, Berezovsky's partner in TV-6, was then appointed as the new VGTRK chief.

Sagalaev did not last long in this post. Soon after the presidential elections, a split in the management of the channel occurred, and some of the company's middle managers accused him of corruption and other abuses. No doubt reluctant to see the scandal spread, and as he himself put it, "wanting to avoid a split in the company's labor collective," Sagalaev resigned. He was replaced as head of the channel in 1997 by Nikolay Svanidze, who was considered close to the "young reformers," and above all to First Deputy Prime Minister Anatoly Chubais, who at that time was in favor. Svanidze had enjoyed a meteoric career with the television channel. A former historian, he began by providing commentaries for news broadcasts and for the program "Podrobnosti." Dressed in a sweater, with thick spectacles and a neat beard, he appeared on the screen like the embodiment of the democratic intelligentsia. His extremely ideological statements were combined on the whole with loyalty to the government, and this gave him a permanent job as host of the tiresome Sunday current affairs program "Zerkalo."

Once appointed general director, Svanidze began by doing away with commentaries by individual journalists. Many of RTR's stars, the most brilliant of whom was Svetlana Sorokina, went over to other channels (NTV in the case of Sorokina, and TV-Center in that of Shashkov). RTR's news broadcasting was restructured on the basis of propaganda techniques; to make managing the company's editorial policy easier, the work of preparing and hosting programs was split between the anonymous editors and a large number of announcers. These changes were accompanied by a transformation in the channel's news presentation, which on the whole became more dynamic and commercially oriented.

It cannot be said that putting a stop to the moralizing by presenters of the old "authorial" school was altogether a bad thing for RTR. Nevertheless, banishing familiar faces from the airwaves was not the best way to combat the channel's low ratings. The net result of the decision by the government to put their stake on Svanidze, in tandem with Mikhail Lesin, who had earlier helped the presidential administration develop links with public opinion as one of the owners of the advertising agency Video International, was that RTR fell even further behind its main competitors ORT and NTV. Perhaps understanding this, and trying to hold onto his Sunday-evening monologues, Svanidze voluntarily resigned following the dismissal of the Kirienko government.

After the crisis of August 1998 and the refusal by the parliament to confirm Viktor Chernomyrdin as premier, a "neutral" candidate was needed to head the television company. The post of VGTRK chief thus fell to Mikhail Shvydkoy, former deputy culture minister and founder of the television channel "Kultura" (this channel filled the niche of "public service broadcasting," which had remained empty for several years since NTV had made morning broadcasts on the fourth channel).

Despite the broad spread of its national coverage, Russian state television in the second half of the 1990s could not compete either with the first channel ORT or with NTV. Its future would thus have remained clouded but for the trend, first under Kirienko and then under Primakov, for the state to play an increasing role in the information system, and as a result, for control over the state media organs to become more concentrated.

The consequence was that RTR not only avoided being privatized, but had its position greatly strengthened. On May 8, 1998, while Kirienko was still premier, Yeltsin signed a decree "On Improving the Functioning of the State Electronic Mass Information Media." Under this decree, a large television holding company began to be set up on the basis of VGTRK. This new structure was to include the local television and radio companies that the federal government owned in almost every region of Russia.

Yevgeny Primakov, who had been under constant attack from the private media holding companies, made considerable efforts to ensure that the influence of the Russian television holding company and the state media in general would increase. An indication of this was the sacking of Sergey Dorenko from the first channel, and the appointment of protégés of the prime minister to posts in the state media. Former resident of Australia Lev Koshlyakov was made VGTRK deputy director in charge of news broadcasting, and press bureau chief Yury Kobaladze became deputy general director of the agency ITAR-TASS.[1]

Nevertheless, the crucial event that determined the fate of the television company, and perhaps of the state media, was the appointment on January 31, 2000, less than two months before the end of the presidential campaign, of Oleg Dobrodeev as director of VGTRK. Dobrodeev had been the founder and director of NTV's news service. The media organs that came under Dobrodeev's control along with RTR included the television channel Kultura; the radio stations Radio Rossii, Mayak, and Golos Rossii (the Voice of Russia, the former foreign service of

Moscow Radio); the news agency Novosti; and dozens of regional television and radio companies and transmission centers throughout the territory of Russia. Former VGTRK head Mikhail Shvydkoy became minister of culture.

Along with Dobrodeev, well-known journalists from other television companies switched to state television. These journalists included Stanislav Kucher, head of the program "Observer" on TV6; the director of Television News Service Aleksandr Gurnov; and also the NTV correspondents Yelena Masyuk, Andrey Medvedev, and Yevgeny Revenko. NTV employees who had already reached their "growth ceiling" in the commercial television company received the chance to establish their own programs.

It is curious that one of the reasons why Oleg Dobrodeyev made the shift to the state channel was his political position; unlike the other Media-Most chiefs, he supported the military operations in Chechnya. With his arrival, the tone of RTR's broadcasting became significantly more dramatized in everything that touched on the war in the Caucasus. Overall, the new VGTRK director managed to raise the professional level of the channel's news reporting and to find the key to viewers' hearts.

The result was that by May 2000 the program "Vesti," for years an outsider, had gained top ratings even in Moscow, and by a wide margin. According to the ratings service NISPI, in May the 8:00 p.m. edition of "Vesti" was seen by 1.73 million people, compared with 1.283 million for the 6:00 p.m. news broadcast and 1.25 million for ORT's 9:00 p.m. program "Vremya." Meanwhile, the 10:00 p.m. and 7:00 p.m "Segodnya" programs on NTV attracted only 1.21 million and 1.145 million viewers, respectively.[2]

Another element in the work of VGTRK was the rebuilding of the documentary film industry. It is interesting that many people well known for their talent as filmmakers took part in this project. They included Vitaly Mansky, who made the films *Studies of Love* and *Private Chronicles*, and who also shot the election campaign film *Leap Year*, about Vladimir Putin. According to Mansky, around a hundred films were being produced at the end of August 2000. Mansky's television projects were supported by the site "Vertov,"[3] devoted to the documentary cinema, whose chief editor was Natalya Manskaya, the wife of the film director. The name chosen for this site is significant. Vertov was one of the most brilliant experimental directors of the Soviet cinematic avant-garde. He rose to fame with such films as *Cine-Eye*, *1/6 of Being*,

Table 6.1

Potential Audience, Coverage, and Viewer Preferences in 1999

Channel	Audience (potential)	Coverage (1st half-year)	Coverage (2nd half-year)	Preferences (Dec. 24–26)
ORT	98	87	88	41
RTR	95	72	77	13
NTV	72	59	58	25
TV6	58	32	37	4
TV-Center	39	15	19	no data
Kultura	36	10	13	no data
CTC	35	16	19	no data
TNT	32	12	15	no data
REN-TV	27	13	11	no data

Source: Sredstva massovoy informatsii Rossii: Auditoria i Reklama. Moscow: Russian Public Relations Group, pp. 86–89.

and *Three Songs about Lenin*, while his industrial film *Donbass Symphony* won the admiration of Chaplin. Vertov is a symbol of the unity, infused with genius, of an innovative, creative approach to cinematography with a propagandist mission of strengthening the state. For the first time in recent decades, the massive concentration of financial resources in state television is making it possible for such a mission to be fulfilled. The "Real Cinema" project that Mansky is heading foresees weekly premieres of documentary films on the state channel RTR.

Oleg Dobrodeev was originally faced with the task of modernizing state television, but unlike his predecessors he not only stands at the head of a vast holding company but also has the full support of an executive power not torn by internal contradictions and ready to assign money to the state media as a top priority.

The only thing the administration lacked in order to restore virtually full control over the information space following the elections was the ability to influence the editorial policy of the semi-state ORT and the private NTV. But before even a year had passed, this problem was solved.

The Story of ORT

ORT is the key to the Russian information space. This channel still has the largest zone of coverage of Russian territory, larger even than the state-owned RTR. Though if we take into account the population covered, this gap does not seem so great; as state channels, ORT and RTR are obliged to cover even the most sparsely populated regions of the country, while all the other channels broadcast to a significantly lesser territory.

The government has always paid special attention to the first channel, and given this, RTR has at times been able to show the independence of its views and the autonomy of its editorial policy to advantage. As chairperson of "Ostankino," Yegor Yakovlev tried to "free up the creative energy of the workforce." It is hard to say whether he might have succeeded in awakening creative forces in the information organ that has probably been the closest to the government and the most cynical, but this effort did not continue for long, because Yakovlev was removed even before the events of October 1993. In Soviet times, the first channel was a powerful tool for inculcating the official picture of reality, and in the whirlpool of political crises not even the first president of Russia could allow himself the luxury of letting go of such a propaganda instrument simply because the director of the channel took an independent position.

The story of the founding of the (closed type) joint-stock company "Russian Public Television" has its beginnings in the autumn of 1994. In this case, "public" is of course an empty word, since ORT has nothing in common with public television as this concept is understood in its European homeland. From all appearances, the use of the term was necessary to convince Boris Yeltsin that the model proposed for the reform of the channel would not arouse objections in society, since it was thoroughly progressive. In addition, the organizers of the reform needed to deal with understandable objections in the state apparatus and the "democratic" press because what was involved was the partial transfer of ownership of the first channel to big business. In the broader reckoning, it was clear to everyone that ORT was supposed to win back for the first channel the ratings and sympathies of viewers, in order then to throw all its resources into supporting Yeltsin and his allies in the parliamentary and presidential elections of 1996.

On December 5, 1994, the Council of Trustees of the joint-stock company ORT was established under the chairpersonship of Boris Yeltsin. On January 1, 1995, a decree of the government of the Russian Federation was issued, listing the representatives of the state in ORT's management organs. On January 24 a founding meeting of the joint-stock company took place. On February 28 ORT was registered in the Moscow registry office. On March 1 the general director of the channel, the television compeer Vladislav Listyev, was murdered.

The killing of this popular television personality shocked everyone and became the subject of much speculation. A period of mourning was declared, and the television showed Listyev's portrait for several days running. To this day the murder has not been solved, but the very fact that such a crime was committed gives an idea of the intensity of the struggle surrounding the first channel.

Various materials from the investigation into the Listyev case have recently started to leak out to the press. These tend to refute the version that the murder had a political motivation. In particular, information published in the newspaper *Sovershenno Sekretno*[4] showed that even before the murder, there were disagreements in the television advertising business; it is well known that Listyev was anxious to restore order to the channel by introducing a moratorium on advertising for several months. Accompanying the article in *Sovershenno Sekretno* were selected summaries of contract killings; these summaries were intended to show how business conflicts were resolved in the world of television advertising.

Another version, making the rounds after Berezovsky's premises were searched in an effort to find clues to the murder, held that Listyev had refused at the last moment to play the role of titular chairperson, instead resolving to become the undisputed boss of the channel. Although the idea of reforming the first channel in order to provide media backing for the election campaigns had evidently come from Berezovsky, the fact that state organs held a controlling packet could have induced Listyev to try to do without an intermediary.

We still have no reliable information on the Listyev case, and it is unlikely that we ever will have. In one respect, however, the murder was significant: the wave of grief that swept over the country following the death of the popular presenter showed how attached people were emotionally to their television heroes. Similar mass outpourings of emotion followed the death of Princess Diana, and a similar veil of secrecy surrounds the murder of President Kennedy. This is still more evidence of the broad and powerful emotional impact of television, of the decisive advantage enjoyed by television over the press as a medium for propaganda and the manipulation of public opinion. A weakness of television is the relatively short-term nature of its impact compared with newspapers. For the most part, however, the government in the 1990s was attempting to solve propagandist tasks of a tactical rather than a strategic character.

On March 20, Sergey Blagovolin was appointed as chairperson of the board of directors of ORT, learning of his appointment by telephone, as

Table 6.2

Founders of the Company "Russian Public Television"*

Founder	Share, %
State Property Committee	36
State Enterprise "Television Technical Center"	3
Russian State Television and Radio Company "Ostankino"	9
ITAR-TASS	3
Joint-stock company "Association of Independent Television Companies"	3
Joint-stock company "Logovaz"	8
National Foundation for the Development of Sport	2
Menatep Bank	5
Natsionalny Kredit Bank	5
Stolichny Bank	5
RAO Gazprom	3
Alfa-Bank	5
Obedinenny Bank	8
Joint Stock Company "Trading Company Mikrodin"	5

*Established January 24, 1996

Source: "Rossiiskie SMI na starte predvybornoi kampanii" [Russian Mass Media at the Beginning of the Preelection Campaign], *Sreda,* no. 3 (1995).

he was in Japan at the time. Arkady Yevstafyev, head of the press service of the State Property Committee (in other words, a member of the Chubais camp) became his deputy responsible for news broadcasting. Blagovolin's other deputy was Boris Berezovsky himself.

The usurping of control over the first television channel under the guise of establishing a "public" channel could not help but arouse objections from the opposition. As early as 1995, the political overtones of the reform of "Ostankino," carried out on the eve of the elections to the State Duma and the presidency, made ORT the target of a multitude of critical articles and the subject of a scandal in parliament. The choice made by the founders of the television channel was, however, borne out. The political resistance failed to stop the new channel from operating— in just the same way, it appears, as the directors of the first channel were not hindered by the publication in the newspaper *Pravda,* on the eve of the presidential elections, of documents from the Accounting Office that dealt with abuses in the television organization.

The only real influence on the channel's policies was that of Berezovsky, even after he formally quit the post of deputy director of ORT and the firm's shares were redistributed. During the time when he was perceived as an intermediary, working on a personal mission from the president and under the patronage of the head of the presidential administration Valentin Yumashev, Berezovsky managed to achieve such influence that he continued to control the channel's information policy even after Vladimir Putin was elected as president of Russia, though not for long.

For Berezovsky, the road to seizing control of ORT lay in the appointing of a weak figure as nominal chairperson, at the same time as Berezovsky seized control over the financial management. After this, everything went ahead according to the model of "Russian privatization" developed by new Russian financiers in industrial enterprises with so-called red directors. The essence of this strategy was to buy the managers rather than the enterprise; once this had been done, the enterprise could be purchased cheaply. It was most likely this goal, as well as habitual and widespread tax avoidance, that was served by the dual wage system at the television channel. The salaries paid to the most important employees were determined personally by Berezovsky or by his protégé Badri Patarkatsishvili.

Sergey Dorenko, after his own fashion, also became a boon to the channel. A military translator by training, and according to Boris Yeltsin "the handsomest announcer on television," Dorenko was guided by the ethical code of a samurai and the moral scruples of wartime where Berezovsky's interests were concerned.

Dorenko was Berezovsky's main weapon. Depending on the circumstances, the anchorman would either appear in the studio or leave the screen to take up a top management position in the channel. To all outward appearances, he always knew why he was leaving and why he was returning, until December 8, 1998, when he was banished without explanation from the airwaves,[5] only to return a year later for what looked like his final mission.

It is interesting to note that Dorenko did not immediately become Berezovsky's samurai. As Giulietto Chiesa put it:

> I recall the reaction by Sergey Dorenko to the canceling of his program "Versii," which had been broadcast on the recently privatized ORT. At that time he was not as thick-skinned, and after talking to opposition journalists, he publicly accused Sergey Blagovolin (the general director of ORT) and Boris Berezovsky (who was then deputy general director) of intervening to censor him. "They imagine," Dorenko said, "that propaganda has to be beautifully polished, like the barrel of a Kalashnikov, so as to shoot the television viewer right in the forehead every day."[6]

It was only after "Versii" had been taken off the air, and an independent project by Dorenko for an economic news program on NTV had collapsed, that he reconciled himself to the role of a propagandist on ORT. During the 1999 parliamentary election campaign, when he returned to the job of anchor on a top-rated weekly current affairs program, he managed the near-impossible task of "drowning" the Fatherland movement and its leaders Yury Luzhkov and Yevgeny Primakov with a series of (unsubstantiated) compromising documents. Primakov, who had been Putin's main rival, did not recover from the blow and refused to be nominated for the presidential elections of 2000. As a politician of the traditional backroom type, he proved unable to withstand a powerful weekly media assault.

It is important to note that Dorenko's poor reputation in professional circles had almost no effect on the trust he inspired in his audience. According to research conducted by NISPI in September 1999, when Dorenko had already taken up his role as muckraker for the government, he was trusted more than any other presenter, with 14 percent of viewers giving him first place. His closest rivals, Yevgeny Kiselev of NTV and Aleksandr Lyubimov of ORT, both of whom tried to show objectivity, garnered 13 and 10 percent, respectively. Nikolay Svanidze, the presenter of an analogous weekly current affairs program on RTR, was supported by only 3 percent.[7]

Berezovsky's last move as de facto owner of ORT, the transferring of shares in the channel to representatives of the creative intelligentsia, received the full approval of the president. After this, the 49 percent controlled by Berezovsky passed into the hands of Roman Abramovich, the owner of one of the largest business empires in modern Russia. That this deal took place was confirmed by Igor Shabdurasulov ("the government has taken control of ORT"),[8] and partly denied by Press and Information Minister Mikhail Lesin.

"According to my information, the companies who owned these shares sold them to other companies," Lesin declared in an interview with Interfax. "Roman Abramovich is not personally associated with these companies." In Lesin's words, these were "not state companies."[9]

No one imagined that Abramovich was buying the ORT shares for himself. As in all stories of this sort, no reliable information on the deals was released. Consequently, we can judge the essence of what occurred only on the basis of the results declared by players in the information field and by rumors. In this particular case, the rumors claim that Abramovich purchased ORT so that the government could control it.

There is reason to suppose that as in the privatization era, an element of mutual favoritism was involved here. On the one hand, ORT went to the state, while on the other Abramovich succeeded in being elected as governor of Chukotka. Meanwhile the company Runikom, which Abramovich controlled, received the status of exclusive trader for the state oil company Slavneft. The amount of clear profit from trading in Slavneft deliveries has been put at $700 million[10] or more, considering the high prices for oil. The cost of 49 percent of the shares in ORT can hardly have exceeded this figure.

It is hard to picture the full degree of control exercised by the state over the mass media without taking into account the personality of the Press and Information Minister, Mikhail Lesin. As explained earlier, before coming to work for the government (from all appearances, this did little to change his mode of operating), Lesin was owner of the agency Video International, which in 2001 held exclusive rights over advertising on ORT, RTR, and NTV. According to the Union of Journalists, Video International controlled around 70 percent of the market for television advertising. Lesin's firm also provided the informal link that makes it possible to speak of total control over the most important television channels on the part of the state (or more accurately, the party of the government). This control substantially exceeded that which had been available to the administration during the 1990s, and closely approximated Soviet practice.

Politicized Capital and Its Evolution

Douglas Gomery of the University of Maryland distinguishes three methods of increasing corporate profits that drive the processes through which the ownership of mass media becomes concentrated. The first of these is the exploitation of economies of scale, the second is the striving for vertical integration, and the third is diversification of capital.[11]

To this list, another factor should be added. This is the effort to win control over the greatest possible number of media outlets in order to increase the political influence of one or another financial or political grouping. In the nineties, this was the prevailing practice in Russia.

The people who began the process of concentration of press ownership in Russia saw the chance to influence public opinion as sufficient cause for investing in one or another media organ. The nonclassical and in some ways even "antimarket" behavior of Russian business entrepreneurs is quite readily explained: political influence provided access to the distribution of assets during privatization, and on a scale compared to which the very modest profits to be made in the Russian media seemed negligible. After 1996, the motive of obtaining property became transformed into the desire to hold onto it. The new owners proved to be interested in maintaining relative political and economic stability—relative, because the main condition for retaining property could only be the existence of a political regime under which property was protected against encroachment from the state. As early as 1997 the interests of the media owners and of the state began coming into conflict, and this soon made its effects felt in the way the media reported the country's political life.

With the help of the mass media, the owners solved problems of two types—within the political elite and within Russian society as a whole. In the first case, the organs employed were mainly elite publications, the so-called influence newspapers. Articles in mass-circulation publications and discussions and commentaries in the electronic media were important but not indispensable elements of such campaigns.

In the second instance, the media were employed to help solve problems on a different scale—in particular, elections. The outstanding example of such use of the media was the presidential election campaign of 1996. In order to shape public opinion, it was essential to make use of the most popular media. The main ace in such campaigns was state television.

During the 1990s, efforts to combine the ability to carry out tasks of both types set the main parameters for the building of the politicized Russian media holding companies. As a rule (at least at the first stage of development of the holding companies), commercial success was viewed as secondary compared to the impact of this or that publication or television channel on one or another (elite or mass) market of influence.

It should be borne in mind that political concentration in Russia has been a local process rather than a national one. The concentration of media ownership in the hands of politicized capital has taken on a much more intensive form in the capital than in the provinces. The lack of return on investments has been a powerful factor limiting expansion of the range of mass communications enterprises taking part in this process. This, however, does not mean that the regional media have been free from any influence whatever. As a rule, control over the mass media in the provinces is exercised by the regional administration and large enterprises, often jointly, as for example in Ulyanovsk Province. Some-times the administration and the enterprises operate separately, as in the Krasnoyarsk Territory, where governor Aleksandr Lebed encountered powerful pressures from the large entrepreneur Anatoly Bykov, who controlled many regional media outlets (in this conflict, victory went to Lebed—his adversary was tried and convicted).

By June 1996, that is, by the time of the Russian presidential elec-tions, there were two media groups in whose formation the political factor had been of primary importance. These were the holding com-pany of the Most financial group (Vladimir Gusinsky), not yet formed into a distinct structure, and several media organs in whose manage-ment and financing Boris Berezovsky took part via the numerous enter-prises, such as Logovaz and United Bank, which he controlled. Among Russian politicians and journalists, these groups had long since been dubbed the "empires" of Gusinsky and Berezovsky.

The Berezovsky Media Group: A Tool of Influence

Boris Berezovsky initially concentrated in his hands large blocks of shares in the first and sixth television channels, that is, in ORT (16 percent) and in the television network TV-6, which was actively expanding in the re-gional television market. He also controls *Nezavisimaya Gazeta* and the magazine *Ogonyok*. It is said that after the presidential elections and the split in the newspaper *Izvestia*, it was Berezovsky who provided credit guarantees for *Novye Izvestia*, published by former *Izvestia* editor Igor Golembyovsky. This is tantamount to controlling the newspaper, since at present *Novye Izvestia*, the only daily newspaper published in color, is not commercially viable.

The outlines of the "Berezovsky empire" are diffuse, and precise data on Berezovsky's participation in various enterprises have always been hard to obtain. Until recently, this information was disseminated not in line with his wishes, but despite them. For example, the list of the founders of ORT was published for the first time in the communist news-paper *Sovetskaya Rossiya*. The lack of openness in the area of media ownership is largely explained by the fact that under the law on the mass media, the question of the transparency of the media is determined through the institution of the official sponsor or "founder," which is now becoming more and more of a formality. None of the owners of the media is obliged to make a show of his or her role unless he or she falls under the provisions of economic legislation requiring public disclosure in joint-stock companies of the open type. This is why the most important media organs in Russia have been registered as joint-stock companies of the closed variety.

The success of Berezovsky's mass media in the influence market was enormously important for him, acting as the foundation of his political and business career. In the 1990s the task set before the managers of his media projects was not so much to make profits as to cut costs. For this reason, the company ORT-Video was established within the framework of the television company ORT; the task of ORT-Video was to operate in the highly profitable home video market. One of the curious consequences of the launching of this company was a campaign against video piracy, headed by ORT general producer Konstantin Ernst.

A change of chief editors in the periodical *Ogonyok* in 1997 (Lev Gushchin was replaced by V.B. Chernov) resulted from dissatisfaction at the fact that the publication needed to be subsidized. The new chief editor was given the task of making the magazine profitable. As a result, *Ogonyok* once again changed its format, acquiring one similar to *Life* after several years in the format of a news weekly (like *Time*). Neither format allowed the magazine to come anywhere near the place in the media system it had enjoyed in the late 1980s, when its circulation reached 3.3 million copies and the magazine itself was considered required reading in broad circles of the intelligentsia.

Of all the Russian media groups, Berezovsky's shadowy holding company best fits the definition of having a "clan" character. Rumors to the effect that the media controlled by the bank SBS-Agro also belonged to this clan were confirmed in September 1998, when SBS-Agro went bankrupt and its media projects fell to Berezovsky.[12] Among these projects were the Internet information agency National News Service and the radio station NSN, broadcasting on the FM band.

The change of ownership of the radio station was followed by radical changes to its name (from NSN to "Nashe Radio") and its repertoire (from commercial jazz to electronic music and Russian pop). The new program director was one of the founders of the popular radio station Maximum, Mikhail Kozyrev. According to a report on the NSN bulletin Mass-Media, Berezovsky's partner in the radio business was Rupert Murdoch,[13] with whom the Russian businessman had established close business ties.

Thanks to Kozyrev's talents, the radio market became an important source of profits for Berezovsky's media group. The setting up of the Nashe Radio network, which held top place in the format of Russian pop and rock music (101.7 FM in Moscow, broadcasting to more than 180 cities), was followed by the opening of the station Ultra, broadcasting quality Western pop and rock (103.4 FM in Moscow).

There was only one media organ to which Berezovsky was not sparing with his cash, and which did not in principle set out to make money. This was *Nezavisimaya Gazeta*, which acted as a sort of forum for the political elite. *NG* can be seen as the exception that proves the rule that the commercialization of the media is a natural requirement of the large media holding companies.

Berezovsky's acquisition in 1999, was the *Kommersant* publishing house (more information on the newspaper *Kommersant* will be given in the next section on the commercial media). By adding to his holding company a group of publications popular in business circles, including the daily newspaper that was the most important in Russia in the second half of the 1990s, Berezovsky significantly strengthened his position on the eve of the elections. In mid-2000, when Berezovsky took up in earnest the project of building a democratic opposition to Putin, the chance of simultaneously influencing the audiences of *NG* and *Kommersant* allowed the businessman to effectively place a political crisis on the agenda; this was during the scandal over the saving of the sailors on board the submarine *Kursk*. The Russian president, who only recently had won election in the first round with the aura of "popular hero," now watched as the drama played out by the mass media hung like the sword of Damocles over his confidence rating.

Gusinsky's Holding Company: From an Influence Newspaper to a Commercial Media Group

If Berezovsky's political intrigues were oriented as a rule toward making profits in other sectors of the economy, Gusinsky's political life became a source for investments in the development of his media business. If it was possible to conclude a deal with the authorities, using the media as a tool to this end, Gusinsky would follow this path, but only on the condition that it led him toward his goal of dominating the media market in Russia and then expanding globally.

The media organs that were united under the control of the Most financial group gave the impression of a civilized and flourishing media group, especially if one bears in mind the comparison with Berezovsky's empire, often more reminiscent of a camp of conspirators than a late twentieth-century media holding company. Most important, many of the media organs that made up Gusinsky's holding company had been founded by Gusinsky himself.

By the time of the 2000 elections, Media-Most included the television company NTV, the talk radio station Ekho Moskvy, the radio stations Sport and RDV (both broadcasting on the FM band), and also the "Sem Dney" (Seven Days) publishing house. The publishing house in turn produced the daily newspaper *Segodnya*, the television weekly "Sem Dney," the monthly "Karavan Istoriy" (History Caravan) and the weekly journal *Itogi* (produced together with *Newsweek*). Also operating within the framework of the holding company was a powerful group of firms devoted to producing and distributing television and cinema films; these firms included NTV-Profit, Most-Cinematograf, and others.

Aside from this, the holding company included NTV-International, aimed at the Russian-speaking audience outside the country; the regional television network TNT; the Internet projects *memonet.ru* and *NTV.ru*; and other businesses.

Gusinsky's crowning achievement was the launching of the satellite system NTV+. In essence, the media magnate succeeded in creating the first working system of digital broadcasting in Russia, with its subscribers already numbering more than 100,000 by the beginning of 2000. Meanwhile, the Media-Most holding company itself founded some of the 53 channels that made up the system's full offering, including the highly popular NTV+ Sport.

The Media-Most group was also the only Russian media holding company to expand actively outside the country. As well as operating the Russian-language channel NTV-International, which had a competitor in the foreign channel of ORT, Media-Most held discussions with the aim of purchasing a Belgrade television channel. This deal did not come off, but another, involving the purchase of shares in the Israeli evening newspaper *Maariv*, the second-largest in Israel after *Ediot Akhronot*, went through and aroused a great deal of controversy in both Israel and Russia.

Amid all the hubbub, it was difficult (as usual) to work out from reports in the Russian press just what Gusinsky had purchased. *Russky Telegraf* reported that he had bought 25 percent, or "according to some reports, 10 percent" of the shares in the newspaper,[14] while according to the journal *Profil*, Gusinsky acquired:

> Twenty-five percent of the shares in the media holding company *Maariv*, the second-largest in Israel. *Maariv* (Evening Prayer) is an information and publishing concern that owns several recording studios, large packets of shares in the Israeli television company Telad, and the cable television network Matav, which publishes the newspaper of the same name and is also involved in film production. For 25 percent of the shares in *Maariv*, Mr. Gusinsky will outlay $255 million. In addition, Most-Media will receive an option on 10 percent of the shares (in addition to its existing 10 percent) in the cable network Matav.[15]

The story of the Most media group begins with the split in the editorial office of *Nezavisimaya Gazeta*. In 1992, roughly half of the editors and journalists founded a new daily newspaper, *Segodnya*, financed by the Most group. The project was initiated by the head of *NG's* economics department, Mikhail Leontyev, and the first chief editor was Dmitry Ostalsky, formerly deputy chief editor of *NG* and head of its politics department.

It is curious to note that immediately after the 1996 presidential election, Gusinsky tried to refashion *Segodnya*, doing away with the remaining elements of the influence newspaper and turning it into a purely commercial mass publication. To this end, the chief editor was replaced, with the post going to Yevgeny Serov from the *Kommersant* publishing house. The journalistic staff were almost all replaced as well; the team was later hired en masse to work on the newspaper *Russky Telegraf*, set up by Oneksim Bank, and later still, many of them switched to the new newspaper *Vremya*. During the "war for Svyazinvest," the newspaper became a weapon in the information war against Oneksim Bank and the government.

The next investment made by the Most group was in the founding of NTV. The new television company started broadcasting in October 1993 over the fifth (St. Petersburg) channel, later sharing the fourth channel with educational television (NTV began broadcasting at 6:00 p.m.). During the presidential elections, NTV commercial director Igor Malashenko was appointed to head Boris Yeltsin's press campaign. Following the elections, NTV received the daytime use of the fourth channel throughout Russia.

The most recent Media-Most project in the field of television broadcasting has been the network TNT, which went on the air in January 1998. The network is aimed at the interests of the regional viewer and features mainly entertainment programming. Appointed to head TNT were Sergey Skvortsov and Pavel Korchagin, who had earlier launched CTC. By offering a number of regional companies more favorable terms than other Moscow channels, TNT managed with one stroke to position itself among the leaders in the Russian regional market. The expansion of TNT did serious damage to the CTC and REN-TV/NVS networks.[16]

In 1994, the radio station Ekho Moskvy became part of the Most group. Ekho Moskvy was notable for its powerful news broadcasting and large audience; the latter had been acquired in Soviet times during the events in Lithuania, when the radio station was the sole source of information on the situation in that republic. Ekho Moskvy retains a high degree of authority and is justly considered one of the best-informed radio stations in Russia. The traditional features of Ekho Moskvy (uncritical liberalism, a democratic orientation, and sympathies with Grigory Yavlinsky) coincide perfectly with the wishes of its investor. This is perhaps why Ekho Moskvy represents an example of an editorial staff retaining its distinct character within a large media holding company.

Ekho Moskvy, meanwhile, has not remained on the sidelines where major political scandals have been involved. Experience has shown that the studio of a radio station can be the ideal place to hold a press conference in conjunction with television; it can provide a guarantee that on-air revelations will be taken up by the mass media. It was thus on a live radio program that Aleksandr Minkin accused Anatoly Chubais of corruption. Minkin claimed to have at his disposal documents indicating that the first deputy prime minister was to receive royalties of around $100,000 for a chapter in a book on privatization (according to rumors, the royalties were in fact for participating in Yeltsin's election campaign). Unlike the usual *kompromat*, this story ended up being proven, and shook the government profoundly. Minkin later won a court case in which Chubais tried to obtain compensation of 250 million undenominated rubles from him on the grounds of defamation.

On November 22, 1998, an American communications satellite was launched from Cape Canaveral. The satellite belonged to Media-Most, and would allow the simultaneous transmission of fifty digital television channels.

It is anticipated that with the help of digital technology, it will transmit television signals to the western regions of Russia and also to Israel, where there is a big demand for Russian-language television. The potential subscribers to this service number 200,000. The satellite will make it possible to broadcast on fifty channels. "Our aim is to open a window onto the world," declared the chairperson of the board of directors of the joint-stock company (closed type) Media-Most, Vladimir Gusinsky. According to Mr. Gusinsky, the new service should begin operating by late December, and the Russian government will not interfere in the selection of programs.[17]

Broadcasts by NTV+ Digital began in February 1999, in parallel with analogue transmissions. The basic packet included the channels:

Cinema World, Our Cinema, MTV-Russia, VH-1, Fashion, Children's World, Nickelodeon (with translations), Discovery (with translations), Animal Planet, Zone Vision (with translations), TNT, and NTV. In the future it is planned to expand the packet to 22 channels. Additional packets will be "007" (hits)—twenty-four hours of topical movies with daily premieres; Late-Night Channel; NTV+ Sport; and NTV+ Football.[18]

Of all the projects announced earlier, Media-Most has so far failed to implement the most ambitious and promising—a round-the-clock Russian-language news channel.

According to estimates by the heads of the Media-Most group, the group's assets were worth around $2 billion. Deputy Director of the holding company, Andrey Tsimaylo, maintained that in three years, following allocation of the shares of the firms making up the holding company, as well as of Media-Most shares held on the open market, Media-Most would be worth around $5 billion.

According to Tsimaylo, the group's debts to Gazprom amounted to $211.6 million. Meanwhile, Gazprom owned 14.3 percent of the shares in Media-Most, as well as two blocks of shares held as security against credits, totaling 48.5 percent. In addition, Gazprom owned 30 percent of the television company NTV.[19]

Tsimaylo added that the holding company had debts to Sberegatelny Bank Rossii of $100 million, which were secured by state bonds. Apart from this, NTV had a debt of $40 million to Gazprombank. The deputy head of the holding company also noted that its debts to Eksimbank under a credit granted until 2009 had diminished from $140 million to $120 million.[20]

After the 2000 presidential elections, government representatives did everything they could to be able to bid for the holding company at a reduced price. Gusinsky was arrested on grounds relating to the company Russian Video and was accused of misappropriating $10 million.

After first declaring in the presence of lawyers that the deal was being concluded under pressure and would thus be null and void, Gusinsky signed an agreement to sell the holding company to Gazprom for $300 million (aside from the cancellation of the debt). Press and Information Minister Mikhail Lesin and the head of Gazprom-Media Albert Kokh appended their signatures to the agreement, which provided Gusinsky with immunity from prosecution. When Gusinsky made his scandalous declaration and the agreement made its way into print (it was first published on the Internet), Lesin escaped with a dressing-down from Prime Minister Mikhail Kasyanov. The purpose of this reprimand was to distance the government from the fact that the press and information minister had accepted the obligation to spare the media owner from prosecution, provided he transferred control over NTV to a semistate monopoly. Naturally, these guarantees testified above all to the arbitrariness that the executive branch had shown during the prosecution of Gusinsky, and also pointed to the real causes. Few people in Moscow had any doubts concerning the latter.

It was another matter entirely that public opinion outside the capital proved unexpectedly to be on the side of Putin. Gusinsky, who as an oligarch and a Jew was not viewed as a winning player, was well suited to be a victim in the populist "law and order" campaign that the administration had unleashed. The Moscow intellectuals once again ended up in the minority.

Nevertheless, the degree of moral superiority that Gusinsky had achieved in this skirmish with the government proved useful to him. A Spanish court refused to hand him over to the Russian government, and Gusinsky was able to fly to Israel. In August 2003 Gusinsky was arrested again at the behest of the Putin government, this time in Greece. The Russian media-political system thus had one less player.

A group of NTV journalists, headed by the presenter of the weekly current affairs program *Itogi* and former deputy general director of NTV Yevgeny Kiselev, went over to Boris Berezovsky's TV-6, provoking a conflict at the latter channel. Deprived of ORT, Berezovsky placed his stake on the NTV team, giving them the task of making TV-6 a force at the national level. Meanwhile, it was already clear that in trying to repeat the success of NTV, TV-6 would rely on a certain oppositional character in its news broadcasting. Unsurprisingly, the license of this channel was revoked upon a lawsuit from a minor owner, the pension fund "Lukoil-Garant," only to be handed back to journalists this time organized in a broad consortium including such political heavyweights as Evgeny Primakov and Arkady Volsky. While Gusinsky lost control over NTV, TNT, and NTV+ to Gazprom, Berezovsky lost both ORT and TV-6. Thus, both were ousted from the Russian media-political system where they used to be major players. This, however, did not happen to Yury Luzhkov, the mayor of Moscow, who controls one of the largest media groups in the country.

The Luzhkov Group as a Unique Type of Regional Holding Company

A report by the Russian Union of Journalists defines two types of regional media systems in Russia: liberal (independent), and paternalistic (state). As examples of such models, the document cites St. Petersburg, where a diverse range of press outlets has continued to exist, and Ulyanovsk Province, where during the 1990s Governor Yury Goryachev controlled most of the regional publications. The authors of the report conclude that the paternalistic model is characteristic of regions where the population holds predominantly to traditional conservative values. Interestingly enough, these are the regions that in per capita terms hold first place in providing their citizens with newspapers and journals.[21]

If we are to use the terminology of the authors of the report, a mixed liberal-paternalistic model held sway in Moscow during the 1990s, with a sector of publications that were either independent or controlled by large holding companies coexisting with a media group financed by the local government.

The press group controlled by Yury Luzhkov was formed without particular controversy during the second half of the 1990s, as the city publications of the Russian capital appealed for financing to the mayor's office, where they never met with a refusal. At times such flexible formulae for collaboration were arrived at as the publication of mayoral documents in the pages of *Moskovskaya Pravda*, an arrangement that provided the newspaper with as much as 10 percent of its revenues.

The result was that Luzhkov, like many heads of administration in the Russian provinces, managed to acquire virtually complete control over the city periodical press and some of the central publications. For example, the Moscow city government became one of the shareholders in Yegor Yakovlev's *Obshchaya Gazeta* (other shareholders in the publication were Gusinsky, Kadannikov, and according to some accounts, National Reserve Bank) and TV-6 (together with Lukoil and Berezovsky's Logovaz). The mayor's office maintained close relations with many independent commercial publications, helping, for example, to attract investments for the *Sovershenno Sekretno* concern's newspaper *Versiya*, and also for *Moskovsky Komsomolets*, which launched regional publications one after another. The latter project was aimed at implementing Luzhkov's strategy, on the eve of the election campaigns of 1999–2000, for penetrating the regional information systems.

The vast financial resources of the Moscow mayor's office made the Luzhkov group one of the most aggressive developers in the all-Russian information market in the late 1990s. When one of the heads of the Russian Television and Radio Company, Anatoly Lysenko, came to work for the Moscow channel, the faceless MTK and the channel 2x2, saturated with advertising segments, were transformed into the television channel TV-Center, which began actively expanding into the provinces.

Well-known television personalities and talented journalists were recruited to work for the channel; they were attracted by the possibility of taking an oppositional stance toward the federal government, under the protection of the Moscow city government. The lively news and current affairs program "Na Samom Dele" thus took its place on the channel; one of its announcers was Mikhail Leontyev, former head of the economics section of *NG* and later deputy chief editor and ideologue of the newspaper *Segodnya*. Little by little "Na Samom Dele" gained momentum and came to occupy a respected place among Russia's news and current affairs programs, even though the aggressively liberal, early 1990s-style position of its announcers was fundamentally at odds with the paternalistic spirit of the Luzhkov media.

Late in 1998, Leontyev was one of Berezovsky's fiercest critics. However, of Leontyev's two main political reference-points—"Great Russia" and economic liberalism—only one corresponded to the political line of TV-Center. In the spring of 1999 Leontyev went over to ORT, taking with him his program, which came to be called "Odnako" (However)—and immediately gained a place at the top of the ratings. Leontiyev later hosted "Another Time," a Saturday night news show on ORT, where one could see the bulk of the senior *Nezavisimaya Gazeta* management team as it was in 1991.

The financial core of the media holding company Metropolis, which united the mass media of the Luzhkov group, was the company AFK-Sistema. In 1997 the holding company was headed by Lev Gushchin, the former chief editor of the weekly *Ogoneyok*.

The holding company Metropolis included the Moscow cable radio Govorit Moskva and M-Radio; the newspapers *Literaturnaya Gazeta* and *Rossiya* (Gushchin considered this a future all-Russian publication, but because of the 1998 crisis, publication of the newspaper had to be stopped); and also the *Metro* group of publications. This latter group consisted of a free weekly newspaper, founded by association with the highly profitable Scandinavian publications and distributed on the Moscow underground railway, and the monthly journal *Metro-Express*.[22] Nikolay Bodnoruk, who earlier had been executive secretary of *Izvestia* and first deputy chief editor of *Obshchaya Gazeta*, was appointed as chief editor to revive *Literaturnaya Gazeta*; the Moscow city government took a 25 percent stake in the newspaper, providing the management with premises (as its property) and an allotment of land (on lease).

Early in August 1998, official reports appeared to the effect that AFK-Sistema had taken over one of the leading Moscow printing works, the *Moskovskaya Pravda* polygraphic and publishing combine,[23] and the large advertising agency Maksima;[24] this allowed observers to speak of a genuinely powerful media group taking shape under the aegis of Yury Luzhkov.

Although the owners of media holding companies usually try to explain the concentration of ownership as the result of commercial considerations, more candid utterances sometimes slip through. For example, Lev Gushchin, who heads the Luzhkov media group's media holding company Metropolis, does not conceal the fact that the concern had political ambitions:

> We have the chance to create the first balanced holding company in the country. It's calculated to have a broader influence than the Media-Most holding company, and other holding companies, if you please, aren't even in the picture. The Oneksim holding company is becoming more and more involved in business, and the question of its impact on public opinion is being ignored. Gazprom is constantly declaring that it has no interests in this area. Berezovsky has either gone cool on the idea, or has decided the time isn't right. So I don't see any others.[25]

Despite having a clear conception of its tasks and achieving a high concentration of its resources, the Luzhkov group did not manage to win the necessary influence on voters in the regions. On the other hand, even if Luzhkov's holding company did not fulfill its "maximum task," its "minimum task" was coped with successfully; on December 19, 1999, Yury Luzhkov was reelected for a second term as mayor of Moscow, with 71.2 percent of the votes. Luzhkov thus reaffirmed his status as an exceptionally influential politician.

After the elections, the press ministry, with Mikhail Lesin at its head, took advantage of the warnings dealt to ORT and TV-Center during the election campaign to refuse to automatically extend their licenses, and announced a competition for the frequencies of these television channels. It took all Luzhkov's influence and three meetings with the press minister in the Pushkin Restaurant in order to keep the license of TV-Center. Meanwhile, the ministry did not cancel the competition, and although none of the television broadcasters lost their frequencies as a result, the effect on them was terrifying. Each of the television channel owners could see himself in the place of ORT and TV-Center, while no other channel could boast of the same political protection. Although in formal terms nothing had happened, and the frequencies remained with their owners, Lesin's ministry had achieved what it set out to do, demonstrating how shaky the position was of any broadcasting company that entered into conflict with the party of the government.

Lukoil and OneksimBank

The domination of the Russian political process by information techniques, a fact that emerged so clearly in the 1996 presidential elections, could not fail to make its effects felt on those businessmen and politicians who still did not have mass media at their disposal during the period of the election campaign. The result was a series of cases in which media outlets were swallowed, and ownership concentrated.

On this level, the story of the seizure of *Izvestia* became symbolic. The players involved were two firms new at that time to the press market—the oil company Lukoil and OneksimBank. After the presidential elections, *Izvestia* remained the flagship of the "democratic media," having managed to retain a relative independence (with numerous reservations) in its editorial policy, along with its respectability and a relatively stable position on the market. A series of commercial failures (such as that of the newspaper *Nedelya*) had made the financial position of the publishing group rather precarious, and the journalists began looking for an investor. After lengthy discussions, the editorial staff reached agreement with the company Lukoil, which was to invest $40 million in a project to establish regional publishing centers, receiving in exchange around 20 percent of the newspaper's shares. The rest of the shares remained in the hands of the newspaper's journalistic collective, its daughter enterprises, and the company Troyka-Dialog (around 15 percent).

On April 1, 1997, a reprint appeared in *Izvestia* of an article from the newspaper *Le Monde* asserting that the capital holdings of Prime Minister Viktor Chernomyrdin were on the order of $5 billion. The article provoked a scandal. Chernomyrdin joked that if he had that much money he would not work but just take it easy. But Vagit Alekperov, the president of Lukoil (35 percent of the shares in this oil company are owned by the state) decided to hit back. He publicly rebuked the journalists for issuing unsubstantiated information.

In the newspaper, the investor's rebuke was interpreted as an "incursion" on the rights of the "Fourth Estate." Beginning on April 15 and each day thereafter, *Izvestia* published venomous commentary articles about Chernomyrdin, Lukoil, and everyone associated with them. The series began with an article by Sergey Agafonov, "The House-Manager's Scheme, or How Political Censorship Is Being Revived in Russia."[26] Other front-page articles then followed one after the other. Their content can be gauged from the headlines: "Oil Games—in Russia, Their Rules Are Dictated by the Apparatus,"[27] "The Cat Is Opposed to a Bell Being Hung Around Its Neck—Why the Premier Made Haste to Defend Natural Monopolies, Calling Them the 'Backbone of the Economy,'"[28] "An Attack on Freedom of the Press Is an Attack on Democracy" (a collective letter by public figures), and "Lukoil Wants to Exert Influence."[29]

As stated in the editorial article "Business and the Press,"[30] Lukoil managed to secure 41 percent of *Izvestia's* stock by buying up shares from other investors. This allowed Vagit Alekperov, meeting with Igor Golembyovsky after the above-mentioned articles had appeared, to take a tough stand. Alekperov offered the newspaper's chief editor the job of chairperson of the board of directors of the joint-stock company, on the condition that the new company president and chief editor were appointed on the recommendation of Lukoil.

On April 22 *Nezavisimaya Gazeta* published several articles on developments in *Izvestia* and also in *Komsomolskaya Pravda*; similar things were occurring in this latter newspaper with the involvement of OneksimBank, but they ended without a major scandal. The *NG* articles provided various assessments of what was happening. A collective letter by chief editors to the president of Russia, with a request to intervene in the situation with *Izvestia*; an interview with Lukoil representative Aleksandr Vasilenko; and an article by Yevgeniya Albats entitled "On the Right to Choose"[31] were published on a single page of the newspaper. They contained three different approaches to the one problem.

The collective letter by the newspaper chief editors used a good deal of the now forgotten rhetoric of the first years of democracy in Russia, with a demand on the president that was similar in spirit: to defend the editorial staff of a newspaper from an investor. The Lukoil representative, by contrast, denied that there had been any attempts by the investor to interfere in the content of the newspaper, rebuking *Izvestia* for whipping up hysteria and for publishing daily libels against Lukoil.

The independent journalist Yevgeniya Albats had been watching the problems of *Izvestia* and *Komsomolskaya Pravda* not as an active participant in events, but from the sidelines. Here is a resume of her article. First of all, *Izvestia* really did publish false information, instead of making its own investigation. The reprint from *Le Monde* was from a foreign political source, which in turn was reproducing information put on record by one of the heads of the American security services at open hearings in the U.S. Congress (an account of these hearings would appear in the newspaper later). Despite the wave of *kompromat* directed at Lukoil, *Izvestia* had not succeeded in proving that Chernomyrdin really did have $5 billion. What was unquestionably involved was a gross editorial error for which someone should bear responsibility.[32] Second, anxious to save face, *Izvestia* then entered into a confrontation with the investor, instead of publishing a retraction; such a retraction was uttered by the chairperson of the board of directors of the joint-stock company in an interview with the journal *Ekspert*, but it did not appear in the newspaper. Third, in the view of Albats the question of whether the president had the right to intervene in such a conflict on the side of the journalists was a quite separate one. And if the president did have the right to intervene, then what would statements concerning the "independence" of the press be worth?

In the next issue of *Nezavisimaya Gazeta*, Vitaly Tretyakov published an article with the headline "A Letter Not to B.N. Yeltsin." *Izvestia*, Tretyakov wrote, was not an independent newspaper, but a party newspaper of the Gaidar-Chubais persuasion, and the loss of its independence would thus mean not so much the weakening of the press in Russia, as a weakening of the media support available to one of the country's political groups. Tretyakov's letter contained a great deal of cruel irony, since he had already had to go through what the *Izvestia* editorial staff was experiencing. It is curious that in the case of *NG*, neither corporate solidarity with the journalists nor letters from public figures made their appearance. The attitude of the *Izvestia* journalists to the problems of *NG* had been one of squeamish condescension; *Nezavisimaia Gazeta* was one thing, while the "fourth estate" was something quite different.

The head of state did not intervene in the conflict between the journalists and the investors, and the *Izvestia* management decided to resort to the help of OneksimBank in order to block the attempts by Lukoil to win control of the newspaper. As a result, OneksimBank bought up a controlling packet of shares in *Izvestia* in record time. Because this was done with the agreement of the chief editor and part of the newspaper's journalistic collective, a little more than 50 percent of the shares in *Izvestia* cost the bank far less than the significantly smaller block of shares that had gone to Lukoil. As in the story of *NG*, the affair was concluded with the participation of armed guards. The investors, however, quickly reached agreement among themselves.

In sum, the only journalist who really gained from all these perturbations was *Izvestia*'s American correspondent Vladimir Nadein, who broke his contract with Lukoil for the purchase of his 0.64 percent of the newspaper's shares, and sold the shares to OneksimBank for twice the sum. His profits from this deal, according to reports in various publications, were between half a million and a million U.S. dollars. Who knows, perhaps he is now worth more than Viktor Chernomyrdin.

Formally speaking, the conflict ended in a truce. An agreement concluded between the investors and the editorial staff was supposed to provide the newspaper's creative workers with a guarantee against day-to-day interference from outside. Before long, however, Igor Golembyovsky and a section of *Izvestia*'s labor collective had founded a new daily newspaper, to feature color printing. This was *Novye Izvestia*, and its design was worked out using the formula of *USA Today*. The new publication was financed by Boris Berezovsky. Golembyovsky was the only person who continued to deny this. The new chief editor of *Izvestia* was Mikhail Kozhokin, the former head of the OneksimBank press service.

Komsomolskaya Pravda was the target of another blitzkrieg by OneksimBank, which managed to buy 20 percent of the newspaper's shares that had previously been meant for Gazprom. For several years Gazprom had financed the newspaper's economic supplement *Delovoy Vtornik*. It is possible that the clash with Berezovsky over *NG* had provided the company's chiefs with a beneficial lesson. In the case of *Izvestia* and *KP*, OneksimBank adopted a *Sturm und Drang* approach.

The alliance with *Komsomolskaya Pravda*, of which the head of the *KP-Segodnya* publishing group Vladimir Sungorkin was appointed chief editor, meant that OneksimBank instantly became one of the most influential media owners. Apart from its stake in *Komsomolskaya Pravda*, whose circulation late in 1997 stood at 2 million copies on weekdays and 3.6 million on Saturdays, OneksimBank became involved in the business of the publishing group, which controls several dozen regional publishing centers and newspapers, as well as two all-Russian weeklies, the sensationalist tabloid *EKSPRESS-Gazeta* and the television guide *Antenna*. OneksimBank acquired enormous political influence, without having to shoulder losses. Not one of the enterprises of the *KP-Segodnya* group was operated at a loss; on the contrary, the group was bringing in profits and developing on a stable basis, especially in the regions.

As well as its shares in *Izvestia* and *Komsomolskaya Pravda*, OneksimBank owns shares in the economics weekly *Ekspert*. The group recently acquired shares in the radio network Yevropa+, though it was later announced that the radio station would not become part of the Prof-Media holding company, formed early in 1998 on the basis of OneksimBank's media assets.[33]

Vladimir Potanin's victory, in alliance with George Soros, at the auction for Svyazinvest made him one of the leading figures in the electronic communications market, and helped ensure him an advantageous position when taking part in future information projects. Although the deal was concluded using mainly Soros's money, Potanin ultimately managed to keep Soros from playing a role in managing the company. Soros later confessed that Svyazinvest proved to be the worst deal he ever made. This perhaps explains why he is best known in Russia not as an investment banker, but rather as a philanthropist. The magnitude of his accomplishments in this capacity, however, by far exceeds what he could ever hope to make out of the communication holding.

Foreign Affairs: The Failings and Success Stories
of Foreign Investors in Russian Media

George Soros was certainly not the only foreigner who "made the worst deal of a lifetime" in Russia. Another billionaire to fail miserably on Russian ground was maverick businessman Ted Turner. He stood behind the rise of channel TV-6. Turner and Jane Fonda were in their hotel room when Eduard Sagalaev, the founder of the channel, told them the bad news.

As the story goes, CNN had been one of the first American TV channels to be broadcast to a Russian audience. It was available at no cost for a while on the band wave receivable with simple antennae. It was also on the air during the events of August 19, 1991, and October 3–4, 1993, when it was rebroadcast by RTR, the second channel. Turner was actively seeking a way to become one of the major players in the emerging Russian media system. And when the opportunity arrived, he jumped at it.

TV-6 was born to be successful, and Ted Turner knew that simply because this was literally the sixth channel in Moscow when there was no seventh. Hence little imagination was needed to promote the channel. Under an agreement that Turner would eventually become a key shareholder in the channel, Turner Broadcasting Corporation (TBC) handed over the rights to dub many American movies made from the fifties to the seventies and to show them on the channel TV-6, instantly winning an enormous audience of Russians hungry for movies they had been unable to see under the Soviet regime. The new audience was not choosy: while the wealthier Russians had had a glimpse of Hollywood films, Hong Kong kung-fu movies, French erotica, and German porno, the bulk of the audience had never seen any of it. Movies were in demand. Old films constituted the bulk of TV-6 programming. While the channel was no smash hit, its ratings went up considerably and continued to grow.

While visiting Russia for one of the Goodwill games he sponsored, Ted Turner met Sagalaev in his hotel room. When Sagalaev asked for more investment, Turner asked in turn for the controlling stake in the company, threatening to revoke the license for the TBC movie library. Sagalaev, however, did not flinch. Instead, he announced that from then on he considered their former agreement void. As he later recalled, Jane Fonda was reaching for a bottle of cola from the refrigerator and from the expression on her face he understood that she would have liked to hit him with it. (She did not.)

After Turner's exit, Sagalaev received 25 percent of the company, and the rest went to Boris Berezovsky, the city of Moscow, and Lukoil. At the end of the nineties Berezovsky managed to acquire the controlling stake in the company and installed the former NTV team there. They made a great start with *Za Steklom* (Behind the Glass), a reality show strongly promoted over the Internet by heavyweight Rambler Internet Holding. In Moscow they were successful enough in the ratings to beat the *Survivor* replica on ORT, and to make it clear that they were on their way to becoming an all-national television channel on a par with NTV.

However, a suit from minor shareholder Lukoil-Garant interrupted their rise. Claiming that its interests had been betrayed, the pension fund of the oil giant demanded bankruptcy for TV-6. This was the second time (the first being the *Izvestia* case) that Lukoil encountered losses while acting in the interests of the state, which controls roughly one-third of the company's stock. The channel's license was revoked. The NTV team went to work for Ekho Moskvy radio station—to stay in shape—and won the license back, this time as a joint-stock company, Media-Socium, under the patronage of Evgeny Primakov and Arkady Volsky, with equity distributed among the founders from the Union of Industrialists and Entrepreneurs. On the TV talk show *Vremena* (The Times), hosted by Vladimir Pozner, Mikhail Lesin claimed that this was one of the first attempts to build a "public" television channel based on the concept of social responsibility. By this he meant that with the dispersal of TV-6 shares no one would have the power to sway the political line of the channel, and knowing how easily the license could be lost, none of the journalists that worked on it would have the nerve to move into the opposition.

Thus the last resource of Boris Berezovsky—one of the few maverick businessmen to discover the power of television and use it in the nineties—was finally ousted from Russian television. Berezovsky is a foreigner too; like Gusinsky, he has an Israeli passport and is forced to live in exile from Russia.

There were many other failures, and many more are mentioned in the Russian edition of this book.[34] But there were success stories also, and it now appears that they outnumber the failures. Peter Gerwe, Andrew Polson, and Derk Sauer are the most successful media entrepreneurs of foreign origin. Peter Gerwe's first venture in the USSR took place in 1982, when he organized a live satellite exchange during a California music festival with financing by Steve Wozniak, one of the founders of

Apple Computer. Gerwe founded his company StoryFirst Communications in 1989, and by then he was no stranger to Russia. At first he worked in film distribution. He invested his profits in one of the first commercial FM stations in Moscow, Radio Maximum. Then he moved on to Ukraine where he founded the International Commercial TV and Radio Network (ICTV); it consisted of a national television network broadcasting in forty-four cities in Ukraine, and two radio stations operating in Kiev.

Later he acquired the sixth channel of St. Petersburg television and built a TV network around it. The network was launched nationwide after he bought Marathon TV in Moscow. The network was called CTC in Russian and is working hard to capture a 10 percent audience share and 10 percent of Russian television advertising revenue. It is claimed that up to 30 percent of CTC belongs to Alpha group.

Andrew Polson suffered a great number of failures. The magazines he chose to publish, *Ponedelnik* and *Vechernyaya Moskva*, both flopped before he came up with *Afisha*, a Russian analogue of *Time Out* that was an overnight success: a magazine about exhibitions, premieres, theaters, and cinema.

It is worth noting that his first attempts failed not because his magazines lacked quality, but because he attempted to start a news magazine in the middle of the nineties (when politics was out of fashion) and a cultural weekly when there was still not a big enough audience for it. *Afisha* repeated *Vechernyaya Moskva* in almost everything but timing. It came to bloom at a time when the tide had turned and the public was switching to entertainment of all sorts in culture and sports. *Afisha* succeeded in an environment in which the queues lined up near the entrances of museums that had stood open but miserably empty throughout the decade. At last there was enough social energy to spill over into leisure activities.

Another bet made by Polson, which looks just as risky as all his previous undertakings, is a free newspaper, *Bolshoy Gorod* (Big City), which he started to publish in 2002. A rough analogue of the *Village Voice*, this newspaper has more articles than advertising so far. However, the articles are of great quality, as are the tourist guidebooks published by *Afisha*—another success story in itself.

However, Polson's stunning success may be due to the fact that, unlike his previous projects, he started this one with a serious partner, Boris Jordan. An American by passport and birth, Jordan is of Russian descent and has integrated himself seamlessly into the higher echelons of the local financial elite, becoming at one point the consultant of Goskomimushchestvo—the state agency, led by Anatoly Chubais, that was in charge of distributing privatized property during the Yeltsin years. He started his career in Moscow as director of the Crédit Suisse First Boston investment office and became the president of Renaissance Capital Group, a major shareholder in Sputnik Group, and a member of the Sidanco board of directors.

Sputnik has interests in Svyazinvest, Sidanco, and Purneftegaz the companies. In the media sector the group has invested in Europa+ radio station, *Afisha* magazine, and *Bolshoy Gorod* newspaper. After Gazprom Media, led by Alfred Koch, took control of NTV, Jordan became general director of the TV company and seemed set to acquire the station, of which Gusinsky still owned 27 percent. In this final accord of the Svyazinvest battle Jordan will probably assemble a full-blown media holding from the shambles of the Gusinsky empire. He could now become one of the key players in the Russian media market.

Unlike Polson, Derk Sauer had a relatively easy start. He came to Moscow with substantial investment funds from his friends, a number of individuals, and VNU, a large Dutch publishing house. After the success of his first publication in Russia, the English-language *Moscow Magazine* (published in a joint venture with the Moscow section of the Russian Journalists Union), he persuaded them to invest in his newly founded company Independent Media, which was about to publish a free English-language newspaper, the *Moscow Times*. At first published twice a week, the newspaper soon became a daily. It reached most of the foreign audience in Moscow and became a "must-read" for fresh arrivals. He started the English-language *Kiev Times* and *St. Petersburg Times* for a similar readership.

Independent Media went on to become a major player in the Russian magazine market where it remains one of the leaders. The secret of success for Sauer was to publish Russian versions of such magazines as *Cosmopolitan, Playboy, Good Housekeeping, Harper's Bazaar, Men's Health,* and *FHM,* as well as a couple of original projects: *Kult Lichnosti* (Cult of Personality) in *Celebrities* format and *Yes* for teenage girls (and now also a *Yes-week* weekly).

The prime achievement of the Independent Media group was the newspaper *Vedomosti,* published in joint venture with the *Wall Street Journal* and the *Financial Times.* Capitalizing on the reputation of Independent

Media as a major and independent enterprise (it is rumored that the only Russian investor was Menatep Bank with only 10 percent), the publishing house was able to establish the newspaper as one of the two leading business dailies.

All the success stories have certain similarities that we will try to summarize here. First, a most important condition: the foreign investor had to be well acquainted with the realities of life in Russia and had to invest some time in building up connections in this country. Then, the initial investment had to be small, but profitable, thus allowing him to learn even more by doing business in Russia. And, perhaps even more important, he had to stay away from all-Russian television and the media-political system, where any conflict with a local player could prove fatal for the undertaking. Foreign investors thus became pioneers of the Russian commercial media.

The New Russian Commercial Media

While some foreign citizens profited by introducing the media culture from the West and others were not so fortunate, key accomplishments were made by local players, one of whom has initiated a quiet revolution in the new Russian media world and, to an extent, has helped to shape it. Vladimir Yakovlev (son of Yegor, the legendary editor of *Moskovskie Novosti* during the Gorbachev era) was first channel general director under Yeltsin, a founding father of the democratic press, and is currently the editor of *Obshchaya Gazeta* weekly. He was a strong reporter who made a name for himself in a series of newspaper scoops and serious investigations. He started his business life by founding a cooperative, *Fact*, created to provide information to business people. Approached by the director of the Cooperative League, Artem Tarasov, who was a celebrity because he became the first of the Soviet millionaires to admit their wealth, he decided to publish a business weekly as the newspaper of the League. The newspaper was so successful that it soon overshadowed the League itself.

The weekly newspaper *Kommersant* first appeared in December 1989. It was a bold and very ironic publication. Every headline was carefully cultivated and bred to maximum effect, and the editorial routine tolerated the fact that sometimes inventing a headline could take just as much time as editing the copy.

The newspaper was one of the first to accept the fact that information has a price and to use all kinds of sources to gather it. A special crime report department was formed that intercepted militia intelligence and reporters instantly drove out to any site where something of interest was happening.

Kommersant was also the first Russian newspaper to fully use the "inverted pyramid" structure and to put leads at the beginning of every article. A rewrite staff put all stories into a distinctive style: business-like, yet with a touch of good humor, and here and there a phrase in Latin. The newspaper was positioned as a quality, yet entertaining, read. Its circulation grew from forty thousand to half a million in one year. In 1992 *Kommersant* expanded to a daily newspaper with a weekly magazine, which in 1997 evolved into two—one devoted to politics and a social agenda (*Vlast* = Power) and another devoted to economics in the most practical sense (*Dengi* = Money).

Dissatisfied with the ideology-centered old school of journalism, Tarasov decided not to hire any professional journalists from outside; instead he opened courses at the newspaper. This enabled his enterprise to identify an enormous base of talented and energetic people who can separate information from comment and focus on facts rather than ideas. It turned out that this was what everyone needed. As one of the first to offer a new kind of journalism, he was able to skim the cream.

Kommersant pioneered one of the four schools of newspaper journalism in Russia: *Nezavisimaya Gazeta*, Independent Media publications, and *Moskovsky Komsomolets (MK)* did the same in their respective domains. *NG* founded a style of reporting political events and commenting upon them, Independent Media introduced trendy glossy magazines, and *MK* dominated the Moscow market with its unique broadsheet tabloid formula of success. *Kommersant* showed what "quality journalism" was about. It was the first newspaper that pronounced itself absolutely neutral, took quality reporting at face value, and made money on that.

While most of the newspapers tried to profit from politics, Vladimir Yakovlev embraced journalism as a business and profited on it, capturing an upscale business audience. This made it possible to raise the price of the newspaper and attract advertising for this and other projects of the *Kommersant* publishing house he founded. Interestingly enough, there were also foreign investments in the beginning, but not for long—they have been bought out.

The *Kommersant* publishing house shares first place in the print press advertising market with Independent Media. Aside from the publications mentioned above it has a car magazine, *Avtopilot*, and a woman's monthly, *Domovoy* (edited by the founder's wife), as well as other publications.

The last and, in a way, one of Yakovlev's most ambitious projects was *Stolitsa* magazine—a cultural weekly that folded. Its failure coincided with Yakovlev's early retirement from the publishing business at the time of the Russian financial crisis. He sold *Kommersant* to Boris Berezovsky.

Polson and Jordan's *Bolshoy Gorod* is believed to be a second attempt to complete *Stolitsa's* mission of issuing a widely read human interest publication. Boris Jordan's media holdings probably belong to this category rather than to that of foreign investment. Here we must add the rumor that Jordan acquired *Metro* daily, free from AFK Sistema group, which is linked to the Moscow city administration.

There are many independent players in the print press market that we should mention. Among them are some undisputable leaders: *Argumenty i Fakty*, *SPiD-Info*, *Moskovsky Komsomolets*, and *Sovershenno Sekretno*, to name just a few.

Argumenty i Fakty became extremely popular during the Gorbachev years. Along with only two other publications—*Moskovskie Novosti and Ogonyok*—*Argumenty i Fakty* became not only a champion of ideological dispute, but at the same time an extremely popular newspaper, with a circulation of 33 million in 1990. In 2000 the readership was only a tenth of that—around 3 million—like that of the Friday edition of *Komsomolskaya Pravda*, but still perhaps the most widely read newspaper in Russia.

The secret of success for this newspaper was a special "Q&A" section on the last page, where newspaper journalists frankly answered questions from readers. Originally, *Argumenty i Fakty (AiF)* was meant to be read by the political workers of the Communist Party. It was for them that this "Q&A" section was designed in the first place. Political instructors had to answer tough questions from their various audiences, so they had to have a place to turn to for the answers to their queries. Strict as it might have been at the beginning of the eighties, by the end of the nineties censorship was relaxed as a result of Gorbachev's efforts to begin dialogue and discussion within society. *AiF* was one of the first publications to react to the new openness, primarily by rediscovering the usefulness of their "Q&A" section and changing the criteria for choosing the letters for publication.

It was a fantastic breakthrough. "Q&A" cut the distance between the journalist and the reader by establishing a dialogue mode that positioned the journalists to see society through the eyes of the reader and always to keep in mind the reader's interests, whatever they might be. It sounds banal, but this was a new and refreshing development, one that would have been impossible within the Soviet political system. Even the "democratic" press at that time did not want to serve the reader, but 'fought to propagate democracy and reform and considered their ability to sway a mass political audience defining for the profession. *Argumenty i Fakty* was one of the few newspapers to avoid this trap and make some money too.

The newspaper expanded into a group of publications that are printed weekly and monthly, with circulations ranging from a few thousand to hundreds of thousands of copies: *AiF-Zdorovie* (Health), *AiF-Dochki-Materi* (Daughters and Mothers), *AiF-Ya-Molodoi* (I Am Young), among others. In thirty-five large cities *AiF* is published with local inserts. In summer 2000 the main *AiF* weekly was second in reach to only one newspaper, albeit a very special one: *SPID-Info* (AIDS Info).

Unlike *AiF*, *SPID-Info* (AIDS Info) never had anything to do with politics. It was a publication devoted exclusively to topics of sexual interest that were explored through a number of perspectives, ranging from popular science to actual stories of sexual liberation and discovery. Yet *SPID-Info* was no *Playboy*—although this newspaper was one of the first to be printed in color (after the "We" joint project of *Izvestia* and the Hearst group that barely lasted a year in 1990). *SPID-Info* dealt with sex mostly through text and tried to explain to the vast Russian audience the basics of sexuality. The popularity of this newspaper is easily explained: under the Soviet regime dissemination of information on this topic was almost completely prohibited.

There was no sex in the Soviet media, and this topic was considered inappropriate for public discussions. This led to a curious, now almost unimaginable situation: people probably spent more time having sex than talking or reading about it or watching it on TV (so perhaps it is not surprising that, since the collapse of the USSR, Russian population figures have continued to slide). Most of the texts on sexuality were circulated as computer printouts (made by dot matrix printers on long paper rolls). Sexual topics thus were confined to *samizdat*. One might argue that they reached a wider audience than other, perhaps more serious, works that were disseminated by the self-publishing industry.

The acronym "SPID" in the newspaper title in Russian means AIDS.

The newspaper used the feeling of urgency and fears raised by the AIDS epidemic to market itself to a wider audience than a sexual liberation monthly could reach. The journalists mastered the art of covering risqué topics without shocking their readership. Just like *AiF*, *SPID-Info* used the success of their newspaper to launch satellite publications. The *SPID-Info* publishing house remains one of the most profitable media enterprises in the Russian media market and enjoys a wide and loyal audience.

There are many other small and medium-sized players in the print press market in Russia worth speaking about, but this is not the place for such a thorough review. Only one of them belongs to the major league of media groups capable of swaying public opinion. This group has grown out of the daily newspaper *Moskovsky Komsomolets*.

Moskovsky Komsomolets is the leading newspaper in Moscow. It is easy to dismiss it as a broadsheet tabloid, but there is certainly much more to this publication than a touch of yellow journalism. In Moscow there are many tabloids, yet none of them has a share of the audience that *Moskovsky Komsomolets* has. The newspaper prints a million copies daily. It is sold at every subway station at dusk and dawn, getting a lion's share of both the morning and the evening newspaper market. This makes it a unique political force by itself. This is the only newspaper in Russia with the political clout of a TV channel. It can decide the fate of almost any electoral campaign in the city of Moscow. Its leading journalists are paid as much as TV anchors.

The secret of its success lies in the unique eclectic formula that *MK* has developed over time. On the front page there is always a scandalous or critical article above the fold, and a huge block of breaking news below. These brief stories probably are the most popular of those read in the city. Most of them deal with killings, robberies, fires, and accidents of all kinds. The rest of the paper offers a collection of thematic pages, ranging from music to literature to women's interests to every other topic imaginable.

Pavel Gusev, the editor in chief and major shareholder in the newspaper, used the elections of 1999–2000 to enlarge his sphere of influence. In return for his political support he received the investment needed to launch regional editions of the newspaper. Some of them became profitable almost instantly, others did not. Yet the influence of *MK* has spread far beyond the capital of the Russian Federation to compete with local publications for advertisers' budgets.

Conclusion

Every new medium that is powerful enough to shape our lives provokes a great deal of disturbance while its popularity is spreading. For Russia in the nineties, television was such a medium.

While under strict control during Soviet times, television could not really develop. It was always confined by the boundaries of the Soviet style and thus reflected all that style's contradictions. Television was strictly censored, like every other medium, and that meant no "live broadcasting." Consumer goods were in short supply, and one had to devise intrigues to get hold of them; hence no advertising. Under the Soviet regime, if there was any juggling with dreams, it was usually by means of clumsy political advertisements.

Many Soviet citizens had never discovered what the TV set was for until the VCR arrived, becoming the new status symbol and bringing with it the Hollywood movies. The USSR was ready to withstand any attack—it had enough nuclear weapons to destroy the planet many times over—but it was not ready for the individualism and consumer mentality that the movie world propelled deep into the Russian soul.

If the democratic press was partly responsible for the rise of Boris Yeltsin, television carries full responsibility for the collapse of the Soviet system. It was the weapon that Gorbachev discovered first, but the one he also never learned how to handle. Live broadcasts of political events during the late eighties and early nineties were designed to become the new source of legitimacy for the reformed USSR, but instead put it in doubt. The nineties thus were a time when television was dangerous, when its potential was discovered, used, and abused to the full. Only on the verge of the new millennium did it fall under the control of something much more powerful, more serious, and more organic to the human being: the ritual.

The blasts of 1999, the Russian analogue of the events of September 11, 2001, started the process of the almost instant reconstruction of the Russian mentality. The war in Chechnya has become one of the instruments in this reconstruction, a way to overcome an age-old weakness in the full-scale onslaught performed as a ritual chase for suspects no one could name.

It looked as if a tide had only been waiting for a sign to open up the deeper levels of collective identity and mentality. The power of the medium to impose meanings was dwarfed and weakened, and TV gradually came under government control. But that does not make a difference anymore, and is only the final safeguard that seals the political system, as it is embodied in the president and the constitution, closed and secure.

Russia has begun to rediscover itself. The uncertainty of the nineties suddenly evolved into a new synthesis, where the old and the new had come to terms. I have tried to trace how it happened and to map some of the sources and reasons for this because I saw these changes happening and saw that the media were a part of them. This book became possible because, by accident and luck, I was able to link politics and the media, to see them intertwined. A "traditional" political history of Russia in the nineties would be incomplete if it did not include media issues and the rise and fall of Russia's first media magnates.

So would our vision on future society be incomplete if we ignore the rising role of the Internet—an alternative information system that is more like a *private* space that develops on its own to become the backbone of the social architecture of the next century. But this is another story.

Notes

Notes to Chapter 1

1. V. Sogrin, *Politicheskaya istoriya sovremennoy Rossii 1985–1994: ot Gorbacheva do Yeltsina* [The Political History of Modern Russia 1985–1994: From Gorbachev to Yeltsin] (Moscow: Progress-Akademia, 1994), p. 11.

2. R. Paasilinna, *Glasnost and Soviet Television: A Study of the Soviet Mass Media and Its Role in Society from 1985–1991* Research Report (Helsinki: YLE/TKMA [Finnish Broadcasting Company], 1995), pp. 148–150.

3. At one point, the audience for serials amounted to as much as 70 percent of Russia's population. See Terhi Rantanen, *The Global and the National: Media and Communications in Post-Communist Russia* (Lanham, MD: Rowman and Littlefield, 2002).

4. The best study of the negative effects of television is probably that by Neil Postman in his book *Amusing Ourselves to Death: Public Discourse in the Age of Show Business* (New York: Penguin Books, 1985).

5. Marshall McLuhan, *Understanding Media: The Extensions of Man* (New York: Signet/New American Library, 1964).

6. This hyper-centralizing function of radio, described so wonderfully by McLuhan, was discovered simultaneously in the USSR and in the Germany of Goebbels.

7. The behind-the-scenes story of how the Soviet press functioned is told best by Sergey Dovlatov in his series of novellas under the general title *Compromise*. See *Sobranie prozy v 3-kh tomakh* (St. Petersburg: Limbus Press, 1993).

8. A. Priepa, "Zadacha dnya: prodavlivat' i ne podstavlyat'sya," *Logos*, 2000, no. 1, p. 4.

9. Sogrin, *Politicheskaya istoriya sovremennoy Rossii*, pp. 68–69.

10. An example is worth noting here. In 1964 Yury Idashkin, the author of the article "Telephone Rights," which appeared in the magazine *Ogonyok* (no. 51, December 1989), was standing in for the chief editor, and was responsible for telephone contacts with government officials. Several times a woman telephoned from the Central Committee of the Communist Party and commented on the contents of the magazine. Idashkin was in a panic. Making inquiries among his colleagues, he tried to discover the woman's status. Only the editor, returning after his stay in the hospital, was brave enough to ask her which department she worked in. She turned out to be a clerk.

11. There are no reliable research findings to show exactly what the ratio of novice and professional journalists was during this period. Simple observations and deductions, however, are arguably enough. While journalists in the USSR had been a tight-knit clan, beginning in the late 1980s the mass media became a growth area that stood out against the general background of depression. Around the end of the decade, new publications created large numbers of jobs. Journalists were needed who could write about political and economic questions in a modern key, and the "professionals," accustomed to dealing in rigid clichés, were unsuited to this role. The result was that 90 percent of the staff of the new print media consisted of novices and of journalists who had earlier written for small publications on "safe" topics such as art and the theater. Some publications, such as those of the Kommersant publishing house, refused as a matter of principle to work with journalists of the old school, preferring to train their staffs independently.

12. Elena Androunas, *Soviet Media in Transition: Structural and Economic Alternatives* (Westport, CT: Praeger, 1993), p. 62.

13. *Izvestia*, February 26, 1992, as cited in Androunas, *Soviet Media in Transition*, p. 63.

14. Androunas, *Soviet Media in Transition*, pp. 63, 64.

15. Ibid., p. 65.

16. Brian McNair, "Media in Post-Soviet Russia: An Overview," *European Journal of Communications*, 1994, vol. 9.

17. Androunas, *Soviet Media in Transition*, pp. 15–16.

18. Sogrin, *Politicheskaya istoriya sovremennoy Rossii*, pp. 157–158.

19. "Parlamentskie vybory v Rossii" (paper presented at the European Institute of Mass Media), *Mezhdunarodnaya Zhizn*, 1994, no. 2.

20. This term is employed here in the sense with which it is used by Murray Edelman in his book *Constructing the Political Spectacle* (Chicago: University of Chicago Press, 1988).

Notes to Chapter 2

1. Denis McQuail, *Mass Communication Theory: An Introduction*, 2d ed. (London: Sage, 1987), p. 12.

2. L.V. Sharonchikova, *Pechat' Frantsii: 80–90ie gg.* (Moscow: Moscow State University Department of Journalism, 1995), p. 50.

3. Ibid.

4. Ibid., p. 53.

5. S.I. Beglov, *Britanskaya pechat' na iskhode veka* (Moscow: Moscow State University Press, 1995), p. 30.

6. Ibid., pp. 31–32.

7. A. Politkovskaya, "Vitaliy Tretyakov prinyal mery. A 'Nezavisimoy Gazety' po-prezhnemu net," *Obshchaya Gazeta*, August 14, 1995.

8. The next project in which Gagua took part was the weekly journal *Ponedel'nik*, founded by Andrew Polson. At first the chief editor was the journalist Stepan Kiselev, but Gagua later replaced him in this post. However, the magazine flopped under Gagua's editorship, and he went to work as one of the editors at Radio Liberty.

9. V. Tretyakov, "Pis'mo ne B.N. Yeltsinu," *Nezavisimaya Gazeta*, April 23, 1997.

Notes to Chapter 3

1. Following is an excerpt from the memoirs of Aleksandr Korzhakov, former head of the Russian Presidential Security Service. The excerpt describes one of the attempts made to remove Oleg Poptsov during the Chechen campaign. It is reproduced here in its entirety, because it is thoroughly typical not just of relations between the press and the government in the early 1990s, but also of the first president of Russia (the electronic version of Korzhakov's book has been used; hence the lack of page references):

> The second, state-owned television channel, RTR, condemned the president in unacceptably vulgar terms for waging military actions in Chechnya. Yeltsin was indignant at all this "negativism," as he described it. There seemed to be only one solution: to sack the head of the television company, Oleg Poptsov. Everyone, however, was afraid of condemnation in the press, since Poptsov had the reputation of being a democrat; moreover, he had founded the second channel.
>
> The chief entrusted the Presidential Security Service with preparing the dismissal order, so that if a big scandal blew up all the blame could be heaped on the "presumptuous" Korzhakov. Incidentally, when a second attempt was made to sack Poptsov, Yeltsin gave the job of preparing the decree to Oleg Soskovets. I understood how delicate the situation was and had readied myself to cope with obstruction from journalists, but just in case I asked that two drafts of the order be prepared. The texts differed from one another in only one phrase; in the first of them Sergey Nosovets was appointed acting head of the channel, while in the second he was named immediately as head of the television company. . . . I took both drafts of the order to Boris Nikolaevich at his dacha in Barvikha, where he was suffering from influenza and depression. Yeltsin read through the papers carefully.
>
> "OK," the president said, "but I need to know what Viktor Stepanovich thinks."
>
> "All right. I'll go and see him now."
>
> I showed the documents to [Prime Minister] Viktor Stepanovich [Chernomyrdin]. Apart from Nosovets, it turned out, the president had no other candidates for the position of head of RTR. Viktor Stepanovich read through both decrees very carefully, and said:
>
> "I'm very well acquainted with Nosovets. Let's appoint him immediately; there's no sense dragging things out with an acting head."
>
> And without hesitation he endorsed the decree appointing Nosovets head of the second channel. I wanted to leave immediately, but Chernomyrdin would not let me go. He invited me to sit down at the table. We sat for a little while and reminisced about my brother. Then I went back to the president.
>
> On the way I had an idea. The Security Council was to meet the next morning. Would it perhaps be worthwhile for the president to discuss his decree on personnel changes in the television industry with the council?
>
> I showed the premier's endorsement to the chief, and suggested that he report to the Security Council on the appointment. Yeltsin agreed immediately: "Yes, that'll be right. . . ."

"I've decided to make another personnel change," Boris Nikolaevich reported to the Security Council. "I've signed a decree to remove Poptsov. I'm appointing Nosovets in his place."

The views of the council members were unexpectedly divided. Rybkin and Shakhrai spoke against the move. Shumeiko made no secret of his astonishment. A discussion began, and proved critical of the decree. Boris Nikolaevich, however, stopped the debate.

"Let's ask Viktor Stepanovich what he thinks."

Caught unawares, Chernomyrdin blurted out: "What's it got to do with me, Boris Nikolaevich? Korzhakov turned up, shoved the decree in front of me, and said, 'here, sign it.' I thought everything was decided, everything had been agreed, that's why I signed it."

The president summed up:

"Well, since everyone's against, we won't remove Poptsov. . . ."

2. R.P. Ovsepyan, *Istoriya noveyshey otechestvennoy zhurnalistiki: perekhodnyy period (seredina 80-kh–90-ie gody)* [The History of the New National Journalism: Transition Period (the Mid-80s to the 90s)] (Moscow: Moscow State University, 1996, pp. 100–101.

3. A.A. Grabelnikov, *Sredstva massovoy informatsii postsovetskoy Rossii* (Mass Media in Post-Soviet Russia) (Moscow: Russian University Druzhby Narodov, 1996), pp. 67–69.

4. Ibid.

5. This was the name of the news program on Poptsov's channel RTR.

6. Grabelnikov evidently has in mind not only demonstrations in support of Chechnya, but also antiwar demonstrations. There is no doubt that for him these were one and the same.

7. Grabelnikov, *Sredstva massovoy informatsii*, pp. 67–69.

8. Ibid.

9. Ibid., p. 56.

10. Ibid. p. 69.

11. Ibid., pp. 72–73.

12. As Aleksandr Korzhakov testifies, the version for the press was thought up on the run and was totally incredible:

"What are we going to do? How are we going to explain what happened?"

"Boris Nikolaevich, say you were very tired. The flight was difficult, and you were jet-lagged. You fell sound asleep, and your bodyguards wouldn't allow you to be woken up. They brazenly declared that the president's rest was more important than diplomatic protocols. And that you'll be sure to punish us for our insolence."

He agreed and repeated all this before the journalists. In Moscow, after he had slept, the president's appearance was more or less fresh, and the journalists had not the slightest idea of the nightmare we had in fact gone through.

From the airport, Boris Nikolaevich was taken straight to the hospital. Naturally, he did not punish anyone. The press made a certain amount of noise, kicked up a din for a while, but then as always calmed down.

13. A. Tsipko, "Prezidentskie vybory v Rossii nado otmenit'. Potomu chto 'vsenarodno izbrannyy'—ne panatseya, a beda" [The Presidential Elections in Russia Must Be Canceled. Because the "Popular Election" Is Not a Panacea, but a Calamity], *Nezavisimaya Gazeta*, February 20, 1996.

14. According to the newspaper *Moskovskie Novosti* (July 16, 1996), the Foundation for Effective Politics was established in the summer of 1995. In the autumn of 1995, it ran the election campaign of the Congress of Russian Communities. In January 1996, it worked out a strategy in the area of information techniques for Boris Yeltsin's election campaign. The leaders and co-owners of the foundation are Andrey Vinogradov (former general director of RIA-Novosti and of the *Ogonyok* publishing house) and Gleb Pavlovsky (former general director of the news agency Postfaktum, consultant to the *Ogonyok* publishing house, and chief editor of the journals *Vek XX i mir* and *Pushkin*). In recent times Pavlovsky has issued several electronic publications, including *Russky Zhurnal*, www.russ.ru.

15. "Prezident v 1996 godu: stsenariy i tekhnologii pobedy," *Doklad Fonda effektivnoy politiki* [Foundation for Effective Politics], March 1996.

16. Ibid.

17. Manuel Castells, *The Rise of the Network Society* (vol. 1 of *The Information Age*), (Oxford: Blackwell, 1996), pp. 330–333.

18. Neil Postman, *Amusing Ourselves to Death: Public Discourse in the Age of Show Business* (New York: Penguin Books, 1985), p. 87. Cited in Castells, *The Rise of the Network Society*, pp. 330–333.

19. Castells, *The Rise of the Network Society*, pp. 332–333.

20. Michael Kramer, "Rescuing Boris: The Secret Story of How Four U.S. Advisers Used Polls, Focus Groups, Negative Ads and All The Other Techniques of American Campaigning to Help Boris Yeltsin Win," *Time International*, July 15, 1996.

21. Ibid.

22. Ibid.

23. Ibid.

24. V. Toporov, "Virtual'naya real'nost' vyborov," *Svobodnaya Mysl,* 1996 no. 11, pp. 24–30.

25. L. Ionin, "Tekhnologii uspekha. Bez politicheskikh analitikov i konsul'tantov vybory v Rossii teper' ne vyigrat'." *Nezavisimaya Gazeta*, July 5, 1996, no. 121.

26. Murray Edelman, *Constructing the Political Spectacle* (Chicago: University of Chicago Press, 1988), p. 39.

27. The theme of writers in Russia as "secular saints" is analyzed in more detail in "The Writer as Secular Saint" by David M. Bethea, in "Literature," in *The Cambridge Companion to Modern Russian Culture*, ed. Nicholas Rzhevsky (Cambridge: Cambridge University Press, 1998), pp. 167–168; or, with reference to the 1990s, by Frank Ellis, *From Glasnost to Internet: Russia's New Infosphere* (Hampshire: Macmillan Press, 1999), p. 130; and, with reference to the Soviet era, in another book by Frank Ellis, *Vasiliy Grossman: The Genesis and Evolution of a Russian Heretic* (Oxford: Berg, 1994).

28. This theme is taken up in more detail in a dissertation by Yelena Kozina, Journalism Department, Moscow State University, "Sredstva massovoy informatsii i vybory: mifotvorchestvo kak element informatsionno-propagandistskikh kampaniy," 2000.

29. This term is used to denote the smearing of an opponent with accusations whether proven or groundless, compromising their reputations.

30. Yevgeny Krasnikov, "Strategi informatsionnoy voyny." *Moskovskie Novosti*, July 16, 1996.

31. To dot all the "i"'s, it should be noted that after an extraordinary scandal in the press, the "cardboard box affair" was dragged out, and on January 1, 1997, was granted an amnesty. This was in connection with the approval of the new Criminal Code, which lacked an article on machinations with hard currency.

32. It is typical that General Korzhakov took his revenge on Yevgeny Kiselev in the traditional style of the *kompromat* wars. In his chapter "Kiselev's 'Dreadful Secret,'" Korzhakov not only unmasks Kiselev as a KGB agent, he also describes in detajl how he (that is, Korzhakov) blackmailed the journalist and how, thanks to Chubais, Kiselev managed to suppress the story, obtaining a denial of this information from the Federal Security Service.

33. A full reconstruction of the strategies of the Berezovsky-Gusinsky campaign and of the government-Potanin countercampaign, including a list of all the publications and television programs, is provided in the Russian first edition of the present study: *Mass-media vtoroy respubliki* (Moscow: Moscow State University Press, 1999).

34. A. Soldatov, "Konverty vskryvali tselyy chas," *Segodnya*, July 26, 1997.

35. Ye. Trofimova, "Vyydet li zavtra v efir ORT? Pervyy kanal riskuet razdelit' uchast' 'Izvestiy' i 'Komsomolki,'" *Segodnya*, July 28, 1997.

36. Yelena Stepanova, "'Vremya' vtorglos' v prostranstvo 'ONEKSIMa,'" *Segodnya*, July 29, 1997. S. Mulin, "Programma 'Vremya' otkryto atakovala Vladimira Potanina," *Nezavisimaya Gazeta*, July 29, 1997.

37. "Boris Nemtsov: khvatit stroit' 'banditskiy kapitalizm,'" *Komsomolskaya Pravda*, 29 July 1997.

38. Yu. Latynina, "Metsenat prevratilsya v svyazista," *Izvestia*, July 30, 1997. "Nemtsov szhigaet mosty," *Komsomolskaya Pravda*, July 30, 1997. N. Yefimovich, "Bitva za 'Svyaz'invest': komu-voyna, komu-mat' rodna," ibid. "Vosem' naivnykh voprosov o skandale vokrug 'Svyaz'investa,'" ibid. The latter article contained a detailed explanation of the reasons for the scandal, plus an explanation by the press service of OneksimBank of how the bank would assist the development of the Svyazinvest holding company.

39. N. Gotova, "Invest ili intsest?" *Moskovsky Komsomolets*, July 30, 1997.

40. "Berezovskiy produmival, kak ubit' Gusinskogo, Kobzona i Luzhkova," *Komsomolskaya Pravda*, 8 August 1997.

41. The reference is to the incident mentioned earlier in which $500,000 was carried out of the main government office building in a photocopier-cardboard box.

42. The issue contained the following articles: A. Kolesnikov, "Svintsovye voyny"; M. Koldobskaya, "My staraemsya ostavat'sya nebogatymi, no gordymi ptichkami. Interv'yu s Nikolaem Svanidze"; V. Novodvorskaya, "U nas v Tekhase"; R. Boretsky, "Chto vmesto Agitpropa"; "Redaktsionnaya PR vo vremya chumy," *Novoe Vremya*, October 26, 1997, no. 42/97.

43. Novodvorskaya, "U nas v Tekhase."

44. I. Budakov, "Zhurnalistskoe presledovanie"; N. Gevorkyan, "Kak Minkin obezglavil Minfin"; A. Sergeev, "Upal, no otzhalsya"; Anonymous: "Vse delo v kampanii"; "Pust' budet stydno tomu, kto plokho ob etom podumaet"; "David Hoffman: tol'ko obshchestvo reshit, chitat' li zhurnalista"; "Yuriy Rost: imya-bol'she, chem uspekh," *Kommersant-Vlast*, November 25, 1997, no. 43 (249).

45. Ibid.

46. Ibid.

47. M. Sokolov, "Televizionnye stekol'shchiki," *Russky Telegraf*, May 21, 1998.

48. D. Dondurey, "Narod ugovorili ne vstavat' s kolen. Informatsionnaya voyna-preddverie grazhdanskoy," *Izvestia*, August 5, 1998.

49. The quotation here is from a speech at the Sixth World Congress of the ICCEES [International Council for Central and East European Studies] in Tampere, Finland, August 2000.

50. G. Vinokurov, "V okopakh informatsionnoy voyny," *Russky Zhurnal*, April 10, 1998. The article can be accessed in the journal's archive at www.russ.ru.

51. Ibid.

52. Ibid.

53. "'Upravlyaemye krizisy' kak neupravlyaemoe oruzhie." Unpublished report of the Foundation for Effective Politics, from around May 1998.

54. G. Pavlovsky, "Voyna elit chuzhimi rukami. Ona konchaetsya myatezhom naemnikov," *Nezavisimaya Gazeta*, 5 December 1997.

55. "Otvetsvennost' sredstv massovoy informatsii," *Nezavisimaya Gazeta*, June 14, 1997.

56. Kh. Main, *Sredstva massovoy informatsii v Federativnoy Respublike Germanii* (Colloquium, 1995), p. 155.

57. This report was prepared in response to a private commission and until now has not been published. Along with other unpublished reports, it was given to the author by Gleb Pavlovsky on July 7, 1998.

58. Ibid.

59. Ibid.

60. Ibid.

61. "Global Media Culture," in Denis McQuail, *Mass Communication Theory*, 3d ed. (London: Sage, 1994), p. 89.

62. Castells, *The Rise of the Network Society*, p. 330.

63. Elena Androunas, *Soviet Media in Transition: Structural and Economic Alternatives* (Westport, CT: Praeger, 1993).

64. Ibid., p. 32.

65. Ibid., p. 114.

66. Ye.L. Vartanova, *Severnaya model' v kontse stoletiya. Pechat', TV i radio stran Severnoy Evropy mezhdu gosudarstvennym i rynochnym regulirovaniem* (Moscow: Moscow State University, 1998), p. 71.

67. It is possible that other scholars would expand the concept of "power" and, as a result, would arrive at a curious conception of the media-political system as the whole totality of communication whose goal is the shaping of public opinion in line with these or other questions (including mass culture). In the present work, however, the media-political system is understood differently.

68. This formula was employed by Uvarov for the first time when he joined with the minister of education in a report on Moscow State University in the winter of 1832–33. It appeared in print for the first time after Uvarov was appointed education minister, taking the form of a directive by the minister in the *Journal of the Ministry of Popular Enlightenment*, 1834, vol. 1, pp. xlix–l.

69. It is not surprising that in an on-air survey only 57 percent of the station's listeners considered that it broadcast news, and 43 percent, propaganda. The survey was conducted on February 11, 1998, during the program "Ricochet," and more than 2,400 people took part.

Notes to Chapter 4

1. A former banker in Nizhny Novgorod, Sergey Kirienko was no. 1 on the electoral slate of the Union of Right Forces, but his brief tenure as politician ended abruptly when he was assigned to govern one of the seven federal districts (in the Volga region) after Putin's administrative reform, thus leaving the party leadership open for Nemtsov.

2. Boris Kagarlitsky, *Restavratsiya v Rossii* (Moscow: Editorial URSS, 2000), p. 305.

3. Ibid., p. 304.

4. Source: Finmarket poll at www.infoart.ru/misc/news/99/05/13_176.html.

5. Source: VCIOM (All-Russia Center for the Study of Public Opinion) of July 1999 at www.polit.ru/documents/106951.html.

6. Kagarlitsky, *Restavratsiya v Rossii*, p. 326.

7. While trying to repair the damage done by his case and clear his name, Borodin decided to run for the post of Moscow mayor against Luzhkov. Although the case against him was dropped in Russia, he was arrested in 2001 in the United States, while on his way to the inauguration of the new American president, on charges issued by Swiss prosecutors.

8. Kagarlitsky, *Restavratsiya v Rossii*, pp. 323–324.

9. Ibid., pp. 322–332.

10. Source: VCIOM poll, published at www.polit.ru 27.08.1999, entitled: "The majority of Russians support increasing salary to the military and want Chechen rebels destroyed in Dagestan and Chechnya."

11. *Itogi* magazine, August 15, 2000.

12. Kagarlitsky, *Restavratsiya v Rossii*, p. 328.

13. Murray Edelman, *Constructing the Political Spectacle* (Chicago: University of Chicago Press, 1988), pp. 78–80.

14. Ibid., p. 64.

15. Laura Belin, "The Media and the Elections of 1999 and 2000 in Russia." Paper presented at the ICCEES conference, Tampere, Finland, August 2000.

16. These paragraphs are based on an interview with Lyudmila Resnyanskaya in August 2000.

17. National Institute for Social Psychology Research, Internews, Russian Public Relations Group, *Russian Mass Media: Audience and Advertising* (Moscow, 2000), p. 26.

18. Mircea Eliade, *The Myth of the Eternal Return: Or, Cosmos and History*, trans. Willard R. Trask (New York: Pantheon, 1954), p. 126.

19. Ibid., pp. 87–88.

20. Ibid., p. 125.

21. The importance of these cultural icons can be judged by the fact that one of the most popular Russian writers of the nineties, Victor Pelevin kicked off his career with a book on Russian civil war hero Chapayev, making him a mystic and making his Watson-style assistant Petka a poet in search of enlightenment. Entitled *Buddha's Little Finger* in English, it is a splendid book indeed. The Russian title was *Petka and the Void.*

22. The popular magazine *Vlast* put both Putin and von Stirlitz on the cover a

week before the elections with the cover story headline "Von Stirlitz: Our President," *Kommersant-Vlast*, March 14, 2000.

23. Elmar Gusseinov (Paris), Boris Lysenko (Berlin), "Unknown Putin," *Izvestia*, January 10, 2000.

24. Murray Edelman, *From Art to Politics: How Artistic Creations Shape Political Conceptions* (Chicago: University of Chicago Press, 1995), pp. 73–90.

25. Another cult figure of Soviet mass culture—a hard-line detective, who went after the gangs in postwar Moscow.

26. Zhukov was a legendary marshal in the Soviet army in World War II.

27. Yekaterina Smirnova, "Shtirlits—nash prezident," *Kommersant-Vlast*, March 14, 2000.

28. Ibid.

29. Edelman, *Constructing the Political Spectacle*, p. 76.

30. Under the Russian media law a warning cancels automatic extension of the frequency leaser, and it is put up for a bid. Although current owners are not barred from participating, and in fact both ORT and TVC kept their licenses, it is important to note how fragile the position of TV broadcasters under the existing legislation is.

31. Elisabeth Noelle-Neumann, *Offentliche Meinung: Die Entdeckung der Schweigespirale* [Public Opinion: Discovering the Spiral of Silence] (Berlin: Ullstein, 1989).

32. Kagarlitsky, *Restavratsiya Rossii*, p. 335. The author cites *Nezavisimaya Gazeta*, November 10, 1999, and *Izvestia*, November 13, 1999.

33. Irina Borogan and Evgeny Krutikov, "Mera prisecheniya," *Izvestia*, June 15, 2000.

34. National Institute for Social Psychology Research, Internews, Russian Public Relations Group, *Russian Mass Media: Audience and Advertising* (Moscow, 2000), p. 16.

35. Dmitry Konovalenko, "Regional'nye sredstva massovoy informatsii kak instrument politicheskoy propagandy na mestnom urovne [Regional Media as an Instrument of Propaganda], in ibid., pp. 9–10.

36. Ivan Rodin, "Kremlyu nuzhny nastoyashchie partii," *Nezavisimaya Gazeta*, August 8, 2000.

37. Jonathan Steele, "Fury over Putin's Secrets and Lies. Russian President Badly Damaged by Series of Blunders over Sunken *Kursk* Submarine," *Guardian*, August 22, 2000.

38. "Inostrannye spasateli ostalis' krayne nedovol'ny organizatsiey rabot v Barentsevom more. Norvezhtsy govoryat, chto ikh postoyanno dezinformirovali [Foreign Rescue Teams Are Upset About the Way Operation Was Organized. Norwegians Say They Were Misled)," Polit.ru, www.polit.ru/documents/301138.html.

39. Karen Gazaryan, "Politicheskoe Vaterloo Putina" [Putin's Political Waterloo], *Utro.ru*, August 24, 2000.

40. Anton Nosik, "Bez prava na pokayanie" [No Right to Do Penance], *Postfactum.ru*, August 24, 2000.

41. Aleksey Kara-Murza, "Putin ne sposoben zhit' chuvstvami svoyego naroda," *Postfactum. ru*, August 21, 2000.

42. Andrey Kolesnikov, "Kak Putin vzyal Vidyaevo," *Kommersant*, August 22, 2000.

43. Ibid.

44. Sergey Kuznetsov, "Minuta nemolchaniya" [A Minute of Nonsilence], vesti. ru, August 26, 2000.

45. Edelman, *From Art to Politics*, p. 104.

46. For more irony, see Vadim Rudnev, *Proch' ot real'nosti* [Away from Reality] (Moscow: Agraf, 2000), pp. 264–270.

Notes to Chapter 5

1. R. Apdzhon and Kh. Raffin. *Internet dlya zhurnalista.* Research Study, Center for International Civil Society (E. Karkenale, translator) (Moscow, 1995) www.internews.ru/books/Internet.

2. *Internet*, no. 1, 1997.

3. A. Malyukov, "Istoriya russkogo interneta," *Zhurnal.ru*, 1998, no. 7, www.zhurnal.ru/7/malukoff.html.

4. The reason behind this was the passing of the "Communication Decency Act" by the U.S. Congress, the introduction of censorship on the Internet.

5. zhurnal.ru/staff/gorny/translat/deklare.html (Evgeny Gorky, translator).

6. www.lib.ru.

7. In August 2000, information about new admission to seventeen electronic libraries appeared at russ.ru/krug/biblio/.

8. Maksim Moshkov, "Shto vyi vsyo o kopirayte. Luchshe byi knizhku pochitali," *Kompyutera* www.lib.ru/COPYRIGHT/computera.txt.

9. www.litera.ru.

10. www.rema.ru.

11. Maksim Moshkov, www.lib.ru/COPYRIGHT/computera.txt.

12. www.metro.ru.

13. madli.ut.ee/~roman_l/hyperfiction.

14. www.guelman.ru/slava.

15. www.vesti.ru/frei.

16. www.litera.ru/slova.

17. www.russ.ru/ssylka. The Russian word "ssylka" means both "exile" and "link." Leybov lives in Tartu, Estonia, where he teaches twentieth-century Russian Literature at the university.

18. www.russ.ru/netcult. Before 2000, this column was led by Yevgeny Gorny, the founder of *zhurnal.ru.*

19. www.cityline.ru.

20. www.russ.ru/netcult/nasnet. Again, a play on words. "NasNet," "We do not exist," can also be interpreted as "Us-Net." The name for this project was selected from suggestions by readers.

21. www.teleportacia.org/war.

22. namniyas.blade.ru/enemy.asp. See also: velikanov.artinfo.ru. Formally the works are signed by Namniyas Ashuratova, Andrey Velikanov's alter-ego. On one of the festivals the artist was accused of manipulating the jury by trying to pass as a member of some kind of ethnic minority.

23. www.cityline.ru/vi/kogot.

24. None other than Aleksey Yatskovsky whose article was published consistently on the mirror side "Kogda," confirms that he successfully tracked down the

organizer of the provocation. In his words, it appeared to be the security administration of the National Reserve Bank.

25. www.ovg.ru/.

26. www.elections99.ru.

27. Raskin's speech to the Russian Panel at the IAMCR 2000 Conference in Singapore is quoted here.

28. www.compromat.ru.

29. www.flb.ru.

30. www.russ.ru.

31. Among the original FEP politician sites are nemtsov.ru and kirienko.ru—made for Boris Nemtsov and Sergey Kirienko, respectively.

32. Yury Granovsky and Pavel Nefedov, "Khvatit portalov!" *Vedomosti*, August 1, 2000.

33. www.talk.ru/forum/talk.ru.poputka.

34. Aside from getting to where you want to go this forum also attracts visitors with opportunities of getting to know someone, maybe even "someone special," as they say in the personal ads. Here this feature is camouflaged yet stands out clearly every time the sex of any given person is defined. Clearly, the most exciting thing about the web is its ability to connect people under all kinds of pretexts including this one.

35. www.rambler.ru.

36. top100.ru.

37 www.ozon.ru.

38. www.yandex.ru.

39. www.km.ru.

40. www.anekdot.ru.

41. *Vedomosti*, August 1, 2000.

42. www.utro.ru.

43. In August 2000, Libertarium called upon the citizens of Russia to take the case of SORM-2 to the Supreme Court of the Russian Federation as a breach of procedure that demanded a court decision or similar action to begin wiretapping.

44. For instance, at www.360.ru.

45. The roundtable took place within the "Pro@Contra" International Conference, organized by the Moscow ArtMediaLab.

46. *Monitoring.ru* discovered that the biggest fans of the Internet were men aged thirty-one, mostly specialists with higher education (35 percent), students (27 percent), and businessmen (10 percent).

Notes to Chapter 6

1. D. Pinsker, "Posledny rezerv," *Itogi*, February 16, 1999.

2. National Institute for Social-Psychological Research, *Nezavisimaya Media-Izmereniya*, June 2000, p. 26.

3. www.vertov.ru.

4. *Sovershenno Sekretno*, 1998, no. 5.

5. "TV Anchor Pulled Off Air," *Moscow Times*, December 10, 1998.

6. G. Chiesa, *Proshchai, Rossiya!* (Moscow: Geya, 1998), quoted by Dorenko in an article in *Sovetskaya Rossiya*, September 28, 1995.

7. *Sredstva massovoy informatsii Rossii: auditoriya i reklama* (Moscow: Russian Public Relations Group).

8. *Znamenitye tsitaty iz zhizni rossiyskih mass-media: vybrasheny i zabyty*; www.osvod.org.

9. Ibid.

10. Ibid.

11. B. Compaine and D. Gomery, *Who Owns the Media? Competition and Concentration in the Mass Media Society* (Hillsdale, NJ: Lawrence Erlbaum Associates, 1993), pp. 47–70.

12. All else aside, this shows the distribution of shares of ORT in a new light: In any event, it became known, because SBS-Agro was headed by a consortium of the banks.

13. "Mass-Media" Bulletin of the National News Service, October 19–25, 1998.

14. T. Plotnikova, "'Media-Most' kupil evreyskuyu 'Vecherku.'" *Russky Telegraf*, May 6, 1998.

15. "Vladimir Gusinsky ovladel 'Vecherney Molitvoy,'" *Profil*, no. 20 (June 2, 1998), p. 92.

16. "Doklad o kriticheskom sostoyanii rossiyskikh sredstv massovoy informatsii" (Moscow: Union of Russian Journalists, September 1997), pp. 48–49.

17. "Mass-Media" Bulletin of the National News Service, October 25–29, 1998.

18. Informational-Analytical Bulletin, *Novosti SMI*, no. 1, January 18–31, 1999.

19. www.cmi.ru/2000/06/27/962111063.html.

20. Ibid.

21. "Doklad o kriticheskom sostoyanii rossiyskikh sredstv massovoy informatsii."

22. I. Shkarnikova and O. Likhina, "'Literaturnuyu gazetu' kupit kholding Luzhkova. A ego dolgi otrabotaet zhyoltaya pressa," *Kommersant-Daily*, April 7, 1998.

23. O. Pestereva, "Vsya Rossiya budet pechatat'sya u Luzhkova," *Kommersant-Daily*, August 6, 1998.

24. O. Pestereva, "Luzhkovsky media-kholding rastyot," *Kommersant-Daily*, August 12, 1998.

25. Ibid.

26. S. Agafonov, *Izvestia*, April 15, 1991.

27. V. Yakov, *Izvestia*, April 16, 1991.

28. Y. Latynina, *Izvestia,* April 17, 1991.

29. *Izvestia*, April 18, 1991.

30. *Izvestia*, April 17, 1991.

31. "Pis'mo prezidentu Rossii B.N. Yeltsin," *Nezavisimaya Gazeta* (April 22, 1997). Signed by: Yu. Belyavsky *(Kultura)*, V. Bogdanov (The Union of Russian Journalists), P. Gutyonov (Committee for the Protection of Free Speech and Rights of Journalists), L. Gushchin *(Ogonyok)*, A. Kolodny *(Vek)*, A. Lisin *(Vechernyaya Moskva)*, V. Loshak *(Moskovskie Novosti)*, S. Muladzhanov *(Moskovskaya Pravda)*, A. Potapov *(Trud)*, A. Pumpyanskii *(Novoe Vremya)*, V. Starkov *(Argumenty i Fakty)*, V. Tretyakov *(Nezavisimaya Gazeta)*, A. Udaltsov *(Literaturnaya Gazeta)*, Y. Yakovlev *(Obshchaya Gazeta)*, Y. Yakunin *(Ekonomika i Zhizn)*.

32. I would like to add, that there is not one mistake here, there are two. The fact is that Chernomyrdin *could* have earned this amount of money if he had not let a month pass after the cancellation of the trust agreement with Gazprom, in which 35

percent of the shares of the concern were bought up by leadership of the company at the reduced price. However, journalists of the paper did not do enough research and could not win the struggle against popular opinion.

33. The following era of reform of OneksimBank was a program of administrative functions of the industrial-finance group "Interros," which was founded on the same basis as the bank, and headed by Vladimir Potanin. As far as the current issue and the events leading up to the formation of the group, the former name of the organization is used.

34. Ivan Zassoursky, *Rekonstruktsiya Rossii* (Moscow: Moscow State University Press, 2001).

Bibliography

Books and Articles in Russian

Agafonov, S. *Izvestia*, April 15, 1991.

Albats, E. "O prave na vybor. Skandal vokrug 'Izvestiy' i 'Komsomolskoy Pravdy' na fone amerikanskogo opyta" [On Election Laws. The Scandal About *Izvestia* and *Komsomolskaya Pravda* in the Mirror of American Experience]. *Nezavisimaya Gazeta*, April 22, 1997.

Aldyon, R., and X. Raffin. *Internet dlya zhurnalista* [Internet for Journalists]. Research by the Center for International Civil Society. 1995. www.internews.ru/books/internet.

Androunas, Elena. *Informatsionnaya elita: korporatsii i rynok novostey* [The Information Elite: Corporations and the News Market]. Moscow State University, 1991.

Arsen'eva, M.Z. "Gazeta the Moscow Times v sisteme stolichnyj pressy" [The *Moscow Times* Newspaper in the Moscow Media System]. Conference thesis, Moscow State University, 1995.

Artyunova, V. "Mikhail Shvydkoy: Ni myi odni govorim pravdu." [Mikhail Shvydkoy: We Aren't the Only Ones Telling the Truth]. *Kommersant-Daily*, August 30, 1998.

Aspin, S. "Reklama v Internete: ataka s otkrytymi glazami" [Advertisement on the Internet: An Attack with Eyes Open]. *Internet*, no. 1 (1998), p. 6.

Barlou, D.P. "Deklaratsiya nezavisimosti kiberprostranstva" [A Declaration for an Independent Cyberspace]. *Zhurnal.ru*, no. 1 (1996). www.zhurnal.ru.

Batalov, A.R. "Referativnoe izlozheniya knigi Alvina Tofflera" [Summarized Exposition of Alvin Toffler's Book]. *Tretya Volna*, no. 8 (November 1982).

Beglov, S.I. *Britanskaya pechatav' na iskhode veka* [The British Press at the End of the Century]. Moscow: Moscow State University Press, 1995.

———. *Britanskaya pechat' na rubezhe tysyachiletij* [British Press at the End of the Millennium]. Griboyedova Institute of International Law and Economics, 1997.

Boretsky, R. "Chto vmesto Agitpropa" [What Replaces the State Propaganda Machine]. *Novoe vremya*, no. 42/97, October 26, 1997.

Budakov, I. "Zhurnalistskoe presledovanie" [Harassed by Journalists]. *Kommersant-Vlast*, no. 43 (249), November 25, 1997.

Charkin, A., and A. Germanovich. "Uzhe ne oligarkhi?" [Are They Not Oligarchs?]. *Vedomosti*, August 12, 2000.

Chiesa, G. *Proshchai, Rossiya!* [Farewell, Russia!]. Moscow: Geja, 1998.

Chyornikh, A. *Stanovlyenie Sovietskoy Rossii: 20-ie gody v zerkale sotsiologii* [The Formation of Soviet Russia: The 1920s in the Mirror of Sociology]. Moscow: Pamyatniki Istorichesky Mysly, 1998.

Dennis, A., and D. Merrill. *Besedy o mass-media* [Conversations About the Mass Media]. Moscow: Vagrius National Press Institute, 1998.

"Doklad o kriticheskom sostoyanii rossiyskikh sredstv massovoy informatsii" [Report on the Critical Condition of the Russian Mass Media]. Moscow: Union of Russian Journalists, September 1997.

Dondurey, D. "Narod ugovorili ne vstavat´ s kolen. Informatsionnaya voyna-predverie grazhdanskoy" [People Will Not Rise from Their Knees: Information as a Prelude to Civil War]. *Ivestia*, August 5, 1998.

"Dva v odnom kanale. ORT i NTV teper´ zavisyat ot VGTRK" [Two in One Channel. ORT and NTV Are Now Dependent on VGTRK]. *Kommersant*, May 12, 1998.

Dzodziev, V. *Problemy stanovlyeniya demokraticheskogo gosudarstva v Rossii* [Problems of the Formation of a Democratic Government in Russia]. Moscow: Ad Marginam, 1996.

Eliade, M. *Mif o Vechnom Vozvrashchenii* [The Myth of the Eternal Return]. St. Petersburg: Aleteiya, 1998.

Fedotov, M. *SMI v otsutstvii Ariadny. Entsiklopediya zhizni rossiyskoy zhurnalistiki* [The Mass Media in the Absence of Ariadne. An Encyclopedia of the Life of Russian Journalism]. Moscow: Union of Russian Journalists, Journalism Foundation of Russia, 1998.

Fomichyova, I. *Pressa na rynke informatsii: provintsial´nyi chitatel´ gazet v Rossii* [The Press in the Information Market: The Provincial Newspaper Reader in Russia]. Moscow, 1992.

Gevorkyan, N. "Kak Minkin obezglavil Minfin" [How Minkin Beheaded the Ministry of Finance]. *Kommersant-Vlast*, no. 43 (249), November 25, 1997.

Golovanova, G.A. *Sredstvo massovoy informatsii SShA* [The American Mass Media]. Moscow: Moscow State University, 1996.

Gordeev, A. "Gazeta *Extra M*: u izdaniya bez statey mnogo chitateley" [The Newspaper *Extra M*: The Paper Without Articles Has Many Readers]. *Kapital*, June 3–9, 1998.

Gouayzer, S., and A. Witt. *Putevoditel´ zhurnalista po oprosam obshchestvennogo mneniya* [The Journalists' Guidebook to Opinion Polls]. Moscow: Vagrius National Press Institute, 1997.

Grabelnikov, A.A. *Sredstva massovoy informatsii postsovestkoy Rossii* [Mass Media in Post-Soviet Russia]. Moscow: Russian University Druzhby Narodov, 1996.

Granovsky, Y., and P. Nefedov. "Khvatit portalov!" [Enough Portals!]. *Vedomosti*, August 1, 2000.

Gurevich, S.M. *Gazeta i rynok: kak dobit´sya uspekha?* [A Newspaper and a Market: How Can One Achieve Success?]. Moscow, 1994.

"Informatsionnoe obshchestvo: vyzov Evrope" [The Information Society: A Call to Europe]. Materials of the Fifth Congress of Ministers of the European Union on Politics in the Region of Mass Media, December 11–12, 1997.

Ionin, L. "Tekhnologii uspekha. Bez politicheskikh analitikov i konsul´tantov vybory v Rossii teper´ ne vyigrat'" [The Triumph of Technology. Elections in Russia

Can No Longer Be Won Without Political Analysts and Consultants]. *Nezavisimaya Gazeta*, no. 121, July 5, 1996.

Ivanov, V.F., and T.V. Ivanova. "Puti povysheniya populyarnosti izdaniy po itogam izucheniya funktsionirovaniya zapadnikh SMI. Zhurnalistika v 1995 godu" [The Road to Increasing the Popularity of a Publication. Results of the Study of the Functions of Western Mass Media. Journalism in 1995]. Thesis from a scientific conference, part 2.

Kachkaeva, A. "Rossiyskie imperii SMI" [The Russian Mass Media Empires]. *Zhurnalist*, no. 6 (June 1998).

Kagarlitsky, B. *Restavratsiya v Rossiy* [Restoration in Russia]. Moscow: Editorial URSS, 2000.

Kappyon, R. *Slovo, ili kak pravila' no pisat' dlya Assoshieyted Press* [The Word, or How to Write Correctly for the Associated Press]. Moscow: TASS.

Khabermas, Yu. *Demokratiya, razum, nravstvennost'. Moskovskie lektsii i interv'iu* [*Democracy, Reason, Morality. Moscow Lectures and Interviews*]. Moscow: Akademia, 1995.

Khachaturov, K. "Informatsionnyi monstr delu ne pomozhet. Uprazdnena vneshnepoliticheskaya propaganda kak funktsiya gosudarstva" [There Is Nothing to Be Done About the Information Monster. The Abolition of Outward Propaganda as a Function of the Government]. *Nezavisimaya Gazeta*, June 5, 1998.

Koldobskaya, M. Interview with Nikolay Svanidze. "My staraemsya ostavat'sya nebogatymi, no gordymi ptichkami" [We Try to Remain Not Wealthy, But Proud Birds]. *Novoye vremya*, no. 42/97, October 26, 1997.

Kolechnikov, A. "Kak Putin vzyal Vidyaevo" [How Putin Took Vidyaevo]. *Kommersant* [n.d.].

Kolesnikov, A. "Svintsovye voyny" [The Lead Wars]. *Novoe Vremya*, no. 42/97, October 26, 1997.

Konkov, V. "Dorenko ne ushli" [Dorenko Hasn't Left]. *Mir novostei*, no. 21, May 23, 1998.

Kornilov, E.A., and V.S. Dyadyushenko. "Stydno chitat' bul'varnuyu pressu?" [Is it Shameful to Read Tabloids?]. *Gorny vozdukh*, no. 1 (1996).

Korzhakov, A. *Boris Yeltsin: Ot rassveta do zakata* [Boris Yeltsin: Sunrise to Sunset]. Moscow: Interbook, 1997.

Krasnikov, Ye. "Strategi informatsionnoy voyny" [The Strategy of the Information War]. *Moskovskie novosti*, July 16, 1996.

Kryukova, A. "'Vremya' prishlo. Kseniya Ponomareva pokidaet ORT" ["Vremya" (the Time) Has Come. Kseniya Ponomareva Is Abandoning ORT]. *Nezavisimaya Gazeta*, September 5, 1998.

Latynina, Yu. *Izvestia*, April 17, 1991.

Main, Kh. *Sredstva massovoy informatsii v Federativnoy Respublike Germanii* [Mass Media in the Federal Republic of Germany]. Colloquium, 1995.

Malyukov, A. "Istoriya russkogo Interneta" [History of the Russian Internet]. *Zhurnal.ru*, no. 7 (1998), www.zhurnal.ru/7/malukoff.html.

Melyukhin, I.S. "Informatsionnoye obshchestvo: problemy stanovleniya i razvitiya (filisofskii analiz)" [The Information Society: Problems of Formation and Development (Philosophical Analysis)]. Doctoral dissertation, Moscow, 1997.

"Mass-Media." *Bulletin of the National News Service*, no. 16, February 4, 1996.

Metodologiya izucheniya regional'noi pechati [Methodology of the Study of Regional Press]. Moscow: Moscow State University, 1993.

Miryazeva, Ye. "Tekhnicheskii informatsionnyy kanal gotov prestupit' k veshchaniyu. Grandioznyy proekt Upravleniya delami prezidenta RF prestavlyaet soboy gibrid Interneta i sputnikovogo televideniya" [A Technical Information Channel Is Ready to Go on the Air. A Grand Project of the President's Administration Is a Hybrid of Satellite Television and the Internet]. *Nezavisimaya Gazeta*, May 14, 1998.

Mitchenkova, I.I. "Sud'ba rayonnikh gazet segodnya" [The Fate of Regional Newspapers Today].

Naryshkina, A. "Slukhi o konchine reklamnogo rynka neskol'ko preuvelicheny. No v sentyabre diagnoz budet utochnen" [Rumors of the End of the Advertising Market Are Somewhat Exaggerated. But in September the Diagnosis Will Be Confirmed]. *Segodnya*, September 4, 1998.

Noiman, N. *Obshchestvennoye mneniye: otkrytie spirali molchaniya* [Public Opinion: Discovering the Spiral of Silence]. Moscow: Progress-Akademia, 1996.

Nosik, A. www.SMI.com. *Internet*, no. 1 (1997).

Novodvorskaya, V. "U nas v Tekhase." *Novoe Vremya*, no. 42/97, October 26, 1997.

"Obzor rossiyskogo televideniya" [Survey of Russian Television]. Information Fund "Obshchestvennoe Mnenie." Research of the Union of Russian Journalists, 1997.

Osnovnyye ponyatiya teorii zhurnalistiki [The Basic Concept of the Theory of Journalism]. Moscow: Moscow State University, 1993.

"Otvetstvennost' sredstv massovoy informatsii" [The Responsibility of the Mass Media]. *Nezavisimaya Gazeta*, June 14, 1997.

Ovsepyan, R.P. *Istoriya noveyshey otechestvennoy zhurnalistiki: perekhodnyy period (seredina 80-kh–90-ie gody)* [The History of the New National Journalism: Transition Period (the Mid-80s to the 90s)]. Moscow: Moscow State University, 1996.

"Parlamentskie vybory v Rossii" [Parliamentary Elections in Russia]. Presentation of the European Institute of Mass Media. *Mezhdunarodnaya Zhizn*, no. 2 (1994).

Pavlovsky, G.O. "Voyna elit chuzhimi rukami. Ona konchaetsya myatezhom naemnikov" [Waging Wars with Mercenaries Leads to Their Rebellion]. *Nezavisimaya Gazeta*, December 5, 1997.

Pavlovsky, G.O. "Strakh 2000" [Fear 2000]. *Pushkin*, no. 4, June 16, 1998, p. 10.

Pechat' Rossiyskoy Federatsii v 1991 godu. Finansy i statstika [Press of the Russian Federation in 1991. Finances and Statistics]. Collection of Statistics. Moscow, 1992.

Pelekhova, Y., and A. Semenov. "Predvybornye kholdingi" [Preelection Holdings]. *Kommersant-Daily*, June 11, 1998.

Pelevin, V. *Pokolenie P* [Generation P]. Moscow: Vagrius, 1999.

Pestereva, O. "Vsya Rossiya budet pechatat'sya u Luzhkova" [All Russia Will Be Published by Luzhkov]. *Kommersant-Daily*, August 6, 1998.

Pinsker, D. "Posledniy rezerv" [Last Reserves]. *Itogi*, February 16, 1999.

"Pis'mo prezidentu Rossii B.N. Yeltsinu" [A Letter to Russian President B.N. Yeltsin]. *Nezavisimaya Gazeta*, April 22, 1997). Signed by: Yu. Belyavsky (*Kultura*), V. Bogdanov (Union of Russian Journalists), P. Gutyonov (Committee for the Protection of Free Speech and Rights of Journalists), L. Gushchin (*Ogonyok*), A. Kolodny (*Vek*), A. Lisin (*Vechernyaya Moskva*), V. Loshak (*Moskovskie Novosti*), S. Muladzhanov (*Moskovskaya Pravda*), A. Potapov (*Trud*), A. Pumpyansky (*Novoe Vremya*), V. Starkov (*Argumenty i Fakty*), V. Tretyakov (*Nezavisimaya*

Gazeta), A. Udaltsov (*Literaturnaya Gazeta*), Ye. Yakovlev (*Obshchaya Gazeta*), Yu. Yakunin (*Ekonomika i Zhizn*).

Plotnikova, T. "'Media-Most' kupil evreyskuyu 'Vecherku'" ["Media-Most" Has Bought the Jewish "Vecherku"]. *Russky Telegraf*, May 6, 1998).

Politovskaya, A. "Vitaly Tretyakov prinyal mery. A 'Nezavisimoy Gazety' po-prezhnemu net" [Vitaly Tretyakov Takes Measures. But No *Nezavisimaya Gazeta* Yet]. *Obshchaya Gazeta*, August 14, 1995.

Presledovanie zhurnalistov i pressy na territorii byvshego SSSR v 1994 godu [The Pursuit of Journalists and the Press in the Territory of the Former USSR in 1994]. Moscow: Foundation for the Protection of Glasnost, 1995.

"Prezident v 1996 godu: stsenarii i tekhnologii pobedy" [The President in 1996: The Scenarios and Technologies of Victory]. Presentation of the Foundation for Effective Politics, March 1996.

Prokhorov, Ye.P., and L.G. Svitich. *Vvedenie v zhurnalistiku: zhurnalistika v sotsialisticheskom obshchestve* [Introduction to Journalism: Journalism in a Socialist Society]. Moscow: Moscow State University, 1989.

Prozorov, I. "Predstavitel' 'LukOila' otkazyvaetsya ot roly tsenzora. Obladetel' kontrol'nogo paketa aktsiy *Izvestiy* khochet videt' vo glave gazety vykhodtsa iz tvorcheskogo kollektiva" [Lukoil Representative Rejects the Censor's Role. The Owner of the Controlling Stake in *Izvestia* Wants Someone from the Newspaper Staff to Run the Paper]. *Nezavisimaya Gazeta*, April 22, 97.

Rodin, I. "Kremlyu nuzhny nastoyashchie partii" [The Kremlin Needs Real Parties]. *Nezavisimaya Gazeta*, August 8. 2000.

"Rossiyskie SMI na starte predvybornoy kampanii" [The Russian Mass Media at the Beginning of the Preelection Campaign]. *Sreda*, no. 3 (1995).

Rudnev, V. *Proch' ot real'nosti* [Away from Reality]. Moscow: Agraf, 2000.

Rybak, S. "Rukovoditeli teleseti TNT idut no zhizni vmeste" [Leaders of the Telecommunication Company TNT Go About Their Lives Together]. *Kapital*, June 3–9, 1998).

Sergeev A. "Upal, no otzhalsya" [Fell Down But Was Pushed Up]. *Kommersant-Vlast*, no. 43 (249), November 25, 1997.

Sharonchikova, L.V. *Pechat' Frantsii (80–90ie gg.)* [The French Press (the 80s and 90s)]. Moscow: Moscow State University Department of Journalism, 1995.

Shkarnikova, I., and O. Likhina. "'Literaturnuyu gazetu' kupit kholding Luzhkova. A yeyo dolgi obrabotaet zhyoltaya pressa" [One of Luzhkov's Holdings Buys *Literaturnaya Gazeta*. And Its Debts Are Being Paid by the Tabloid Press]. *Kommersant-Daily*, April 7, 1998.

Shmitter, F.K., and T.L. Karl. "Chto takoe demokratiya?" [What Is Democracy?]. Translation from *Journal of Democracy*, vol. 2, no. 3 (Summer 1991), pp. 75–88. The Russian version can be found at www.russ.ru.

Sibert, F.S., U. Shramm, and T. Peterson. *Chetyre teorii pressy* [Four Theories about the Press]. Moscow: Vagrius National Press Institute, 1998.

Sigal, A. "Obzor rossiyskogo televideniya" [A Survey of Russian Television]. Prepared for the U.S. Agency of International Development by the Internews news agency, April 1997. www.internews.ras.ru/report/tvrus/tv_bib.html.

Smirnova, Ye. "Shtirlits—nash prezident" [Von Stirlitz—Our President]. *Kommersant-Vlast*, March 14, 2000.

Sogrin, V. *Politicheskaya istoriya sovremennoy Rossii 1985–1994: ot Gorbacheva do Yeltsina* [The Political History of Modern Russia 1985–1994: From Gorbachev to Yeltsin]. Moscow: Progress-Akademia, 1994.

Sokolov, M. "Televizionnye stekol'shchiki" [The Television Glaziers]. *Russky Telegraf*, May 21, 1998.

Sovremennaya sovetskaya zhurnalistika [Modern Soviet Journalism]. Moscow: Moscow State University, 1983.

"Taina diskety pogibshego zhurnalista" [The Mystery of a Dead Journalist's Diskette]. *Komsomolskaya Pravda*, November 26, 1997.

"Televidenie na mylo: media-imperii vstupili v bitvu za regional'nogo telezritelya" [Television on Soap: The Media Empires Battle for the Regional Audience]. *Ekspert*, no. 15, April 20, 1998.

Teshkina, P.Yu. "Tipologicheskaya klassifikatsiya politicheskoy pressy Rossii" [A Typological Classification of the Russian Political Press]. *Zhurnalistika v 1995 Godu*. Thesis from a research conference, part 3.

Theses from a research conference entitled "Journalism in 1996: the Mass Media in Post-Soviet Society," organized by the Department of Journalism and associated instructors and researchers of journalism. Moscow: Moscow State University, 1996.

Theses from a conference entitled "Journalism in a Period of Transition," conducted under the initiative of organizations with the participation of the Department of Journalism and UNESCO.

Theses from a student research conference at the Department of Journalism of Moscow State University, April 5, 1997.

Theses from speeches and recommendations made at a Gosdum hearing. Available at: 194.226.22.151/gd/NEWS.HTM#3>.

Tipologiya periodichskoy pechati [A Typology of Periodical Press]. Moscow: Moscow State University, 1995.

Toporov, V. "Virtual'naya real'nost' vyborov" [The Virtual Reality of Elections]. *Svobodnaya Mysl*, no 11 (1996).

Tretyakov, V. "Pis'mo ne B.N. Eltsinu" [A Letter Not to B.N. Yeltsin]. *Nezavisimaya Gazeta*, April 23, 1997.

Tsipko, A. "Prezidentskie vybory v Rossii nado otmenit'. Potomu chto 'vsenarodno izbrannyy—ne panatseya, a beda" [The Presidential Elections in Russia Must Be Canceled. Because the "Popular Election" Is Not a Panacea, but a Calamity]. *Nezavisimaya Gazeta*, February 20, 1996.

"U nas s Borisom ochen' khoroshie otnosheniya" [We Have a Very Good Relationship with Boris]. *Kommersant-Daily*, no. 188, October 31, 1997.

"U pervogo kanala zhenskoe litso" [Channel One Has a Feminine Face]. *Obshchaya Gazeta*, no. 42, October 23–29, 1997.

"'Upravlyaemye krizisy' kak neupravlyaemoe oruzhie" ["Crisis Management" as an Uncontrollable Weapon]. Moscow: Foundation for Effective Politics, unpublished, May 1998.

Urina, N.V. *Sredstva massovoy informatsii Italii* [The Italian Mass Media]. Moscow: Moscow State University Department of Journalism, 1996.

Vartanova, Ye.L. *Severnaya model' v kontse stoletiya. Pechat', TV i radio stran Severnoy Evropy mezhdu gosudarstvennym i rynochnym regulirovaniem* [The Northern Model at the End of the Century. Press, TV, and Radio of the Nations of

Northern Europe Amidst Governmental and Market Regulations]. Moscow: Moscow State University, 1998.

Vinokurov, G. "V okopakh informatsionnoy voyny" [In the Trenches of the Information War]. *Russky Zhurnal*, April 10, 1998. www.russ.ru.

Vishnevsky, A. *Serp i rubl'* [The Sickle and the Ruble]. Moscow: OGI, 1998.

"Vladimir Gusinsky ovladel 'Vecherney Molitvoy' [Vladmir Gusinsky Has Seized the *Evening Player*]. *Profil*, no. 20, June 2, 1998, p. 92.

Yakov, V. *Izvestia*, April 16, 1991.

Yavlinsky, G.Ya. *Ekonomika Rossii: nasledstvo i vozmozhnosti* [Russian Economics: Inheritance and Opportunities]. Moscow and Kharkov: EPI Center-Folio, 1995.

Zassoursky, I. *Stanovlenie rossiyskogo instituta SMI v kontekste global'nykh informatsionnykh protsessov* [The Condition of the Russian Mass Media Institution in the Context of Global Information Processes]. Moscow: Moscow State University, 1995.

———. *Mass-media vtoroy respubliki* [The Mass Media of the Second Republic]. Moscow: Moscow State University Press, 1999. Also available at www.smi.ru/1999/09/30/938635529.html.

———. *Rekonstruktsiya Rossii* [Reconstructing Russia]. Moscow: Moscow State University Press. Published by *Russky Zhurnal* at www.russ.ru/politics/20001114_0.html.

Zassoursky, Y.N., ed. *Sistema sredstv massovoy informatsii Rossii* [The Mass Media System in Russia]. Moscow: Moscow State University Department of Journalism, 1995.

Zemlyanova, L.M. *Sovremennaya amerikanskaya kommunikativistika* [Modern American Communication]. Moscow: Moscow State University, 1995.

Zemtsov, A., T. Plotnikova, and V. Tsypin. "Al'fa SV" ili "Prem'er TV" [Alpha SV or Premier TV]. *Russkii Telegraf*, May 21, 1998.

Zhanry sovetskoy gazety [The Genre of Soviet Newspapers]. Moscow: Vyshaya Shkola, 1972.

Zhurnalist i pressa rossiyskoy provintsii [Journalists and the Press of the Russian Provinces]. Moscow: Nachala-Press, (September–December) 1994.

Zhurnalistika v 1995 godu. Theses from a Scientific Conference, part 3. Moscow: Moscow State University Department of Journalism.

Books and Articles in Other Languages

Androunas, E. *Soviet Media in Transition: Structural and Economic Alternatives*. Westport, CT: Praeger, 1993.

Alexander, A., J. Owers, and R. Caverth, eds. *Media Economics: Theory and Practice*. Hillsdale, NJ: Lawrence Erlbaum Associates, 1993.

Altschull, J.H. *Agents of Power: The Role of the News Media in Human Affairs*. New York and London: Longman, 1984.

Bagdikyan, B. www.econet.apc.org/fair/extra/best-of-extra/corporate-ownership.html.

Bertrand, C-J. *Le Deontologie des medias. Que Sais-Je?* Paris: Universite de Paris-2, 1997.

Bird, S. Elisabeth. "Facing the Distracted Audience: Journalism and Cultural Context." *Journalism*, no.1 (2000), p. 30.

Bourdieu, P. *The Field of Cultural Production*. New York: Columbia University Press, 1993.

Breton, P. *L'utopie de la communication*. Paris: La Découverte, 1997.

Breton, P., and S. Proulx. *L'explosion de la communication*. 2d ed. Paris: La Découverte, 1996.

Castells, M. *The Information Age: Economy, Society and Culture*, vol. 1, *The Rise of the Network Society* (1996), vol. 2, *The Power of Identity* (1997), vol. 3, *The End of the Millennium* (1998). Oxford: Blackwell.

Changing Media and Communications. Moscow: Moscow State University Department of Journalism, 1998.

Chalaby, Jean K. "Journalism Studies in an Era of Transition in Public Communications." *Journalism*, no. 1 (2000), p. 34.

Chomsky, N. "Media control." *Alternative Press Review* (Fall 1993). www.worldmedia.com/archive/talks/9103–media-control.html.

Cook, T.E. *Governing with the News: The News Media as a Political Institution*. Chicago: University of Chicago Press, 1998.

Debord, G. "Society of the spectacle." *Black and Red*. Detroit, MI: 1970. www.nothingness.org/SI/debord.

———. *Treatise on Secrets: Commentaires sur la societe du spectacle*. London: Verso, 1990. www.geocities.com/CapitolHill/1585/CommentSocietySpectacle.-html.

Edelman, M. *Constructing the Political Spectacle*. Chicago: University of Chicago Press, 1988.

———. *From Art to Politics: How Artistic Creations Shape Political Conceptions*. Chicago: University of Chicago Press, 1995.

Eliade, M. *The Myth of the Eternal Return: Or, Cosmos and History*, trans. W.R. Trask. New York: Pantheon, 1954.

Flichy, P. *Une histoire de la communication moderne: espace publique et vie privée*. (Paris: La Découverte, 1991.

Global Report Series. International Institute of Communications, 1996.

Gomery, D. "Who Owns the Media?" In *Media Economics: Theory and Practice*, ed. A. Alexander, J. Owers, and R. Carveth. Hillsdale, NJ: Lawrence Erlbaum Associates, 1993.

Guillauma, Y. *La Presse en France*. 2 édition. Paris: La Decouverté, 1990.

Hartley, John. "Communicative Democracy in the Redactional Society: The Future of Journalism Studies." *Journalism*, no. 1 (2000), p. 43.

Journalism, Theory, Practice and Criticism, ed. Michael Bromley, Howard Tumbler, Barbie Zelizer, no. 1 (2000).

Kramer, M. "Rescuing Boris: The Secret Story of How Four U.S. Advisers Used Polls, Focus Groups, Negative Ads and All The Other Techniques of American Campaigning to Help Boris Yeltsin Win." *Time International*, July 15, 1996.

Krug, P., and M.E. Price. *Russia: Media Ownership and Control in the Age of Convergence*.

Last Rights: Revisiting Four Theories of the Press. Urbana: University of Illinois Press, 1995.

Lauristen, M. *Contexts of Transition // Return to the Western World: Cultural and Political Perspectives on the Estonian Post-Communist Transition*. Tartu: Tartu University Press, 1997.

Lévy, P. *L'Intellegence collective: pour une anthropologie du cyberspace*. Paris: La Découverte, 1994.

———. "CÑyberculture, Rapport au Conseil de l'Europe." *Editions Odile Jacob// Editions du Conseil de l'Europe* (November 1997).

Luhmann, N. "The Concept of Society," *Thesis*, vol. 11, no. 31 (1992).

McChesney, R. *Corporate Media and the Threat to Democracy. The Open Pamphlet Media Series*. New York: Seven Stories Press, 1997.

McLuhan, M. *Understanding Media: The Extensions of Man*. New York: Signet/ New American Library, 1964.

McLuhan: Hot and Cool. A collection of essays with responses by Marshall MacLuhan. New York: New American Library, 1967.

McNair, B. *Glasnost, Perestroika, and the Soviet Media*. Routledge, 1991.

———. "Media in Post-Soviet Russia: An Overview." *European Journal of Communications*, vol. 9 (1994).

McQuail, D. *Mass Communication Theory: An Introduction*. 2d ed. London: Sage, 1987.

———. *Mass Communication Theory: An Introduction*. 3d ed. London: Sage, 1994.

McQuail. D., and S. Windahl. *Communication Models for the Study of Mass Communications*. 2d ed. London and New York: Longman, 1993.

Media and Politics in Transition: Cultural Identity in the Age of Globalization. Leuven, Belgium: Acco Leuven-Amersfoort, 1997.

Media Economics: Theory and Practice. Hillsdale, NJ: Lawrence Erlbaum Associates, 1993.

Media Ethics. 5th ed. London: Longman,1997.

Media in Transition. Moscow: Moscow State University Faculty of Journalism, 1996.

National Institute for Social-Psychological Research, Internews, Russian Public Relations Group. *Russian Mass Media : Audience and Advertising*. Moscow, 2000.

Nordenstreng, C. "Professional Ethics: Between Fortress Journalism and Cosmopolitan Democracy." Written in May–April 1997 for *Festschrift* to Denis McQuail.

Paasilinna, R. *Glasnost and Soviet Television, a Study of the Soviet Mass Media and its Role in Society from 1985–1991*. Research report 5. Helsinki: YLE/TKMA [Finnish Broadcasting Company], 1995.

Postman, N. *Amusing Ourselves to Death. Public Discourse in the Age of Show Business*. New York: Penguin Books, 1985.

Sigal, I. *Internews*. www.internews.ras.ru/report/tvrus/index.html.

Sparks, C., and A. Reading. *Communism, Capitalism and the Mass Media*. London: Sage, 1998.

Steel, R. *Walter Lippmann and the American Century*. New York: Vintage Books, 1981.

Steele, J. "Fury over Putin's Secrets and Lies. Russian President Badly Damaged by Series of Blunders over Sunken *Kursk* Submarine." *Guardian*, August 22, 2000.

Toffler, A. *Powershift: Knowledge, Wealth and Violence at the End of the 21st Century*. New York: Bantam, 1991.

Tunstall, J., and M. Palmer. *Media Moguls*. London and New York, 1991.

Webster, F. *Theories of the Information Society*. London: Routledge, 1998.

Winston, B. *Media, Technology and Society. A History: From the Telegraph to the Internet*. London: Routledge, 1998.

Wolgensinger, J. *L'Histoire à la Une: La grande Aventure de la Presse*. Paris: Découvertes Gallimard, 1989.

Interviews (in chronological order)

- Editor in chief of *Obshchaya Gazeta*, Yegor Yakovlev, November 25, 1996.
- Dean of the Moscow State University Faculty of Journalism, Yassen Zassoursky, December 25, 1997; April 13, May 15, and August 31, 1998.
- President of the Foundation for Effective Politics, Gleb Pavlovsky, July 7, 1998.
- Creator of the Internet project "Liberatarium," Anatoly Levenchuk, August 25, 2000.

Index

Journalist **Ivan Zassoursky** is well acquainted with the inner workings and nuances of contemporary media. Since his first job at age 16 as a newspaper reporter for the Studinformo News Agency, Zassoursky (Ph.D. 1998, Moscow State University) has worked for independent newspapers *Nezavisimaya Gazeta* and *Obshchaya Gazeta* and won numerous journalism awards.

He is currently the director of the Laboratory for Media, Culture, and Communications at the Faculty of Journalism, Moscow State University.